# Imagining Surveillance

## Eutopian and Dystopian Literature and Film

Peter Marks

D1615516

EDINBURGH
University Press

Edinburgh University Press is one of the leading university presses in the UK. We publish academic books and journals in our selected subject areas across the humanities and social sciences, combining cutting-edge scholarship with high editorial and production values to produce academic works of lasting importance. For more information visit our website: edinburghuniversitypress.com

Edinburgh University Press Ltd
The Tun – Holyrood Road
12(2f) Jackson's Entry
Edinburgh EH8 8PJ

First published in hardback by Edinburgh University Press 2015

Typeset in 10/12pt Goudy Old Style by
Servis Filmsetting Ltd, Stockport, Cheshire,
and printed and bound in Great Britain by
CPI Group (UK) Ltd, Croydon CR0 4YY

A CIP record for this book is available from the British Library

ISBN 978 1 4744 0019 0 (hardback)
ISBN 978 1 4744 0020 6 (webready PDF)
ISBN 978 1 4744 2655 8 (paperback)
ISBN 978 1 4744 0446 4 (epub)

# Contents

# Acknowledgements

First and foremost, to Jo Watson and Ella Watson Marks, with gratitude for the patience and love that got me through.

To my friends and colleagues in the Surveillance in Everyday Life group (Pat O'Malley, Charlotte Epstein, Mehera San Roque, Harriet Westcott, Garner Clancey and Pete Brown) thanks too for your intelligence, support and companionship. A special thanks to Gavin Smith for encouragement and libations far above the call of duty.

Institutionally, thanks to the Faculty of Arts and Social Sciences for the grant that got the Surveillance in Everyday Life group going. Versions of the arguments presented here were given, among other places, at the University of Sydney; Clare Hall, Cambridge; University of Michigan; and Queen's University, Ontario. My especial thanks to Rowell and Penny Huesmann and to David Lyon for asking me to come by.

# Introduction

In May 2013, a young American fled Hawaii, bound initially for Hong Kong. He planned to seek political asylum in Ecuador, knowing that massive amounts of classified information he had leaked to liberal newspapers in the United States and the United Kingdom about surveillance carried out by the National Security Agency (NSA) and the Government Communications Headquarters (GCHQ) would lead to his arrest. Rather than escape in total secrecy, he conducted a television interview in Hong Kong with the journalist Glen Greenwald. His name, he told Greenwald, was Edward Snowden. Snowden justified passing on the restricted material by saying that citizens needed to know about the scope of surveillance carried out by their governments, surveillance that accessed their personal information and communications to an unprecedented degree. He argued that the public should be in control of the decision-making processes on mass surveillance. Snowden understood, he told Greenwald, that as a result of his actions he might be 'rendered' by United States security agencies, and that possibly his life was at risk. Within days, the previously unknown operative was a global celebrity, denounced as a traitor by some, lauded as a courageous whistle blower by others. Revealingly, his defenders came from across the political spectrum, as did his accusers.

Ultimately, the United States government ensured that Snowden was denied access to Ecuador. At one point, Bolivian President Evo Morales's jet was held up in Europe on suspicion that Snowden might be on board, secretly *en route* to Ecuador. This incident temporarily threatened diplomatic relationships between the United States and several Latin American countries. By the end of 2013 Russia had granted Snowden asylum, to the obvious annoyance of United States officials. Many suspected that the Putin regime had aimed for just that effect, part of a larger, self-assertive diplomatic push. The Snowden revelations created a rolling sequence of international and internal scandals, inquiries and debates. Commentators, politicians and citizens in the United States decried what they saw as the violation of the Fourth Amendment of that country's constitution, which prohibits unreasonable searches. US President Barack Obama was forced to apologise to German Chancellor Angela Merkel after it was revealed that her personal mobile phone had been tapped. China expressed possibly disingenuous outrage at the scale of United States monitoring, warning that it threatened Sino-US ties. Global corporations denied allowing governments access to information their customers believed was private.

This thriller scenario – with mass surveillance, deception, clandestine flights, international diplomatic intrigue and embarrassing public revelations – eerily reprised the Cold War, its plot twists and characters worthy of John Le Carré or Graham Greene, writers whose tales of espionage and realpolitik had defined the spy genre for much of that period. But the author most commonly invoked by Snowden's actions was George Orwell. Sales of Orwell's novel *Nineteen Eighty-Four* spiked sharply in the United States as Snowden's disclosures became widely known. Mass media and public forums repeatedly employed Orwell's totemic creation, Big Brother, and the adjective 'Orwellian' as shorthand for the state intrusion that leaks by Snowden appeared to uncover. The book simultaneously measured and fed public anxiety. *Time Magazine* reported Barack Obama using *Nineteen Eighty-Four* to fight off criticism of the 'Prism' programme, by which the NSA gained access to the systems of Google, Facebook and Apple. 'In the abstract you can complain about Big Brother and how this is a potential program run amok,' Obama claimed, 'But when you actually look at the details, I think we have struck the right balance.'[1] A *New Yorker* article asked rhetorically, 'So Are We Living in *1984*?'[2] (The implications of treating the novel's title as a date are considered in Chapter 3.) Snowden himself, in an alternative Channel 4 Christmas message to the Queen's traditional BBC message, observed that Orwell had 'warned us of the dangers' of mass surveillance.

Yet much of what Snowden revealed – the tracking of mobile phone metadata; the monitoring of computer use, including through Google; the interception of unfathomable amounts of information carried through cables under the Atlantic – bore little resemblance to what Orwell imagined in a novel first published in June 1949. We need not fault Orwell for this, for computer technology was still in its infancy. And Orwell died barely six months after the publication of the work that would ensure his posthumous reputation and which in time be recognised as a 'touchstone' of surveillance (Nellis 2009: 178). The brave new World Wide Web, social media, mobile phones and body scanners, identity theft and GPS tracking, let alone the aggregation and assessment of Big Data by governments and corporations, was unknown and unknowable to the author of *Nineteen Eighty-Four*. To this we might add, among other developments, the rupture caused by the events of September 11, 2001. That attack, incessantly replayed on television screens around the world, helped reset the security coordinates (and some would argue the moral coordinates) of many nations. It gifted government agencies in supposedly liberal countries new and controversial surveillance powers and resources, contributing significantly to what Torin Monahan labels 'the time of insecurity' (Monahan 2010). Did the rush

---

[1] Available at <http://newsfeed.time.com/2013/06/11/sales-of-george-orwells-nineteen-eighty-four-soar> (last accessed 23 October 2014).

[2] Available at<http://www.newyorker.com/online/blogs/books/2013/06/so-are-we-living-in-1984.html> (last accessed 23 October 2014).

to reference *Nineteen Eighty-Four* in the post-Cold War, post-September 11, hi-tech scenario exposed by Snowden signal a failure of public and media imagination? Is it time to move beyond Big Brother?

This book answers 'yes' to those questions. Surveillance scholars regularly complain that the concept of Big Brother is 'out of date' (Gilliom and Monahan 2013: 7), and that 'no single Orwellian Big Brother oversees [the] massive monitory effort' that is surveillance in the twenty-first century (Haggerty and Ericson 2006: 5–6). In technological terms, Oceania certainly is profoundly outmoded. Yet we might temper this dismissal by accepting surveillance expert Benjamin Goold's statement that:

> Looking at the discourse of surveillance and technology over the past fifty years, it is difficult to overestimate the impact that Orwell's novel *Nineteen Eighty-Four* has had on the popular and academic imaginations. (Goold 2004: 208–9)

This admission suggests that if we aim to understand the scope and impact of surveillance in the contemporary world, evaluate its history and speculate on its future, *Nineteen Eighty-Four* still has something to teach us. The world Orwell projected remains the most emblematic depiction of state monitoring in all literature, a still-terrifying case study of the dehumanising effects of surveillance on individuals and groups, and a compelling warning against the type of society that might evolve, given a complacent, fearful or compliant citizenry. The novel continues to stimulate and perplex readers, its ongoing centrality to public debate saying much about the power it retains to entertain, provoke, inform and, on occasion, to activate. David Lyon, one of the world's leading authorities on surveillance, recognises this:

> How do we know what being under surveillance, or engaging in surveillance, is really like? Why do we experience surveillance in specific ways? It is possible that we have been deliberately watched . . . Equally it is possible that we have studied surveillance . . . Far more likely, however, that we know about surveillance because we have read about it in a classic novel such as *Nineteen Eighty-Four* (1949) or that we have seen a film depicting surveillance such as *Enemy of the State* (1998). Such movies and novels help us to get our bearings on what surveillance is all about and – because they are usually negative, dystopian – give us a sense of the kind of world we wish to avoid. (Lyon 2007: 139)

Lyon indicates the important way in which novels and films offer vicarious experiences of surveillance. They provide us with scenarios, narratives and characters through which we can imagine surveillance worlds similar to, or intriguingly different from, our own, and in which we see individuals, groups and societies responding to the existence or development of surveillance regimes, technologies and protocols.

Surveillance often is presented in terms of rapidly evolving technology and overwhelming, impersonal systems. Certainly these are powerful, important and consequential elements of what Lyon calls our *Surveillance Society* (2001). The impact of technology becomes even more apparent and pressing in the age of Big Data, when computers have come to supplement and in many instances to supplant cameras as the key instrument of surveillance. Individuals can be considered less important than their 'data doubles', aggregates of 0s and 1s that are collated with those of countless others to produce mass information that can be sorted, sold and assessed by state agencies and corporations. Surveillance scholars have underlined the ubiquity of disembodied transactions and interactions in a world where identification systems rely less on our actual selves than on our digital profiles (Solove 2004; Lyon 2010, among many others). Gilles Deleuze's provocative term 'dividual' (the individual shorn of distinctiveness and merged into 'samples, data, markets or "banks"'(Deleuze 1992: 5), captures this potential loss or absence of embodied selfhood. Yet the reality of actual humans being under surveillance as opposed solely to their digital doppelgängers has not been discarded. Lyon begins his synoptic account, *Surveillance Studies: An Overview*, by stating plainly that 'Surveillance is about seeing things and, more particularly, about seeing people (Lyon 2007: 1), while John Gilliom and Torin Monahan 'define surveillance as *monitoring people in order to regulate or govern their behaviour*' (2; original emphasis). We might further underline the italicised 'people' in that quotation to suggest the distinctive value that literature and films retain in conceptualising surveillance. They supply a critical human dimension, dramatising conflicts about individual and social identity, tackling ethical problems and ideological debates, investigating why people comply with or rebel against monitoring, and supplying creative projections on the shape of surveillance things to come. In their variety and inventiveness they illustrate the critical interplay between people and processes, supplying judgements, options and possibilities at the personal and societal levels. Literature and films have regularly been used by surveillance scholars to illustrate specific aspects of surveillance, or to measure the impact monitoring has or might have. Monahan acknowledges that 'Because the topic of surveillance seems to lure creative minds, the field [of surveillance studies] has been in a loose conversation with artists, fictions, and their robust material for a while' (Monahan 2011: 501). This study aims to transform loose conversation into productive dialogue by contributing to what Monahan labels the 'emerging "cultural studies" of surveillance' (503).

The present study concentrates on utopian novels and films, employing 'utopian' as an umbrella term that encompasses eutopias ('good' places) and dystopias ('bad' places), as well as texts that mix both places. These works provide immensely rich source material for dealing with the creative representation and critical assessment of surveillance. Other genres suggest themselves, most obviously spy, detective or police procedural fiction, as Mike Nellis documents (2009). D. A. Miller's influential *The Police and the Novel* (1988) presents an account of social discipline in terms of Victorian fiction, while more recently, David Rosen and Aaron Santesso in *The Watchman in Pieces* (2013) venture energetically and lucidly across the centuries from Shakespeare to postmodernism, charting connections between surveillance, literature and liberal notions of personhood. Sébastien Le Fait offers a thematic account of surveillance over a range of genres in contemporary film and television in *Surveillance on Screen* (2012), explaining the effect surveillance has had on our watching patterns. But no single genre depicts and assesses surveillance with the creative vitality, social engagement and historical sweep of utopian texts. Spy novels and detective fiction potentially can deal with larger social questions, though they tend to be tightly focused. They tend not to investigate in any sustained or encompassing way how societies are organised or might be organised differently in the future as do utopian texts. Surveillance is pervasive and consequential in contemporary life, constantly morphing and expanding as new technologies and social situations arise. The future arrives early, so to speak, and we need ways of thinking inventively about the challenges and questions surveillance continues to raise. Modern utopian works overwhelmingly project forward, initiating imaginative thought experiments that can feed into social awareness and discourse. Surveillance is integral to questions of identity and privacy, the maintenance of social processes and order, to social interaction through sites such as Facebook, and to questions of border protection and crime prevention. Twenty-first century consumer capitalism could not function without the collection, storage, processing and transmission of personal information; the same could be said about modern social welfare. Gilliom and Monahan accept that 'our lives as citizens, students, employees, and consumers are fully embedded in interactive and dynamic webs of surveillance', adding that 'such transformative changes require a complete reimagining of social life' (vii). The complete reimagining of social life functions as a serviceable working definition of the utopian genre, and the endless diversity of those projections incorporate options and possibilities, hints, warnings and aspirations.

Placing *Nineteen Eighty-Four* within this larger generic field maps on to developments in the academic study of surveillance itself. As later chapters explain in more detail, the novel was referenced in some of the earliest scholarly accounts of surveillance, most notably James Rule's foundational *Private Lives and Public Surveillance* (1973). Rule employed *Nineteen Eighty-Four* as a Weberian ideal model by which to measure the degree and tenor of surveillance in the United States and Britain at the time. Two decades later, another key text, David Lyon's *The Electronic Eye: The Rise of Surveillance Society* (1994), devotes much of a chapter to Orwell's text, noting that 'the majority of surveillance studies is informed by either Orwellian or Foucauldian ideas' (79). Lyon thoughtfully observes, though, that 'Powerful metaphors lie relatively unexamined in various films as well as novels such as Franz Kafka's *The Castle* or Margaret Atwood's *The Handmaid's Tale*' (78). By 2007 he had extended that list to include films such as Terry Gilliam's *Brazil*, Ridley Scott's *Blade Runner*, Peter Weir's *The Truman Show* and Steven Spielberg's *Minority Report* (Lyon 2007: 139–58). Sean Hier and Josh Greenberg take a similar line in the introduction to the 2009 collection *Surveillance: Power, Problems and Politics*, connecting *Nineteen Eighty-Four* with a network of texts: Kafka's *The Trial*, Aldous Huxley's *Brave New World*, Ray Bradbury's *Fahrenheit 451*, and *The Handmaid's Tale* (Hier and Greenberg 2009: 4). Zygmunt Bauman's and David Lyon's *Liquid Surveillance* (2013) acknowledges that 'the utopian and dystopian muses still offer scope for imaginative critiques' (Bauman and Lyon 2013: 115). Bauman observes that 'The authors of the greatest dystopias of yore, like [Yevgeny] Zamyatin, Orwell or Aldous Huxley, penned their visions of the horrors haunting denizens of the solid modern world' (108) which has been replaced by the 'liquid world', his metaphor for fluid contemporary society. This fleeting account of references to *Nineteen Eighty-Four* and a small selection of utopian texts suggests their potential value in exploring the complexities, nuances and development of surveillance. But while surveillance scholars have regularly alluded to these works, they have yet to interpret them fully or systematically. This is no damning criticism, given that most major surveillance researchers traditionally have come from the social sciences. The current book brings a humanities perspective to the topic, concentrating intensively and extensively on literature and films that represent and assess surveillance. It evaluates how, individually and collectively, these creative works extend and enhance our understanding of surveillance, and how they supply provocative speculations about what lies ahead.

We need to stipulate at the outset what the term 'utopian' means and to sketch in pertinent distinctions within the genre. Gregory Claeys and Lyman Tower Sargent suggest using the encompassing term 'utopianism', which they define as 'the imaginative projection, positive or negative, of a society that is substantially different from the one in which the author lives (Claeys and Sargent 1999: 1). Utopianism embodies what they see as 'social dreaming'. Elsewhere, Sargent distinguishes three subgroups of social dreaming: utopian thinking, utopia as a literary genre and real world experiments in utopian living, or so-called intentional communities (Sargent 2010). In its literary manifestation, utopianism incorporates a range of subgenres including dystopias – nightmares, after all, are types of dreams. This gives us the following classifications: eutopias or positive utopias; dystopias or negative utopias; utopian satires; anti-utopias and critical utopias, all of which fall within the boundaries of the term 'utopia'. Sargent defines the root term as applying to 'A nonexistent society described in considerable detail and normally located in time and space.' So, a eutopia or positive utopia is a 'nonexistent society described in considerable detail and normally located in time and space that the author intended a contemporaneous reader to view as considerably better than the society in which the reader lived'. Given that this study also deals with films, we can modify this definition to include the contemporaneous reader or viewer. A dystopia or negative utopia, obviously enough, is a considerably worse non-existent society, while a utopian satire is 'a criticism of that contemporary society'. These are distinguished from the anti-utopia, which is a 'criticism of utopianism or some particular eutopia', and the critical utopia, which, though 'better than contemporary society', has 'difficult problems that the described society may or may not be able to solve and which takes a critical view of the utopian genre' (Sargent 2000: 15). Tom Moylan and Rafaella Baccolini would later add the 'critical dystopia' to this list, a subgenre in which a generally dystopian environment contains a eutopian enclave. Such works, they observe, incorporate narratives of resistance (Baccolini and Moylan 2003). For purposes of clarity and consistency, these definitions will be employed in the following chapters, the words 'utopias' and 'utopian' being used to encompass positive and negative projections.

The term 'social dreaming' might immediately trigger a charge against utopianism, that such thinking is divorced from the real world. Friedrich Engels, in *Socialism: Utopian and Scientific*, first published in 1880, argues that utopian ideas put forward by committed socialists such as Henri de Saint-Simon, Charles Fourier and Robert Owen, in essence are disconnected from social, economic and political realities. As a consequence, Engels suggests, the energy that might usefully be targeted at transforming actual social reality gets dissipated in comforting but unattainable dreams of better worlds. Utopianism is appealing but dangerously misguided, not comprehending the world with the necessary rationalism. As a consequence, utopianism cannot fundamentally change the world. 'To make a science of socialism', Engels contends, 'it had first to be placed upon a real basis' (Engels 1972: 616). From a very different perspective, the contemporary political philosopher John Gray charges in his polemical account, *Black Mass: Apocalyptic Religion and the Death of Utopia*, that utopian thinking fuses Christian apocalyptic thought with fantasies of human perfection. 'The core feature of all utopias', he contends, 'is a dream of ultimate harmony' that 'discloses its basic unreality' (Gray 2007: 17). Gray uses 'utopia' here to designate what this study labels eutopias. A card-carrying realist, he considers that some utopian visions are memories 'of a lost paradise rather than a glimpse of an achievable future', adding that 'Utopianism was a movement of withdrawal from the world before it was an attempt to remake the world by force' (15). For Gray (and he is far from alone in this line of thinking), utopianism in 'remaking the world' remains passionately and destructively uncompromising. Worse, it is founded on a basic misreading of human nature, which Gray takes as irredeemably flawed and impossible to improve. 'Conflict', he asserts, 'is a universal feature of human life' (17). Gray's rhetorically insistent argument sweeps from the dawn of Christianity to George W. Bush's war on terror, tracing what he sees as discernable and incriminating lines of similarity in the assurance by utopianists that they and their actions are sanctioned, owing to some form of higher knowledge about the fate of humanity.

Gray rarely touches on literary examples of utopia, except to invoke their negative power: 'If we want to understand our present condition', he advises, 'we should read Huxley's *Brave New World* or Orwell's *1984*, Wells's *Island of Dr Moreau* or Philip K. Dick's *Do Androids Dream of Electric Sheep?*'. These and other works, he comments, are 'prescient glimpses of the ugly reality that results from pursuing unreliable dreams' (20). Literary dystopias function for Gray as instructive and necessary antidotes to utopian poison. Lucy Sargisson counters that Gray:

> oversimplifies the case: not all utopianism is about realizing dreams (or progress or harmony) and not all utopianism is driven by perfectionism. This is important and [Gray] unnecessarily flattens the concept of utopianism, failing to show how complex, powerful and interesting it really is. (Sargisson 2012: 29)

We might think that, as an expert on utopias real and imagined, Sargisson has a larger sense of generic territory and possibility than does Gray. H. G. Wells's *A Modern Utopia*, for example, published in 1905, calls for endlessly creative and progressive utopias, substantiating Sargisson's understanding of utopianism, although Aldous Huxley openly warns against the dangers of achieving perfection at the cost of freedom. Part of the genre's remarkable energy and longevity come from such contestation about its basic purpose. Despite Gray's sustained attack upon utopianism, his sense that literary dystopias can do valuable work by stimulating critical think-ing, with the consequent rejection of excessive eutopian schemes, unwittingly dem-onstrates the appeal and significance of utopias generally and generically. For just as dystopias focus a searching eye upon the negative potential of certain ideas, eutopias offer critiques of the shortcomings or excesses in actual worlds. They also critically challenge the status quo. Whether or not that challenge is taken up is less important than that it takes place at the instigation of such works. This is to understand the genre not simply in terms of the content of individual texts, but from the standpoint of the reader, or, in the case of films, the viewer. Or, better, readers and viewers, for these texts can be interpreted in different ways, especially if they are treated as thought-provoking projections, rather than as limiting blueprints.

This more open-ended sense of how we might use utopias to enrich rather than to foreclose thinking fits with a long-standing tradition that sees the genre as both lib-erating and activating. A brief overview of this perspective might start with Darko Suvin's argument that utopias and science fiction are genres 'whose necessary and sufficient conditions are the presence and interaction of estrangement and cogni-tion, and whose main formal device is an imaginative framework alternative to the author's empirical environment' (Suvin 1979: 7–8). Presenting the reader or viewer with a possibility based on different principles than those of the world they inhabit can produce a form of what Suvin labels 'cognitive estrangement', a productive dislocation that opens up new thoughts and possibilities for them. Fredric Jameson suggests something similar, arguing that utopian discourse provides 'an object of meditation . . . whose function is to provoke a fruitful bewilderment and to jar the mind into some heightened but unconceptualisable consciousness of its own powers, functions, aims, and structural limits' (Jameson 1988: 87–8). Tom Moylan proposes that the utopia provides a 'manifesto of otherness' (Moylan 1986: 37) that can generate new ways of understanding contemporary society. These manifestoes are oriented towards the future, Moylan indicates, finding that 'in the estranged vision of another world lie the seeds for changing the present society' (35). Ruth Levitas – drawing on *The Principle of Hope*, the hugely influential work of the philosopher Ernst Bloch, which 'represents utopia as a kind of anticipatory consciousness' (Levitas 2013: 6) – argues that:

> The core of utopia is the desire for being otherwise, individually and col-lectively, subjectively and objectively. Its expressions explore and bring to debate the potential contents and contexts of human flourishing. It is thus better understood as a method than a goal – a method elaborated here as the Imaginary Reconstitution of Society, or IROS. (Levitas 2013: xi)

Michael Marder and Patrícia Vieira suggest that the concept of dystopia might also be anticipatory, heralding 'a promise of its own: in replacing the fake neutrality of social facts with a negatively charged value judgment, built into the very interpre-tation of the world, it evinces an intense sense of discontent with, and indeed a rejection of, the status quo' (Marder and Vieira 2012: ix). Pronouncements such as these reflect a far more exploratory and energised sense of what utopias might aim to achieve than the programmatic and repressive objects conjured up by Gray. They are not merely depictions of other societies, and analyses of the current failings of current societies, but are attempts to persuade readers and viewers, striving to activate critically aware responses. Taking Thomas More's *Utopia* (1516) as a starting point, the genre has undertaken this task of provocation for five centuries. That extended history has significant implications. In a purely literary sense, the utopia precedes the novel as a form in English, if we take Daniel Defoe's *Robinson Crusoe* (1719) as a starting point, or even if we trace prose fiction in English as far back as George Gasgoine's *The Adventures of Master F.J.* (1573). Beyond the merely pedantic noting of the genre's longevity, this fact reminds us that utopias are not purely, or not merely, works of fiction. While many of the utopian literary texts considered in this book are novels, several crucial texts – including *Utopia* itself, and Jeremy Bentham's *Panopticon Writings* – are not. The ramifications of this are dealt with more extensively in Chapter 2, which considers the history of surveillance in utopian texts before *Nineteen Eighty-Four*, but the extensive contribution of literary works in this broader sense to the imagining of surveillance can be exemplified by *Utopia*. Its narrator, Raphael Hythloday, makes clear that on the eponymous island of Utopia there are 'no hiding places; no spots for secret meetings. Because [the inhabitants] live in the full view of all' (More 2002: 59). To this explicit example of visual surveillance we can add other elements that would alert a contemporary surveillance scholar: the doors of dwellings on the island of Utopia spring open automatically, and the houses and cities themselves are identical. Utopians are required to obtain authorised passes in order to travel beyond their usual environs, and must travel in groups. An individual who travels without permission is made a slave. The germinal utopian text, then, incorporates consciously suggestive elements that herald the challenges the genre brings to an understanding of surveillance. While not all utopias depict or are materially concerned with surveillance, in tracing some of the genre's extensive and inventive engagement with the topic over nearly five hundred years, particularly from the late nineteenth century onwards, we gain a broader appreciation of how surveillance has been understood and imagined historically.

That historical sweep encourages and enables a longer temporal perspective than might be gained from considering a single text, allowing for an expansive survey of imaginative representations of surveillance. One benefit of considering the topic from a generic viewpoint is that continuities, contrasts and changes can be observed and analysed. Take the houses in *Utopia*: the identical nature of these buildings reflect the communitarian and egalitarian ideology underpinning the island's initial construction; Utopians abhor individual showiness and possessiveness. Yet that same principle of uniformity can make characters visible to each other. Peter Weir's 1998 film, *The Truman Show*, set on the fictional reality television island of Seahaven, also has nearly identical buildings, based on the New Urbanism model of architecture and town planning. The dwellings here, though, impose a middle class conformity, and because everything on the show is for sale to the audience, prompt material consumption based on a *faux* sense of an integrated community. Architecture places the film's protagonist, Truman Burbank, in view of his neighbours, who are part of an elaborate peer monitoring system of which he is unaware. Or we might consider the need for passes on Utopia, also a requirement in Michael Winterbottom's 2003 film *Code 46*. Travelling without the requisite pass is as punishable in the global world depicted by Winterbottom as it is in *Utopia*, although the differentiation between spaces is far more graded in the film. Additionally, *Code 46* deals with the trade in illegal passes that exposes holders to risks and that subverts the division of the world into eutopian enclaves and dystopian deserts. These comparisons are addressed more substantially in Chapter 4, which considers the surveillance of spaces, but the overlaps and distinctions are immediately apparent between these historically distinct texts.

Although *The Truman Show* satirically plays with American nostalgia for a mythic, utopian 1950s, it is set in a near future where a whole town is created for a show that has run for over 20 years. *Code 46*, by contrast, projects a few decades ahead of its initial release date. For much of its history, the utopian genre (including *Utopia* itself) depicted utopian and dystopian lands far away over the horizon, but situated in a contemporaneous world to that of initial readers. Fátima Vieira makes the distinction between the eutopia, the good place, and the euchronia, in which the idea of a better place shifts from geography to temporality, to something existing in the future. This difference is registered, for Vieira, in a change in more modern texts from a utopian wish for something different, though not achievable, to a utopian hope of a better world that can be created by human effort. The bulk of the selected texts considered here come from the late nineteenth century onwards, so tend to point towards the future. Because of the interests and expertise of the current writer, they also are primarily Anglophone. There are exceptions, as with Yevgeny Zamyatin's *We* and Fritz Lang's *Metropolis*, works that have had important and undoubted influence in the Anglophone world. Undeniably, as Vieira indicates, important works from other nations such as France and Italy (7) and elsewhere exist, but to aim for international comprehensiveness would have been beyond the scope of any one volume. Although most of the texts considered are modern, the generic focus employed here also incorporates earlier texts, from at least as far back as More's *Utopia*. Many of the key concepts, figure and narrative structures in those early works are renewed, revived or consciously rejected by later texts. Understanding these changes promotes a richer awareness of how surveillance has been understood and analysed.

That said, the innumerable texts produced since *Utopia* make anything like a complete account of surveillance in Anglophone eutopias and dystopias impossible. Lyman Tower Sargent's *British and American Utopian Literature 1516–1975* (1979) lists over 200 works for the 1890s alone. The current study necessarily is highly selective, focusing primarily on texts produced over the last century, while sampling texts from earlier times that illuminate surveillance in significant ways. The last century itself contains thousands of possible works, requiring energetic sifting of potential candidates. Yet the dozens of literary and cinematic texts that are considered furnish a rich supply of material. While there are many works not looked at that deserve extended critical attention, the texts that are interpreted have been chosen because they introduce new ideas and interpretations, or extend or challenge established concepts relevant to surveillance. The generic connections enable historical developments in the depiction and analysis of surveillance to be assessed, helping to explore salient connections between utopian texts. As John Frow writes, while genre is 'amongst other things, a matter of discrimination and taxonomy: of organising things into recognisable classes', something that draws on models developed in the sciences, 'no real-world system meets these requirements: in every system principles are mixed, and there are anomalies and ambiguities which the system sorts out as best it can' (Frow 2005: 51–2). This acknowledgement of anomalies and ambiguities undercuts any sense that genres are static or ahistorical phenomena. Moylan and Baccolini suggest, for instance, that 'the typical dystopian text is an exercise in a politically charged form of hybrid textuality' and that critical dystopias 'allow both [audiences] and protagonists to hope by resisting closure: the ambiguous, open endings of these novels maintain the utopian impulse *within* the work' (7; original emphasis). Utopias are varied as well as vivid.

Surveillance scholars have used some of these works to illustrate their ideas and arguments, and have made telling assessments. But closely examining utopias through the lenses of literary and cinematic scholarship extends our understanding of their nuances and intricacies. Torin Monahan, a social scientist, recognises this possibility, making the intellectually generous point that:

> There are many other possible avenues for the study of surveillance as cultural practice. The creation and study of artistic interventions are clearly fruitful . . . as artists provide imaginative resources that oftentimes channel latent concerns and anticipate future worlds in ways that social science would have difficulty doing without deviating from disciplinary norms. (Monahan 2011: 501)

This study has no pretensions to be comprehensive. The sheer number and astounding variety of utopian novels and films that depict and dissect surveillance regimes, processes, threats and promises makes that impossible. Nevertheless, we must start somewhere and this book takes preliminary steps down one of Monahan's possible avenues.

# 1 Surveillance Studies and Utopian Texts

Orwell's 'Big Brother' and Foucault's understanding of the Panopticon should be in no sense thought of as the only, let alone the best, images for yielding clues about surveillance. Powerful metaphors lie relatively unexamined in various films as well as in novels such as Franz Kafka's *The Castle* or Margaret Atwood's *The Handmaid's Tale*. (Lyon 1994: 78)

Benjamin Goold's acknowledgement of *Nineteen Eighty-Four*'s immense historical importance to public and academic imagination of surveillance, noted in the Introduction, comes with a sting in the tail. Accepting that Orwell and Michel Foucault 'have been instrumental in shaping the way many criminologists and social theorists now think about questions of surveillance and its role in contemporary society', Goold, a self-confessed empiricist, advises those criminologists and social theorists to concentrate their research on the actual rather than on the imagined world. He warns the alternative might be that the 'theoretical literature of social control will become increasingly divorced from reality' (Goold 2004: 212). Goold's point is entirely valid methodologically, but does not seem to have been honoured by some of his fellow social scientists. As well as numerous references to Orwell, a brief survey of works published after Goold's advice quickly discloses an array of works where utopias are referenced: seven chapters in *The New Politics of Surveillance* (2006); five chapters in *Theorising Surveillance: The Panopticon and Beyond* (2006); the chapter 'Surveillance, Visibility and Popular Culture' in Lyon's *Surveillance Studies: An Overview* (2007); four chapters in *Surveillance: Power, Problems and Politics* (2009); John McGrath's and Dietmar Kammerer's respective contributions to the *Routledge Handbook of Surveillance Studies* (2012), and the more recent examples mentioned in the introduction from Lyon and Bauman in *Liquid Surveillance*, among others. Goold himself is not averse to others examining surveillance through cultural lenses. In *New Directions in Surveillance and Privacy* (2009), he and co-editor Daniel Neyland introduce Mike Nellis's 'Since *Nineteen Eighty-Four*: Representations of Surveillance in Literary Fiction' (Nellis 2009: 178–204) with a brace of questions: 'we have the opportunity to ask whether writing about futures of surveillance can be seen as one of the sets of resources through which readers of texts orient their contemplation of surveillance activities? Through fiction can we see the ways in which surveillance concepts are becoming part of the world?' (Neyland and Goold 2009: xxiv). This book answers 'yes' in both cases. Neyland and Goold acknowledge that 'the field of surveillance studies continues to expand at a rapid pace' (xxv), the implication being that integrating literary and cinematic texts can be critical to that expansion. Indeed, as this chapter demonstrates, those imaginative texts have been critical from the outset of surveillance studies, providing models, concepts and dramatic situations that have been drawn from or argued against since Rule's *Private Lives and Public Surveillance* in the 1970s. Orwell presents surveillance scholars with only one model – and that a contested one – from the packed utopian library. The regularity with which surveillance scholars draw from those shelves demonstrates the genre's diversity and sustained utility.

David Lyon's 1994 assertion above in his critically acclaimed *The Electronic Eye* acknowledges the significance of *Nineteen Eighty-Four* while hinting at the interpretive possibilities in other dystopias. Lyon comments that the novel's influence 'has been felt well beyond the literary', adding that 'the metaphor of "Big Brother", in particular, now expresses profound cultural fear in areas quite remote from what Orwell originally had in mind. The impact of Orwell's dystopia has also been sociologically significant' (11). Although Lyon recognises the sociological potential of such works, he remains throughout *The Electronic Eye* securely within the compass of sociology. His reticence is understandable given the territoriality of academic research, the very notion of academic 'fields' evoking conceptual and methodological boundaries and the intellectual equivalent of land wars. It says much for the evocative power of a novel nearly half a century old when *The Electronic Eye* appeared, though, that Lyon sees *Nineteen Eighty-Four* influencing academic thinking on surveillance. He indicates that that influence is not entirely beneficial, for while accepting that 'Much surveillance theory is dystopian', he counters that 'the unmitigated negativism of the dystopian misleads. Surveillance has two faces' (201). Yet, if Lyon understands *Nineteen Eighty-Four* as presenting a 'dystopic vision' along the lines of Kafka and Atwood (he also mentions Charlie Chaplin's *Modern Times*, 119), he does not develop the generic links between these texts, and those like them. Nor does he consider in any substantive way the possibility of eutopian visions of surveillance. This is entirely understandable given the vast territory Lyon surveys from a sociological standpoint, and the many cogent insights he makes as a consequence. The sense of the dystopian genre as purely negative, though, understates the capacity and indeed the intention of works such as *Nineteen Eighty-Four* to generate responses; in warning against the possibility of the world of Oceania and Big Brother, that novel confronts readers with the necessity for fresh thinking and counteraction. Moylan's and Baccolini's delineation of critical dystopias, energised by resistance narratives, hints at the activating potential of *Nineteen Eighty-Four*. Lyon later incorporates that potential into his understanding of dystopias (Lyon 2007: 150–1). Far more surprising is that in the two decades after *The Electronic Eye* cultural scholars largely failed to explore the suggestive paths to which Lyon points.

Nor, for the most part, did they pick up on the continued presence of dystopian works in surveillance theory over the last forty years.

Concentrating on eutopias and dystopias mines by far the richest seam of literature and film with surveillance implications. The following chapter demonstrates how they repeatedly draw on symbols, narratives, characters and metaphors from at least as far back as the Old Testament, most pertinently, in terms of surveillance, the notion of an all-seeing God. The utopian genre is intensely interactive, later works often referencing and responding to precursors. Wells's A Modern Utopia, for example, explicitly names utopias by Edward Bellamy, William Morris and others, if only to criticise their deficiencies. He updates the Guardians from Plato's The Republic into an ascetic monitoring class, the Samurai. Wells's speculative works in turn inspired three major twentieth century dystopias with surveillance implications: Zamyatin's We, Huxley's Brave New World, and Nineteen Eighty-Four, the first two of which are examined in the following chapter. The chapter subsequent to that, devoted to Nineteen Eighty-Four, underlines that novel's importance to surveillance studies, especially through the first three decades as scholars mapped the field's territory.

James Rule's generative Private Lives and Public Surveillance makes that importance clear, opening with the question, 'Why do we find the world of 1984 so harrowing?' (19). Beyond its centrality to the investigation he undertakes, Rule acknowledges the novel's personal impact: 'As with most people, my first sensitivity to the issues [surrounding surveillance] came on reading Orwell's 1984' (19). Rather than closing down though, that harrowing novel instigates it for Rule. In the ground-clearing exercise at the beginning of his sociologically rigorous study, Rule explains that he 'is concerned with the workings of systems of mass surveillance and control, systems which rely heavily upon documentation in order to deal with numerous clientieles' (29). The five bureaucratic systems he examines – police criminal record keeping, vehicle and driver licensing, and National Insurance in Britain; consumer credit reporting and the BankAmericard in the United States – had all 'developed elaborate means of collecting, processing and maintaining pertinent data about their clients' (29). Rule comprehends variations between systems, but judges that decisions made are done so on the basis of 'who has complied with the rules', and involve 'some form of punitive or preventative action against clients' who have not complied. He then makes a telling connection:

> In these respects, present day systems of mass surveillance and control like those studied here share many of the sociological qualities of the single mass surveillance system depicted in 1984, though of course they are much less powerful and they do not necessarily pursue the same malevolent purposes. (29)

Several points are worth probing in a preliminary fashion here, not least Rule's use of Nineteen Eighty-Four as a model for mass surveillance society. For while processed information, the basis of a real world surveillance society, plays a part in the novel – such as the news and historical records that Winston must adulterate to fit Party directives – there is no evidence that the sort of personalised data held by the

National Insurance is collected, processed and maintained by the Party in Oceania. Admittedly, Winston Smith is shouted at by the physical instructress on the tele-screen, who uses the formulation, '6079, Smith, W!' (Orwell 1997b: 39), something later repeated by a voice at the Ministry of Love (238). These isolated examples hint at some form of bureaucratic identification system, something central to Zamyatin's *We*, from which Orwell took some elements. But data on individual citizens is not integrated into *Nineteen Eighty-Four*'s plot or characterisation. Even under torture in the Ministry of Love, O'Brien still refers to Winston by his first name, where the dehumanising '6079' would seem the appropriate substitute. Rule does make an incisive point, though, about compliance with surveillance protocols, something vital to the power of the Inner Party. The compliance of most Party members who proclaim their love for Big Brother often gets neglected in interpretations accentu-ating Winston as rebellious protagonist. But the level of surveillance is variable in Oceania. The proles, for example, are under lower levels of surveillance than Party members, and Winston finds spaces such as the countryside that are not monitored as rigorously as his apartment or workplace. A general surveillance system applies in Oceania, but, critically, the intensity of monitoring is graded.

Rule employs the novel as a worst-case scenario by which to measure the growth of mass surveillance and control. He asks, 'Is the association between rigid mass surveillance and authoritarian rule accidental or inevitable?', answering that 'one recalls uneasily the very large scale controlled world of 1984'. He develops this comment, labelling Orwell's novel the paradigm of 'a *total surveillance society* (sic)'. Yet he argues that while aspects of this fictional world might survive for a short time, no society exactly like *Nineteen Eighty-Four* could continue indefinitely. Instead of understanding the novel in terms of simple and flawed prediction, Rule recognises that:

> The usefulness of the paradigm lies in its making it possible to compare systems of surveillance and control now in existence to this theoretical extreme, and to one another in terms of their proximity to the extreme. (30)

He rightly emphasises the novel's effectiveness as a catalyst rather than worrying overly about where its projection of a future world might be true in any objective sense. Rule understands the larger point made by utopian scholars such as Lyman Tower Sargent that the act of projection itself entails critical reflection on the contemporary world of readers (or, in the case of films, of viewers). In imagining futures, either better or worse than our own, we initiate a dialogue of possibilities that can stimulate fresh thought, Moylan's manifestos of otherness. As with all manifestos, utopias are open to dispute. Although Rule deals with social realities, he understands that his sociological approach involves broader implications, for 'what good sociology should contribute is an accurate and pertinent view of how the social world *works*' (345; original emphasis). Having set out the findings of his exhaustive investigation over 350 pages, he accepts the need 'to confront directly the moral and social issues implicit in the growth of mass surveillance and control' (350). From the methodological perspective the factual material he sets out with clarity and in great detail needs to precede the moral case, partly to 'avoid the impression that the factual material…was gathered simply to justify a preconceived argument' (350). Nonetheless, his judgement that the rise of surveillance implicitly raises moral questions exposes an important line of thinking in surveillance scholarship.

Having to ask and attempt to answer ethical questions in part explains the value of novels and films generally to the full consideration of what surveillance entails. The sorts of choices characters are required and sometimes forced to make under the fierce scrutiny of surveillance systems – the mutual betrayal of Winston Smith and Julia in *Nineteen Eighty-Four* being one of literature's most emotionally complex and potent examples – project to readers and viewers what lived experience might be like in such systems, and the situations and developments by which such systems could be imposed. David Lyon's view that we might in part come to 'know' about surveillance having read about it in a novel such as *Nineteen Eighty-Four* captures something of that educative function. Rule argues in 1973 that contemporary mass surveillance practices 'are sufficiently undesirable in themselves and in certain of their potential consequences that we would do well to curtail them whenever possible', approximating the impulse behind many dystopias. A critical factor lies in the possibility that in the future, the 'political disposition of those who control these systems might change' (351). Balancing pessimistic and optimistic assessments of those future dispositions, Rule concludes that any confidence 'seems to require a political and historical clairvoyance not given to men' (352), implying that *Nineteen Eighty-Four* provides a graphic and persuasive warning of what might happen given a malevolent future government. Such a government need not create all aspects of Orwell's dark speculation, of course, need not create a total surveillance state, to push society in a worrying direction. Although Rule announces that he has 'reservations about the tendencies of other writers to assume that the present direction of change points unambiguously to a 1984 world', he also notes that 'some of the available signs are disquieting' (42). Gary T. Marx, himself a pioneer in surveillance studies, describes *Private Lives and Public Surveillance* as 'the first scholarly book to empirically examine the social implications of the computer databases that large organizations had started to use' (Marx 2012: xxii). Beyond examining the real world of databases, Rule finds *Nineteen Eighty-Four* – in which there are no such databases – a key tool to measure the surveillance situation in late 1960s and early 1970s Britain and the United States. He notes that 'Journalists, legislators, jurists and others have identified in the growing collection and use of personal information both the seeds of the destruction of privacy and the beginnings of 1984-style authoritarianism' (31). Rule is less pessimistic, but using *Nineteen Eighty-Four* reveals his acceptance of its heuristic worth. That utility in part explains the novel's centrality to public discourse, something that would come to frustrate those later surveillance scholars eager to escape the shadow of Big Brother.

Stanley Cohen's *Visions of Social Control* (1985) a decade after Rule constitutes a more expansive approach to creative pieces. Cohen openly situates his investigation of crime control within 'the wider context of utopian and dystopian visions', explaining that he takes this approach 'not to indulge in cheap futurology but rather to show how social-control ideology is deeply embedded in these more general predictions, fantasies, visions and expectations' (Cohen 1985: 198). For Cohen, then, such visions are not simply attractive window-dressing, or flights of fancy detached from social reality. As Rule had shown with *Nineteen Eighty-Four* alone, they help explain ethical and social questions embedded in that reality, taking the assessment of surveillance beyond the merely instrumental. The question, Cohen writes,

> is not whether these things could 'really' happen. As with Orwell's *Nineteen Eighty-Four*, or any species of anti-utopian thinking, these visions help clarify our values and preferences. Every form of social control, actual or idealized, embodies a moral vision of what should be . . . the system's sense of the future is not at all restricted to technical possibilities such as thought control, electronic surveillance or psychotechnology. I am talking about ideological rather than mechanical visions. (204)

Cohen's use of 'anti-utopian' here accords with how dystopian is used in this book, but the significant point is that Cohen encourages readers to stay attentive to important moral and ideological questions that might go unanswered if technology remains the sole or primary focus. Critically, he understands that if forms of social control contain a moral vision, as well as an ideological one, imaginative texts can provide a platform from which these visions can be proposed. By extension, the visions also can be rejected.

This contestation often takes place within text themselves, even those that might be seen broadly as dystopian. Moylan's and Baccolini's distinguishing of the 'critical dystopia' proves valuable here. Individual characters or groups regularly challenge dominant ideologies, as with Connie Ramos's struggle to escape invasive brain surgery designed to neutralise her in Marge Piercy's *Woman on the Edge of Time* (1976). Even in Peter Weir's far more playful *The Truman Show*, we track Truman Burbank's heroic sea voyage to and literally through the edge of his known world. These examples encompass environments determined by sexist and neo-liberal economic forces, respectively, reflecting some of the ideologies depicted in individual works. While resistance does not always prove successful, the attempt itself remains revealing, encouraging and enabling. A cumulative understanding of threats, practices and possibilities gets created by linking similar texts. That understanding need not come only from dystopian visions that are meant to forewarn. Cohen himself describes B. F. Skinner's 1948 projection *Walden Two* as a vision of 'perfect social control: an observed, synchronized society' (205), a description that might imply a dystopian vision. Skinner, though, saw the work essentially as a eutopian vision of a community in which the shortcomings of his contemporary American society had been addressed and overcome. Not for the first time (Edward Bellamy's 1888 *Looking Backward 2000–1887* is a standout example) actual communities were set up using Skinner's text as a blueprint (see Kuhlmann 2005). But characters within *Walden Two* itself trenchantly and repeatedly attack the ideals propounded. Utopias prompt rather than mandate responses even within their own narratives.

*Undercover: Police Surveillance in America*, published three years after *Visions of Control*, touched only lightly on the topic of utopias, but Gary T. Marx's observations signalled rethinking about the impact of new forms of surveillance, and the ways that they might become integrated into social norms. Marx declares from the outset that he approaches 'the topic of covert practices as a sociologist interested in the criminal justice system and in the nature of social control' (Marx 1988: xx). Despite what he finds and comes to understand about the increase in undercover tactics by police, so that 'Undercover means have become a prominent and sophisticated part of the arsenal of American law enforcement', he assures his readers early on that 'George Orwell is not yet around the corner' (14). The qualify-ing 'not yet' is instructive, marking *Nineteen Eighty-Four* as a form of sociological trip wire. Marx concludes that, in the contemporary world, what the final chapter labels 'The New Surveillance' obtains, one in which 'Powerful new information-gathering technologies are extending ever deeper into the social fabric and to more features of the environment' (206–7). The characteristics of this emerging form of surveillance – which include that it transcends distance and time; that records can be stored and communicated; that it is often involuntary; that prevention is a major concern; that it involves decentralised self-policing, as well as shifting the target from the suspicious individual to the 'categorical suspicion of everyone' (217–19) – indicate a trend, for Marx, 'toward, rather than away from, a maximum-security society' (Marx 1998: 221). He cites Jeremy Bentham's *Panopticon or the Inspection House* (1791), which 'offered a plan for the perfect prison' (220) as in some ways anticipatory, given that society in general might become 'the functional alternative to the prison' (221). As well as providing an incisive account of covert policing in the United States, Marx is finely attuned to the complications and nuances of this emerging surveillance world, including its ironies. Noting that the new surveillance 'is likely to increase the power of large organizations', he also observes that because of the increasing accessibility of databases in the 1980s, 'the personal computer can break the state's monopoly of information' (224). He sees this as 'nicely illustrated by the USSR's unwillingness to make personal computers easily available to its citizens', something that creates 'The seeming paradox of computers perceived in the U.S. as a symbol of Big Brother and in the U.S.S.R. as a symbol of liberation is partly resolved by separating large, institutionally controlled mainframe computers from the small, privately owned microcomputers' (224). Marx is perhaps referencing Apple Computer's acclaimed 1984 advertisement that adapts imagery and language from *Nineteen Eighty-Four* to associate IBM with the desire for totalitarian control (though only of the computer industry). In the final section of *Undercover*, titled 'Concern For the Future' (229–33), however, Marx argues that the emergent forms of surveillance power that involve deception and manipulation based on informa-tion control, rather than merely on overt violence, reveal that

> What Orwell did not anticipate and develop was the possibility that one could have a society where significant inroads were made on privacy, liberty, and autonomy, even in a relatively nonviolent environment with democratic forms and the resumed bulwarks against totalitarianism in place. The velvet glove is replacing (or at least hiding) the iron fist. Huxley may be a far better guide to the future than Orwell. (222)

Although Marx does not extend the analysis, invoking *Brave New World* as a better guide than *Nineteen Eighty-Four* exchanges one dystopia for another. Admittedly, at a surface level the world imagined by Huxley is far less oppressive, far more the velvet glove, than what Orwell depicted. The prevailing World State's motto is 'COMMUNITY, IDENTITY, STABILITY' (Huxley 1994: 1), a subtle combination of the innocuous and the ominous, and different forms of surveillance guarantee and impose those determining ideas. In *Brave New World*, monitoring critically takes place at the genetic as well as personal and social levels. The next chapter examines those aspects and suggests that Wells's earlier *A Modern Utopia* offers a more instructive point of comparison with 'new surveillance'.

A fault line that emerged in theoretical disputes about surveillance in the 1990s, and that continued beyond, ran along the distinction between a Foucauldian disciplinary model and the control model based on the work of Gilles Deleuze, the key text being Deleuze's 'Postscript on the Societies of Control' (1992). In this short but germinal essay Deleuze posits a 'societies of control' model as more explanatory than Foucault's 'disciplinary societies' model. Deleuze argues that Foucault knew disciplinary societies to be transitory, having themselves replaced the 'societies of sovereignty'. For Deleuze, the disciplinary societies 'reach their height at the outset of the twentieth [century]. They initiate the organization of vast spaces of enclosure' with the prison as the analogical model. A fascinating part of Deleuze's explanation is that in choosing an example to illustrate his point, he chooses not only a literary example, but something akin to a dystopia: Franz Kafka's *The Trial* (1926). 'In *The Trial*', Deleuze writes,

> Kafka, who had already placed himself at the pivotal point between the two types of social formation [disciplinary and control] described the most fearsome of judicial forms. The *apparent acquittal* of the disciplinary societies (between two incarcerations); and the *limitless postponement* of the societies of control (in continuous variation) are two very different modes of juridicial life, and if our law is hesitant, itself in crisis, it's because we are leaving one in order to enter another. (Deleuze 1992: 5; original emphasis)

Deleuze's observation that Kafka placed himself between two types of social formation is debatable, but *The Trial* certainly describes a fearsome judicial form. What Kafka does in the pages of that novel is not only to describe the effects of such forms, but also through the hapless or hopeless (in the sense of someone without hope) figure of Joseph K., to endlessly deny the acquittal that the system seems to hold out as a possibility. *The Trial*'s awful power, its capacity to intrigue and repel readers by binding them, even at one remove, to Joseph K.'s fate, comes from the unnatural power imbalance between the individual and the system, the putatively accused and The Law. That power imbalance is not, however, consistent or constant – there are moments in *The Trial* when Joseph K. thinks he will be set free, at other times when he demands that he be set free, while elsewhere he despairs of ever being set free. This requires tightening and loosening of dramatic pressure, so that Joseph K. feels oppressively monitored, then bafflingly left alone, alternating between everyday

states and those of existential threat, the full meaning of one reinforced by the actuality of the other. Kafka achieves his effects partly through characterization, but also
by endlessly deferring the narrative conclusion both readers and, one would expect,
Joseph K. desire.

Yet the novel's final action reveals hitherto unknown mysteries, dark depths that
are partly unfathomable, perhaps or particularly to Joseph K. himself, as he is knifed
through the heart:

> With his failing sight K. could still see the gentlemen [his assassins] right in
> front of his face, cheek pressed against cheek, as they observed the decisive
> moment. 'Like a dog!' he said. It was as if the shame would outlive him. (Kafka
> 1994: 178)

This violent and degrading acceptance of personal annihilation contrasts massively
with a central element of Deleuze's argument, that in societies of control individuals as such do not exist, that the individual signature has been replaced by a code,
and that 'the numerical language of control is made of codes that mark access to
information or reject it'. As a consequence, 'Individuals have become "viduals", and
masses [that comprised the other pole from individuals in societies of discipline],
samples, data, markets or "banks"' (5). We need not fully accept Deleuze's distinction as applicable in all circumstances to see its validity at times, and to quickly
name eutopian and dystopian examples that deal with something similar.

In Yevgeny Zamyatin's We, for example, the names of the characters are made up
of alpha-numerics, with males, such as the protagonist D-503, coded with a conso-
nant, while females such as O-90 or the subversive I-330 are designated by vowels.
Secret personal passwords, along with passes or 'papelles', allow or prohibit access
to eutopian spaces in Code 46. Its protagonist, William Geld, has the ability (drug-
assisted) to break the personal codes, an ability that allows him access to a factory in
which the passes are being manufactured and later stolen for illicit use. His surname
alludes ironically to the genetic code (we are made up of 23 pairs of chromosomes)
embodied in the film's title. In an increasingly mobile world where various forms of
biological advance – including cloning and in-vitro fertilization on a massive scale
– have increased the possibility of couples unwittingly committing incest, 'Code 46'
also names the law that forbids sexual relations between people with close genetic
connections. Genetic codes also determine chances to access eutopia in Andrew
Niccol's Gattaca (1997). There, the genetically inferior Vincent Freeman uses black
market blood samples from a genetically superior being, Jerome Morrow, who has
been maimed in an accident, to access the heavily monitored and elitist Gattaca
Corporation. Without samples of blood, as well as defoliated skin and urine from
Morrow that Freeman uses to deceive the surveillance system in a future determined
by genetic apartheid, he would be denied access to Gattaca. There, he dreams, he
will overcome the supposed deficiencies of his genetic code. The Corporation's
name itself is a code made up from the letters G, A, T and C that act as shorthand
for the four nucleobases found in DNA: Guanine, Adenine, Thymine and Cytosine.
That genetic code functions as the key identifier in Gattaca. As Morrow explains

to Freeman, as long as Freeman presents samples of blood, skin and urine with Morrow's DNA code, 'they don't see you, they see me'. The body, and identity itself, is 'read' and valued primarily at the level of genetic codes.

Deleuze posits a new control mechanism that gives 'the position of any element at any given instant', declaring that the state of affairs 'is not necessarily one of science fiction'. He adds that his colleague Félix Guattari

> has imagined a city where one would be able to leave one's apartment, one's street, one's neighbourhood, thanks to one's (dividual) electronic card that raises a given barrier; but the card could just as easily be rejected a given day or between certain hours; what counts is not the barrier but the computer that is making sure everyone is in permissible place, and effecting a universal modulation. (7)

A prototype of Guattari's imagined system can be seen nine decades earlier in Wells's A Modern Utopia, where personal information is collected, assessed and transmitted instantly around the globe on transparent cards. This allows, among other things, authorities to manage the free movement of people, but implicitly also to restrict that movement. Edward Bellamy's late-nineteenth century projection Looking Backward employs credit cards to distribute wealth and goods equally amongst American citizens in 2000, while Atwood's The Handmaid's Tale exposes the negative side of card control: credit cards held by women are rendered useless by patriarchal Christian fundamentalists, a crucial early marker of their takeover of the United States. Wells's card system also ensures, for example, that those intending to marry are fully aware of the past of those they intend to wed, something Wells takes as an improvement of the actual pre-marital situation in the early twentieth century. In the real world, Oscar Gandy's provocative study, The Panoptic Sort (1993), details and evaluates the implications of data use towards the end of that century. Like Gary T. Marx, Gandy's references to dystopias are very occasional, but again they reveal ways in which these works function viably as comparative examples. Gandy admits the 'substantial' influence of Foucault on his work, to the extent that it 'threatens to dominate the construction of my arguments about power and social control' (Gandy 1993: 9), one of many markers that Foucauldian ideas were rapidly overtaking the Orwellian model in 1990s surveillance studies. Foucault's Discipline and Punish (1977) had quickly become and would remain a commanding and profoundly stimulating text for surveillance scholars, but Gandy acknowledges the importance of Bentham's Panopticon scheme to Foucault's conception of panopticism. He notes that Bentham's Pantopicon named 'the design for a prison that would facilitate the efficient observation or surveillance of prisoners by guards', before adding that 'In Foucault's view, the panoptic design need not be limited to prisons but would apply equally well too other institutions that share a disciplinary, educational, or rehabilitative purpose' (Gandy 1993: 9). He later notes that 'Bentham's vision was not limited to the use of the panoptic forms of prison, per se; he also thought that it might serve a dual function as a self-sufficient, even profitable workhouse for the indigent and unemployed who were unwilling or unable to join the emerging proletariat' (22). But, as the next chapter shows, Bentham believed that the basic architectural principle could be valid in manufacturing, Mad-Houses, hospitals, and schools, improving in various ways the lots of those who functioned within such environments or institutions. Indeed, for Bentham, the Panopticon essentially is a eutopian project, which he thought and hoped would have immense and lasting social benefits.

For Gandy, Foucault's 'panopticism serves as a powerful metaphorical resource for representing the contemporary technology of segmentation and targeting, which involves surveillance of consumers, their isolation into classes and categories, and their use in market tests that have the character of experiments' (10). While putatively objective, the surveillance of information activated by such processes discriminates systematically against certain groups and individuals, because 'classification always includes an assessment, whether expressed or not' (17). Gandy chooses the term 'panoptic sort' to incorporate Foucauldian notions of the power imbalances built into panopticism with the key contemporary element that the classifying function built into modern technology, both government and corporate, privileges the few while 'eliminating' the many. 'The panoptic sort', Gandy writes, 'is a screen that excludes, a filter that blocks, a magnet that ignores fine wood in preference for base metals' (18). His 'primary focus', he states 'is on inequality' (3), and he argues that,

> The panoptic sort institutionalizes bias because the blind spots in its visual field are compensated for by a common tendency to fill in the missing with the familiar or with what is expected. When the paradigmatic vision the panoptic machine is linked with the futures of bureaucratic organisations and the individuals who stand at their helms, the incentive to find precisely what has been predicted is often too powerful to resist. (16–17)

Gandy warns of the 'strategic rationalism' of new technology 'which is designed to identify, classify, evaluate, and assign individuals on the basis of a remote, invisible, automatic, and comprehensive sensing of personhood' (3). He writes that the type of identification enforced and administered by the panoptic sort 'will never move to the level of personhood as we may understand the person as the subject of religion, philosophy, and idealised systems of justice. The attention of the panoptic sort moves only to levels of identification that have administrative and instrumental relevance' (16). Gandy's definition usefully distinguishes a boundary line between the identification and identity, between personhood as rich, if messy, lived experience and personhood as a set of administrative and administered categories.

Gandy explains systematically and persuasively that the panoptic sort can have determining if unrecognised disciplinary power, delineating it as

> the identification of persons with histories, records, and resources when those persons or agents of those persons present a card, form, signature, claim, or response, or when they present themselves at a particular place or time. Identification is associated with authorization and authentication of claims.

Identification is associated with the assumption of responsibility for actions, transactions, interactions, and reactions, which may be recorded by the panoptic system. (16–17)

This power, influential as it is, remains intermittent relative to an actual individual's totalising awareness of personhood that incorporates religion, philosophy, and idealised systems of justice, as well, we might add, as emotion, desire, interpersonal relations and personal history, among other markers of identity. This fuller sense of personhood gets stress-tested in many utopian novels and films, in terms of individuals themselves and in their relations with other characters. Forms of identification necessarily feed into this evolving and interactive sense of identity, but can at times be at odds with that internal sense of self, along a gradient of acceptance and resistance. Gandy notes that 'The same technology that threatens the autonomy of the individual seems destined to frustrate attempts to re-establish community and shared responsibility because it destroys the essential components of trust and accountability' (3). Sometimes, but not always, so that – in *The Handmaid's Tale*, for instance – the shared oppression felt by the handmaids initiates subversive social practices that draw them together, maintaining a basic individuality within a collective identity as oppressed young women. There are occasional betrayals of that communal solidarity in Atwood's novel, as there are in other works, but the possibility of betrayal by others serves to ground those texts in a complex and nuanced world of human interaction.

Early on, Gandy criticises Jacques Ellul's fear of 'technology as guaranteeing a dystopic future. Ellul's is an untempered pessimistic view' (Gandy 1993: 5). But Gandy also recognises the power of dystopian thought more generally, noting that 'Public policy deliberations about privacy in Congress, or the spectre of the much-feared "1984" and the domination by "big brother," can be seen to be linked closely to increases in the numbers of the citizens who are concerned with privacy' (140). Gandy cites research by James Katz and Annette Tassone that asked 'respondents to indicate how close we had come to the society that George Orwell described in his book *1984*'. He notes that Katz and Tassone 'found the proportion who thought that we had already arrived at that society to have more than doubled between 1983 and 1988 and to have tripled between 1983 and 1989' (140). This striking increase should be put in perspective, the tripling involving a move from 6 per cent to 19 per cent, meaning that four out of five Americans in the 1990s did not think that the United States approximated Oceania. Still, Gandy's willingness to allow the novel to work as a sociologically valid point of reference for national opinion, as do Katz and Tassone, speaks to its integration into public awareness and judgement of surveillance. Gandy concludes *The Panoptic Sort* with a short section titled 'What is to be Done?', a reference to Lenin's 1902 incendiary pamphlet of the same name. This section begins with Ellul's description in *The Technological Society* (1964) of a future that reads very much like a utopian fusion, one of 'human passion . . . lost amid the chromium gleam' where '[our] deepest instincts and most secret passions will be analysed, published and exploited. We should be rewarded with everything our hearts ever desired. And the supreme luxury . . . will be to grant the bonus of useless reward of an acquiescent smile' (Ellul 1964: 427). The tension between eutopian fulfilment and dystopian reality suggests either that Ellul's dystopian pessimism is overwhelming, or that he intends the sarcastic tone to jolt readers into thought and action in order to stave off a looming though not inevitable prospect. Pessimism need not eradicate agency. Ironically, George Gerbner links Gandy's own study to a dystopian text, observing in his approving notice on the back cover of *The Panoptic Sort* that it 'will take its place on a shelf of the significant books of the decade and alongside *1984* and *The Power Elite*'. The comparison with Orwell was meant to be favourable, and reinforces how Orwell's novel especially embedded itself in the emerging academic field.

Published just a year after *The Panoptic Sort*, David Lyon's *The Electronic Eye: The Rise of Surveillance Society* established itself as a key text in the rise of surveillance studies. It also initiated Lyon's ongoing series of individual and collaborative works that disclosed and examined diverse forms of surveillance across a range of environments. As earlier searchers had done, Lyon work regularly shows a concern with situations and possibilities that have moral implications. Like Rule, Lyon situated his interest in Orwell at the personal level, admitting that 'when I tell people that I'm studying surveillance, and in particular investigating ways that our personal details are stored in computer databases, the most common reaction is driven by George Orwell; 'This must be the study of "Big Brother". A perfectly understandable response' (Lyon 1994: 57). The disclosure comes at the beginning of a chapter titled 'From Big Brother to the Electronic Panopticon' (57–79). Lyon recognises the novel's influence, beyond the literary, as something sociologically significant. James Rule, Lyon notes, 'explicitly refers to *Nineteen Eighty-Four* as the situation of "total surveillance" from which he derives the concept of "surveillance capabilities". Others such as Christopher Dandeker, in *Surveillance, Power and Modernity*, carry the same concepts into sociological analysis of the 1990s' (11). Lyon quotes the chairman of the British Data Protection Committee, who commented in 1978 that 'we did not fear Orwell's 1984 was just around the corner, but we did feel some pretty frightening developments could come about quite quickly and without most people being aware of what was happening' (12). Lyon had already addressed Orwell's novel, commenting that 'The vexed question of computers, power and domination conjures up a variety of sinister images. The best known of these is Orwell's dystopia *Nineteen Eighty-Four*, where telescreens constantly monitor all activities' (11). Chapter 3 offers a slightly different reading, noting how telescreens do not function everywhere or to the same effect. Lyon is alert to the potential explanatory value of Orwell's novel, though, for while 'No single metaphor or model is adequate to the task of summing up what is central to contemporary surveillance . . . important clues are available in *Nineteen Eighty-Four* and in Bentham's panopticon' (78). He presents a sensible and sensitive reading of the novel, recognising how 'technologically rather dated' Orwell's depiction is in the 1990s, but acknowledging that 'its focus on human dignity and on the social divisions of surveillance . . . remain instructive' (78). Importantly, as earlier surveillance scholars had done, sometimes fleetingly, Lyon argues that:

Powerful metaphors lie relatively unexamined in various films as well as in novels such as Franz Kafka's *The Castle* or Margaret Atwood's *The Handmaid's Tale*. (78–9)

He later makes the perceptive statement that in *The Handmaid's Tale* 'the gender dimension of categorisation, and its implications for stunted citizenship for women, is vividly portrayed' (78–9), although he does not move beyond this suggestive assertion to any deeper analysis. Earlier, he recommends 'the abandonment of the merely negative, dystopian perspectives. They act as a hindrance to both adequate social analysis and appropriate ethical practice' (20). This book, by contrast, argues that dystopias need not be read as totally negative.

The tension between dystopian texts that both provide powerful metaphors and hinder analysis and practice runs through whole sections of *The Electronic Eye*. Lyon devotes part of Chapter 5, 'From Big Brother to the Electronic Panopticon', to *Nineteen Eighty-Four*. His treatment of Orwell is circumscribed by his awareness that the novel 'has in many ways been superseded technologically'. He admits that 'limited, but important aspects of its account of a surveillance society still remain relevant today' (58). As the chapter title illustrates, Lyon notes the rise of another model for surveillance, Jeremy Bentham's Panopticon as reoriented by Foucault. He makes the telling point that:

Ironically, the Panopticon, now the major alternative to Big Brother, started life as a utopian scheme for social reform, and a long time before Orwell. Indeed, Orwell wrote *Nineteen Eighty-Four* partly as a *dystopian* critique of such enterprises. (58; original emphasis)

While Orwell never wrote specifically against Bentham (Bentham's name does not appear in the 20-volume *Complete Works of George Orwell*), Lyon's general point holds true, with Orwell (as Huxley had done) especially writing consciously against certain literary speculations by H. G. Wells. As well as understanding the repeated interaction between utopian texts, Lyon observes that while *Nineteen Eighty-Four* is a dystopia depicting an 'undesirable . . . but conceivable future', that future is also 'avoidable' (59). This is a critical point, reflecting Orwell's definitive statement that 'the moral to be drawn from this dangerous nightmare situation is a simple one: *Don't let it happen. It depends on you*' (Orwell 1998f: 134; original emphasis). The novel was intended by its author to activate responses in its readers, rather than to dishearten them by presenting the world of Oceania as inevitable. Yet Orwell's need to make this public statement immediately after its publication exposes the fact that it was being misinterpreted as though that was the case.

Lyon thoughtfully examines ways in which Orwell's creative account did not accord with 1990s reality, most obviously because of the novel's restriction of surveillance power to the state and its emphasis on violent modes of enforcement. He notes how those on the fringes of consumer society are excluded disproportionately, and agrees with Gary T. Marx's views from *Undercover*, that 'more subtle, less coercive means have become increasingly prominent' and that electronic means allow for 'less conspicuous surveillance' (61). Chapter 3 proposes a reading that argues a more graded sense of surveillance in *Nineteen Eighty-Four*, but here Lyon aims to contrast Orwell's dystopian vision with what he reads as Bentham's utopian Panopticon. He is alert to how the Panopticon has been 'recently mediated in the work of Michel Foucault' (62), but emphasises 'Bentham's apparently utopian enthusiasm' (63). The qualifier 'apparently' is apt, scholars still arguing over what utopian might mean for Bentham. Lyon connects Bentham's panopticon to Julien Offray La Mettrie's mid-eighteenth century work *L'Homme Machine*, with its 'clockwork image of being human', adding a utopian link (depending on whether La Mettrie is read as satirising the idea or not), one that might be extended over two centuries to Anthony Burgess's incendiary dystopia, *A Clockwork Orange*. Lyon credits Bentham with a better understanding than Orwell of how power works or might be employed through the instructive notions of the panoptic 'normalising discipline', 'the exaggerated visibility of the subject, the unverifiability of observation, the subject as bearer of surveillance' and 'the quest for factual certainty' (72).

A revealing term Lyon uses here is 'the subject', one that contrasts with the more 'literary' concept of 'the character'. Do we understand Winston as a subject or as a character, and what might be the difference? The question is particularly pertinent for utopian texts, often derided for being populated by two-dimensional figures fashioned merely to satisfy a predetermined plot, to take their places in a static, predetermined world. H. G. Wells makes this criticism from within the genre in *A Modern Utopia*, attacking utopian speculations whose 'common fault is to be comprehensively jejune. That which is the blood and warmth and reality of life is largely absent; there are no individualities, but only generalised people' (Wells 1994: 7). Wells's own capacities as a fiction writer raised the modern standard for characters in such works (not that two-dimensional figures have been eradicated), so that twentieth and twenty-first-century novels and films are more likely to contain fleshed out characters, who struggle, successfully or otherwise, to maintain or reclaim their individuality and their humanity. Alex DeLarge, for example, fights in *A Clockwork Orange* against attempts by various institutions to transform him into the dehumanised object of the novel's title. He wins, but his victory is only one in a range of outcomes depicted in modern and contemporary utopias. As much recent utopian work is dominated by the 'dystopian turn' (Baccolini and Moylan 2003: 3), this should come as no surprise. Naomi Jacobs observes that 'much of the repulsive force of classical dystopia comes from its portrayal of a world drained of agency – of an individual's capacity to choose and to act, or a group's capacity to influence and intervene in social formations' (Jacobs 2003: 92). She adds that:

> The classic dystopian text . . . speaks from and to the humanist perspective, in which the unique, self-determining individual is the measure of all things. Against the perversion of dystopia is set the model of a 'truly human' life in which self-expression and self-determination are relatively unconstrained. (Jacobs 2003: 93)

The 'truly human' life may not be enjoyed, but it does provide the model for what might be achieved. Dystopian negativity can inspire the hope of something better, the absence of agency in a creative text provoking the reader or viewer to act otherwise.

Lyon in *The Electronic Eye* devotes a whole chapter, titled 'Against Dystopia: Distance, Division' (199–217) to criticising the negativity of the dystopian sub-genre. He claims that such texts 'are unable to articulate, except by implication, what might be a desirable state of affairs' (201). Interestingly, he grants that *Nineteen Eighty-Four* 'may under some circumstances galvanise action and resistance – "Big Brother is Watching You" must be the best known anti-surveillance slogan', but agrees with Raymond Williams's response that by creating a largely passive mass of proles, 'Orwell created the conditions for defeat and despair' (Lyon 1994: 201; Williams 1971: 79). While Orwell presents a 'possible but preventable future', Lyon argues, Foucault's dystopian reworking of Bentham's eutopian Panopticon makes the darker interpretation seem 'imminent and inevitable' (204). For all their heuristic power, however, Lyon considers both are deficient, a comment that prompts a revealing declaration:

> Herein lies the challenge for surveillance theory. I propose that such theory often depends for its criterion of judgement, its normative basis, upon dystopian visions. These have the virtue of directing our attention to the negative, constraining, and unjust aspects of surveillance, and of helping us to identify which kinds of trends are especially dangerous from this point of view. But their disadvantage is that they may thus exaggerate the negative by seeing only one side of surveillance, promote pessimism about whether such negative traits can be counted, and fail to offer any indication as to what the content of an alternative might be. (Lyon 1994: 204)

Lyon then sets out the options, but his admission of the power of dystopian visions in surveillance theory is telling. It marks a slightly aggravated response to such visions in terms of surveillance theory, especially allied with Lyon's admission that the 'common reaction' (which we can assume includes those outside the academy) is to assume that he is studying 'Big Brother'. As the study of surveillance began to establish itself as an academic territory, in the main dominated by social scientists, the need arose for a more grounded and nuanced reading of surveillance. Yet Benjamin Goold's call a decade after *The Electronic Eye* for surveillance scholars to deal with reality exposes the way in which utopian texts continued to haunt the space those scholars were mapping so assiduously.

Different maps were being drawn, so while Foucault proved the dominant model in surveillance studies as it developed in the 1990s, the Panopticon model itself was challenged from several theoretical angles. William Bogard, in *The Simulation of Surveillance: Hypercontrol in Telematic Societies* (1996), while acknowledging aspects of Foucault's work, concentrates on Jean Baudrillard's simulacrum as a model for a totalising form of 'hyper-surveillance'. He describes simulation technology as part of the 'imaginary of surveillance control – a fantastic dream of seeing everything capable of being seen, recording every fact capable of being recorded, and accomplishing these things whenever and wherever possible, prior to the event itself' (6). For Bogard, as for Baudrillard, the 'real' was less important than the simulated, if the real existed at all. Bogard labels his perspective a social science fiction, a conjunction of 'social science and science fiction' (6). He references *Star Trek: The Next Generation* as part of this social science fiction as well as Philip K Dick's *Do Androids Dream of Electric Sheep?*, the latter to explain the 'panic over the precipitous loss of agency that comes with the development of simulated forms of control' (128). Dick's novel and its film adaptation, *Blade Runner*, suggest to Bogard that in a world of hyper-surveillance, humans, like the replicants in the film who strive to detach themselves from their programmed 'retirement', find it impossible to 'unplug' themselves from the machines that determine them. Human efforts to do so, Bogard argues, remain 'a fantasy of crossing over to a side (agency) we have already left behind' (128). *Do Androids Dream* operates as suggestive text here, but Bogard uses it only as fleeting illustration.

He gives *Nineteen Eighty-Four* more space, acknowledging it as a 'popular metaphor for surveillance in telematic society' (138). Bogard defines a 'telematic' society – 'tele' is Greek for distant – as one that aims 'to solve the problem of perceptual control at a distance through technologies' (9). He proposes that a cyborg vision of the future is 'far more complex' than anything Orwell imagined, for in a telematic society,

> you watch Big Brother watching you watch Big Brother, in a continuous reversal or oscillation of poles of observation and power. And not only that. In this oscillating space of watching and control, Big Brother definitively disappears, and so do you, into the very technology and practice of watching, which themselves dissolve into simulation. The cyborg model goes Orwell one better. Big Brother doesn't just place you under surveillance anymore, but you become a fully integrated component of an encompassing network of surveillance, both its target and support. In a cyborg world, *Big Brother is you and you are Big Brother*. (136; original emphasis)

The looping formulations indicate that *Nineteen Eighty-Four* is not so much being analysed as being utilised to substantiate Bogard's poststructuralist position. Clearly, the novel works mainly to measure the distance between conventional awareness of surveillance, based on accepted notions of reality, and the simulated hyper-surveillance Bogard sees emerging. In *Nineteen Eighty-Four*, he comments, privacy is still of political and social value, where the 'love affair between Julia and Winston ... at least asserts this value against the forced betrayal of each other's secrets' (137). Another reading might be that Julia and Winston betray each other without betraying each other's secrets; this reading is advanced in Chapter 3. Bogard adds that *Nineteen Eighty-Four* 'points to the paradoxes of the totalisation of surveillance, where not even thought (especially thought!) escapes the machineries of inspection, confession, recording and indoctrination' (137). Chapter 3 questions the extent of that totalisation, as well as the degree to which Winston's thoughts are ever truly known. Bogard's interpretations are valid, and he does recognise that 'Big Brother is a projection, a screen, not a watcher, but only the sign and image of a watcher' (137–8). Big Brother is more than that, though, being also the focus of self-obliterating love, but he is, as Bogard suggests, akin to Bentham's Inspector. Winston never 'sees' Big Brother because there is no Big Brother to see. The novel's deficiency for Bogard is that it 'appeals to a strong principle of reality', not to the hyperreality of the telematic society. 'In hyper surveillance', he declares, 'there is no question of a return to some private realm' (138). Even so, he admits it is the 'tension between the actuality and virtuality of privacy, the actuality and virtuality of free, criminal thought, that animates *Nineteen Eighty-Four*', and that makes it such 'popular metaphor' (138) for surveillance. Where Goold criticises the novel for being divorced from reality, Bogard decries it for being too embedded in actuality.

Kevin Haggerty and Richard Ericson mount a more influential counterargument to Orwell and Foucault in their key article 'The Surveillance Assemblage' (2000), working off the insights from the work of Deleuze and Guattari. Haggerty and Ericson argue that though Orwell's and Foucault's metaphors have commandeered much of the discussion of contemporary surveillance, and provide useful insights, both miss 'some recent dynamics'. They explain that they employ the work of Deleuze and Guattari to 'analyse the convergence of once discrete surveillance systems' (605), into the assemblages of their article's title. 'Surveillance technologies', they explain, 'have surpassed even [Orwell's] dystopic vision. Writing on the cusp of the development of computing machines, he could not have envisaged the remarkable marriage of computers and optics that we see today' (606). They see another deficiency in that Orwell concentrates too heavily on the state as the 'agent of surveillance', something they take to be 'too restricted' in a world also monitored by 'non state institutions'. Furthermore, his 'prediction that the "proles" would largely be exempt from surveillance seems simply wrong in the light of the extension and intensification of surveillance across all sectors of society' (607). While they feel that Foucault's treatment of society-wide surveillance surpasses Orwell's, Haggerty and Ericsson note Foucault's failure 'to directly engage contemporary developments in surveillance technology' (607). Their alternative, the surveillant assemblage, they note, is not a stable entity with fixed boundaries, but instead exists 'as a potentiality, one that resides at the intersection of various media that can be connected for other purposes' (609). For them, 'surveillance is driven by the desire to bring systems together, to combine practices and technologies and integrate them into a larger whole'. Where *Nineteen Eighty-Four* depicts state-centred control, 'this assemblage operates across state and extra state institutions' (610). Orwell and to a lesser extent Foucault offer a top down representation of surveillance, but Haggerty and Ericson favour Deleuze's and Guattari's rhizomatic metaphor. Their search for a new direction in how surveillance might be conceived and studied is both astute and inventive.

A more aesthetically-oriented account of surveillance came with *CTRL SPACE: Rhetorics of Surveillance from Bentham to Big Brother* (2002), based on a major 2001 exhibition at the ZKM Centre for Art and Media in Karlsruhe, Germany. The exhibition and subsequent book comprise an intelligent intersection of surveillance, art and theory, with around 100 short, zesty entries including essays as well as reports on artistic projects that attempt to survey 'what could be called the arts of surveillance' (Levin et al. 2002: 11). Contributions from or about leading figures such as Michael Foucault (from a 1970s interview), Gilles Deleuze (his 'Postscript on Control Societies'), Lev Manovich and Slavoj Žižek were included, as well as work by surveillance artists such as Sophie Calle and the Surveillance Camera Players. As the title suggests, some writers considered Orwell and Bentham, although the editors note that the book is 'Not simply Orwellian in its focus' and 'explores an array of different surveillance cultures'. While the exhibition's and the book's consideration of art, rather than literary or cinematic utopias, makes it an interesting study of an important and highly creative adjacent field, it is noteworthy that one of the editors, Thomas Y. Levin, references *Nineteen Eighty-Four* in his own entry:

> Not least since Orwell's 1949 vision of an aggressively authoritarian 1984, our sense of the future – and increasingly of the present – has been marked by the fear of being watched, controlled, and robbed of our privacy. Indeed, one could argue that one of the hallmark characteristics of the early twenty-first century is precisely the realization of Orwell's worst nightmare. (Levin 2002: 578–9)

Many surveillance theorists would disagree emphatically with that last argument, perhaps favouring Žižek's position in the same volume that in contemporary culture we have the 'tragic-comic reversal of the Bentham-Orwell notion of the Panopticon-society', in that the modern 'anxiety seems to arise from the prospect of NOT being exposed to the Other's gaze all the time' (Žižek 2002: 225). Whether as positive or negative model, *Nineteen Eighty-Four* stimulated Levin, Žižek and others.

Orwell and Foucault, then, as well as Bentham, continued to cast resilient shadows in the twenty-first century. In their introduction to *The New Politics of Surveillance and Visibility* (2006), for example, Haggerty and Ericson reaffirm that 'The concept of the surveillant assemblage ... points to the disconnected and semi-co-ordinated character of surveillance. No single Orwellian Big Brother oversees this massive monitory effort' (4). And in the David Lyon-edited *Theorizing Surveillance: The Panopticon and Beyond* (2006) Haggerty begins his chapter 'Tear Down the Walls: On Demolishing the Panopticon' with a blunt accusation: 'The panopticon is oppressive', he writes, adding that 'the panoptic model has been over-extended to domains where it seems ill-suited, and important attributes of surveillance that cannot be neatly subsumed under the "panoptic" rubric have been neglected' (Haggerty 2006: 23). Haggerty presents a forceful if frustrated case against Foucault for having provided a Kuhnian paradigm that now needs demolishing if new and better models are to emerge. There is even talk of intellectual regicide, Foucault being designated conceptual king whose head 'it is perhaps time to cut off'. Haggerty acknowledges Foucault's lineage, observing that Bentham's utopian panopticon 'still retains pride of place in studies of surveillance' (27). He also repeats the criticism that Foucault largely ignores surveillance technologies, before noting,

that the most lasting and prescient image of the place of surveillance technologies in contemporary surveillance was provided by Orwell (1949), who wrote
decades before Foucault and the full flowering of new visualizing technologies.
(33)

That said, Haggerty warns against 'forms of dystopian technological determinism
that are often apparent in surveillance studies literature' (41). He adds that citizens
need to be understood as 'active agents', and that the field needs analyses of 'the
experiences of the subjects of surveillance' (42). David Lyon's answer a year later, in
*Surveillance Studies*, to his own rhetorical questions about how we know what it is like
to be under surveillance, and why we experience surveillance in specific ways – that
in part our understanding comes from novels and films – extends what counts as experience. Foucault and to a lesser degree Orwell still haunt the corridors of *Theorizing
Surveillance*, six of the collection's chapters making reference, even if only in passing,
to *Nineteen Eighty-Four*. Other dystopian texts are also touched upon, Greg Elmer and
Andy Opel in one chapter, and Didier Bigo in another, examining the film *Minority
Report*. Bigo notes that the film 'has undoubtedly had enormous success because
it recalls this ambiguity [about the virtualization of the real], this uncertainty of
political security and more particularly of contemporary antiterrorist policies to try to
foresee the future' (Bigo 2006: 62–3). And Kirstie Ball employs a quotation from the
film *Gattaca* as an epigraph to her chapter on resistance (Ball 2006: 296), returning to
comment briefly on the film's treatment of managed embodiment (309).

   *Theorizing Surveillance* marked only one instance where surveillance scholars
more generally began to utilise utopian novels and films beyond the usual subjects.
William Bogard discussed *Brave New World*, *The Trial* and *Gattaca* along with
*Nineteen Eighty-Four* in *The New Politics of Surveillance*, while John Gilliom touched
on Terry Gilliam's *Brazil* in that volume. It is important to admit that most of the
references were fleeting, the point being not to exaggerate the importance of these
creative works to the dominant sociological tenor of the volume. Even so, they
retained their place in the minds and the arguments of sociologists. David Lyon,
in *Surveillance Studies: An Overview*, devotes a whole chapter to 'Surveillance,
Visibility and Popular Culture' (139–58). Of all surveillance scholars, Lyon has
maintained the most concerted interest in literary, cinematic and televisual representations of surveillance, and the chapter extends and updates ideas and examples
from his previous studies. He acknowledges Gary T. Marx's work in the area, particularly Marx's suggestion that 'a kind of *verstehen* – or sympathetic understanding
of intentions and contexts – of surveillance experiences can be gleaned from popular
media' (141; original emphasis). (Marx's 'Electric Eye on the Sky: Some Reflections
on the New Surveillance on Popular Culture' from as early as 1996, which deals
among other things with Doonesbury and Dali, Hitchcock, Dylan and 'Santa Claus
is Coming to Town', provides an inventive and early venture into this area). Lyon
weighs the value of such culture, observing that:

   While some people may have read social science or philosophical work on
   surveillance, a much larger audience will have seen a surveillance movie, so

knowing how surveillance is framed in popular cultural forms such as film should at least be a rough guide to public perceptions. (141)

Lyon is right to emphasise the 'rough guide' element, it being impossible to quantify in any way acceptable to a social scientist a simple correlation between a film and its impact, especially given the intensely personal aspect of many interpretations. Yet *Nineteen Eighty-Four* demonstrates the enduring importance cultural texts can have in supplying starting points for individual and social awareness of surveillance and of how it might develop. Lyon concentrates on the most productive forms, novels and films, while also venturing into the domestic space through his analysis of the *Big Brother* reality show. He notes that:

> Novels are an important source of metaphor and simile, then, and help to alert us to significant dimensions of surveillance as well as helping the reader imaginatively to get inside characters who are either the surveillors or, more frequently, the surveilled. However, in the twenty-first century it is probably true that the novel is being supplanted by the film as a means of understanding surveillance. But while the medium of film may provide insights unavailable elsewhere, it is likely that the key question of the surveillance metaphor . . . will still have to be sought in literary contexts. (145)

He makes the qualified comment about television that 'it would be foolish to imagine that anything definitive let alone optimistic could be said of the chances of popular media contributing to a thoroughgoing assessment of contemporary surveillance', but the positive attention he gives films and novels especially validate the focal texts of this study.

James Rule returns briefly to Orwell more than three decades after *Private Lives and Public Surveillance*, arguing in *Privacy in Peril* (2007) that:

> As the year 1984 approached, and as computing became an everyday tool of government, the warnings of George Orwell's classic work helped inspire privacy legislation in virtually every prosperous democracy. (42–3)

Possibly because personal information was misused in the Second World War, Rule contends that Northern European countries created privacy codes in the lead up to what some called 'Orwell's Year'. Despite the fears and the actual misuse of information, Rule reasons that 'surveillance capabilities are morally neutral', adding that 'systems for orienting state power to individual lives can serve any purpose that prevailing political climates dictate, life-giving or the opposite' (43). The implication here is that works such as *Nineteen Eighty-Four* offer some form of moral perspective on surveillance technology and programmes, or allow readers to consider moral questions surrounding surveillance that the systems themselves do not and cannot enable. He considers this general theme again later, declaring,

> that massive surveillance sweeps like the Bush administration's NSA surveillance of millions of Americans' telecommunications transmissions can

somehow be carried out with respect to privacy does violence to the English language. It brings eerie reverberations of the Party slogans in 1984: 'War is Peace; Freedom is Slavery; Ignorance is Strength'. (190)

Orwell's fictional slogans provide Rule with a means to measure government duplicity in the real world. Something similar might be said of utopias generally, which describe and critically examine alternative societies, the individuals and groups that inhabit them, questions of organisation and the distribution of power, and their relation to the worlds of readers and viewers.

Mike Larsen and Justin Piché also demonstrate the remarkable applicability of *Nineteen Eighty-Four*'s imaginative take on surveillance, in this instance to theoretical considerations. It is important to remember, they argue, that Winston Smith,

> lives in mortal fear not only of Big Brother but also of his fellow citizens. All citizens in Oceania monitor each other's activities and most of them are willing to report 'symptoms of unorthodoxy.' The panoptic gaze of 'Big Brother' is diffused through society; a combination of fear and suspicion reinforces the authoritarian status quo. (Larsen and Justin Piché 2009: 187)

They explain in an extended footnote that while they recognise the value of Haggerty's and Ericson's 'surveillance assemblage' position, and use it in their analysis, 'we also utilize the concepts of "Big Brother" and the "panoptic", which retain their validity and utility, particularly in theorizing the relationship(s) between the surveillance assemblage and practices of power and control' (footnote 2, 242–3).

In the same collection, Dwayne Winseck comments that 'it was not surprising that a 1965 proposal in the United States to create a National Data Centre conjured up fears of Big Brother, while blueprints for wired nations sparked anxiety about civil liberties and people's privacy. George Orwell's *Nineteen Eighty-Four*, Aldous Huxley's *Brave New World*, and films such as *Blade Runner* and *Brazil* anchored dystopian images even deeper in the public mind' (Winseck 2009: 153). With the end of the Cold War and technological innovations in the late 1980s and early 1990s, though, including desktop computers, new media and net-based applications, Winseck judges that the reality was 'anything but the menacing colossus contained in the dystopian visions of *Blade Runner* and *Brave New World*' (153).

Taking a broader, disciplinary views in the 'Conclusion' to *Internet and Surveillance: The Challenges of Web 2.0 and Social Media* (2012), one of the collection's editors, Kees Boersma, declares that 'Internet Surveillance Studies is a growing subfield of Internet Studies and Surveillance Studies'. He begins his summing up of the state of play in this emerging research concern, noting that 'Internet Studies is currently shaped by a debate about the effects of web 2.0 on society.' He distinguishes opposed takes on web 2.0: the 'utopian and dystopian', suggesting that 'The new utopian view of web 2.0 parallels the web 1.0 optimism of the 1990s before the dotcom crisis.' Boersma then subdivides dystopian views into the 'strong' and the 'less apocalyptical'. The former echo, a tradition of technological pessimism: the expanding force of technology will result in a total institution, in which we are completely encapsulated. Well-known dystopian ideas about our future technological society are expressed in Huxley's *Brave New World* . . . Orwell's *Nineteen Eighty-Four* . . . and Kurt Vonnegut's *Player Piano* . . . In their own way, each emphasizes the dark side of out times: our individual autonomy, privacy, and our right to be left alone are at stake. (Boersma 2012: 300–1)

The less apocalyptic thinkers, he indicates, 'argue that the Internet makes us – the current generation – less creative, more stupid, and narcissistic', 'or even violent'. He adds that 'there is more: the web 2.0 social media like Facebook and Youtube are increasingly defining our identity: Who are you? Where are you? And: What is in your mind?' For the apocalyptics, 'web 2.0 is mastering the body, mind and soul'. Boersma himself argues the need 'to go beyond dystopian approaches', quoting from David Lyon's *Surveillance Studies*: 'A careful exploration of the social and material realities of cyberspace does induce cynicism about utopian visions, but this by no means paints social analysis into a dystopian corner' (Lyon 2007: 100; cited in Boersma 2012: 300). Leaving to one side the validity or otherwise of Boersma's position, his use of utopian and dystopian as rubrics under which to consider the emerging field of Internet Surveillance Studies underscores the value of the sorts of distinctions made in the chapters that follow.

The resilience and utility of utopian thinking to surveillance gets warranted attention in *Liquid Surveillance: A Conversation* (2013). In this flexible interchange, Zygmunt Bauman and David Lyon discuss surveillance relative to Bauman's concept of 'liquid modernity', a state in which social forms and identities are fluid and moving. They feel that the utopian and dystopian muses still offer scope for imaginative critiques of surveillance and, for Bauman, Michel Houellebecq's novel *The Possibility of an Island* presents 'the most insightful dystopia thus far of our deregulated, fragmented and individualized modern society'. Where writers such as Zamyatin, Huxley and Orwell had produced projections tailored to their own times, one of excessive or expected state domination of power, Bauman argues that in the world of 'liquid modernity' new rules apply:

If Houellebecq's predecessors [Zamyatin, Huxley and Orwell] were concerned about what the agents at the command post of 'major social changes' might do to stifle the irritating randomness of individual behaviour, Houellebecq's concern is about where that randomness of individual behaviour will lead in the absence of command posts and the agents willing to man them with 'major societal change' in mind. It is not the excess of control and coercion – its loyal and inseparable companion – that worries Houellebecq; it is the dearth that renders all worry toothless and superfluous. (110)

The current study acknowledges the weirdly compelling affectless quality of Houellebecq's novel, but its concentration on the Anglophone tradition means that *The Possibility of an Island* goes unconsidered here. But this book does deal with other contemporary texts Bauman and Lyon deem worth considering, among them *Minority Report*, where 'security has morphed into a future-oriented enterprise' and which 'works through surveillance by attempting to monitor what *will* happen, using digital techniques and statistical reasoning' (5).

Summarising Bauman's position, Lyon notes his collaborator's recognition of and response to the uncertainties of the liquid world, the response involving the 'spurning' of 'lifeless rules and regulations' and 'the stress on the significance of the lived experience of the Other. Realizing our responsibility for the human being before us is his starting point' (7). One might guess that Lyon is highly sympathetic to this attitude, one that leads him to specifying two issues that 'confront surveillance ethics':

> One is the distressing tendency towards what Bauman calls 'adiaphorization' in which systems and processes split off from any consideration of morality. 'It's not my department' would be the quintessential bureaucratic response to queries about the rightness of an official assessment or judgement. The other is that surveillance streamlines the process of doing things at a distance, of separating a person from the consequences of an action. (7)

Lyon adds another aspect of adiaphorization arising from 'the way that data from the body (such as biometrics, DNA) or triggered by the body (think of logging in, using access cards, showing ID) are sucked into databases to be processed, analysed, concatenated with other data, then spat out again as a "data double"' (8).[1] The supposedly 'personal data' linked to the data double may affect that person's life chances and choices, Lyon continues, and 'tends to be trusted more than the person, who prefers to tell their own tale'. The creative texts examined in this book often reintroduce the 'human factor' lost in these accounts, proposing the sorts of ethical questions Lyon feels are often left unasked and that go unanswered. This chapter has charted how some influential surveillance scholars (but by no means all) have regularly used utopias for a variety of purposes since the early 1970s when the field was in its infancy. The chapters that follow aim to interpret these texts more intensively and to fill in the gaps between these creative texts, establishing interactive connections in an attempt to broaden and deepen our understanding of what imaginative literature and films have to offer.

---

[1]  Zygmunt Bauman and David Lyon, *Liquid Surveillance: A Conversation* (Cambridge: Polity, 2013), 8.

# 2 Surveillance Before Big Brother

And God saw every thing that he had made, and, behold, it was very good. (Genesis 1:31)

Every house has a front door to the street and a back door to the garden. The double doors, which open easily with a push of the hand and close again automatically, let anyone come in – so there is nothing private anywhere. (More 2002: 46)

*Looking Backward* provoked *News From Nowhere*, which in turn provoked *A Modern Utopia*. What George Orwell called 'the chain of utopias' was strengthened with every addition of a link, whether this took strictly a utopian or an anti-utopian form. (Kumar 2000: 253)

Dating the birth of the utopian genre is simple enough – Thomas More's *Utopia* (1516) gives us the name and the model for innumerable later speculations. Dating the birth of utopian thinking is far more contested. Krishan Kumar (Kumar 1987) argues forcefully that discussion of utopias should be confined to the period from More's work onwards. Yet the titles and contents of authoritative studies such as *Utopias of the Classical World* (1975), *Utopian Thought in The Western World* (1979) – the first part of which details 'The Ancient and Medieval Wellsprings' – or the anthology *Utopia: The Search for the Ideal in the Western World* (2000), with chapters on 'Ancient, Biblical and Medieval Traditions', and Plato, all suggest a far longer historical pedigree. Utopian authority Lyman Tower Sargent notes in his contribution to *Utopia: The Search for the Ideal* that 'while More invented the word utopia and the literary genre, utopianism as social dreaming long predated the book'. He concedes the difficulty of 'specifying the first appearance of utopianism', but observes that 'early expressions are found on Sumerian clay tablets, in the Old Testament, and in the poetry of Hesiod of the eighth-century B.C.E., and utopian speculation played a central role in the philosophic and political debates of fifth-century B.C.E. Athens' (Sargent 2000: 8). In their sweeping account of utopian

thought in the Western world, Frank and Fritzie Manuel note the resilient connections between utopia and paradise:

> Though utopia proper remains the creation of the world of the Renaissance
> and the Reformation, the visions of two paradises (Eden and the World to
> Come) . . . have so tenacious a hold on Western consciousness that they are a
> constant presence – in multiple variations – in all utopian thought. (Manuel
> and Manuel 1979: 33)

Kumar's choice of More as his starting point for the utopian genre rests on the distinction between those projections that might arise for the efforts of humans (which
More introduced) and those that are merely wish fulfilments produced by some fantastic gesture or power and simply deemed to exist already in some ahistorical realm.
Those that humans produce, by contrast, respond to perceived deficiencies in social
organisation that require annulling or improving. Implicit in this latter sense is the
possibility that the society so produced might in time itself prove insufficient, so that
utopian thinking can entail constantly striving for progress without ever achieving
a complete state of perfection.

It is not necessary to rehearse the long, complex and inventive history of utopian
texts before *Utopia*. What is undeniable, though, is that modern novels and films
regularly draw symbols, narratives, character types and themes from works that
embody forms of social dreaming. While the set of texts considered in this chapter is
highly selective – a comprehensive account would require a small library of studies
– those chosen do exemplify the long historical interplay between surveillance and
utopias. Not all utopian novels and films, it needs to be re-emphasised, deal in a
substantive way with surveillance. The repeated reference by some surveillance
scholars to utopian texts considered in the previous chapter, though, does indicate
their explanatory value. Much of that scholarship deals with *Nineteen Eighty-Four*
and works produced post-Orwell. This chapter, though, explores and explains some
of that value by retrieving and examining a small but indicative sample of utopian
works created before Orwell, some of which influenced his own thinking. Kumar, in
one of the epigraphs to this chapter, notes how Edward Bellamy's *Looking Backward:
2000-1887* provoked William Morris's *News From Nowhere*, which in turn prompted
H. G. Wells's *A Modern Utopia*. Kumar comments that Orwell recognises a 'chain
of utopias', adding that additional links strengthen that chain. (Kumar's definition
of 'anti-dystopia' above is the equivalent to the term dystopia used throughout this
account.) We enhance our understanding of *Nineteen Eighty-Four* by recognising it
as part of a chain (or, perhaps better, an interactive network) of such texts. That
awareness of genre prepares the ground for the close examination of that novel in
the next chapter and the subsequent interpretation in later chapters of texts that
take us well beyond Big Brother.

We can begin, aptly enough, with Genesis. Viewing Eden as a eutopian space is
relatively unproblematic, and even in the secular world utopian artists often pla-
giarise elements from Eden: interaction with pristine Nature, for example, along
with, initially at least, the absence of want or of troubling desires. But if a little

levity can be allowed briefly, the Genesis tale does have surveillance elements, most obviously an omniscient God (a prototype Big Brother). Art historian Astrit Schmidt-Burkhardt explores the idea of 'God's Eye as Proto-Surveillance' in writing that 'The idea that gods have eyes, or even more, are eyes, reaches back before antiquity. Divine symbolism should be seen as a relic of hieroglyphic knowledge that also had Greek and Roman authors . . . . The eyes of God are mentioned often in the Bible.' For Schmidt-Burkhardt, though, 'anthropomorphic illustrations of the organ signifying divine omnipresence and omniscience cannot be traced prior to the sixteenth century' (Schmidt-Burkhardt 2002: 18). She interprets an early example, Hieronymous Bosch's *Seven Deadly Sins*, in which Christ sits in the pupil of a 'lidless divine eye [that] is always open, sees all'. Schmidt-Burkhardt explains that ' "Caue caue d[omin]us videt" is the threatening warning in the centre of the picture', the translation reading: '"Take care, take care, God sees you".' Here, God's all-seeing eye observes the seven deadly sins being carried out as a prelude to punishment, and as a caution against transgression for those who see the painting. Were the pre-emptive call heeded, the everyday dystopian reality might be replaced by a utopian improvement. Bosch, Schmidt-Burkhardt makes clear, represents pictorially some of the primary and determining forces in surveillance.

Gary T. Marx, for one, has noticed the links between Eden and surveillance, tracing an historical line back through important contributors to surveillance studies such as Foucault, Max Weber, Bentham and Thomas Hobbes. Marx acknowledges that you could go 'even further back to the watchful and potentially wrathful (although also the loving and protective) eye of the Biblical God of the Old Testament' (Marx 2012: xxvi). As well as the Big Brother analogy above, we might develop the Old Testament and surveillance connections further, recognising that for twenty-first century readers The Tree of Knowledge approximates an entic-ing database. By eating of that fruit of that tree, the serpent tells Eve, 'your eyes shall be opened, and ye shall be as gods, knowing good and evil' (Genesis 3: 5). The erring Eve and her less adventurous or more susceptible partner Adam succumb to tempta-tion and eat the fruit (hack the database). Naturally, because of his omniscience, God finds them out. Where Winston and Julia in *Nineteen Eighty-Four* are arrested and forced to betray each other, Eve and Adam are expelled from the eutopian space in Christianity's most consequential instance of border security. There is no chance of repatriation for them given the angels with flaming swords who guard Eden, and they (along with all their progeny) must suffer and scratch existences outside in the dystopian spaces east of Eden. Their expulsion also reminds us that Eden is not a global phenomenon, but the ultimate gated community, in a divided world patrolled by angels and an all-seeing and omnipotent deity.

Lyman Tower Sargent develops the notion of two strands in the history of utopias: those 'brought about without human effort, such as Hesiod's Golden Age or Eden, and utopias brought about through human effort, such as the *Laws* of Plato' (Sargent 2000: 81). He later includes Plato's *The Republic* among the second strand, a text that presents an influential secular model for surveillance. Plato constructs his Republic on a foundation of justice, but understands that the ideal needs to be enforced for the Republic to succeed. To this end he creates a supervisory class, the

Guardians, to rule and to administer the city-state. Socrates, whose dialogue with Glaucon makes up the bulk of *The Republic*, uses the metaphor of the 'well-bred watchdog' to suggest the qualities required of the Guardians: strength, courage, keen perception and the ability to be 'gentle towards their fellow citizens, and dangerous only to their enemies' (Plato 1987: 128). The Guardians are selected and trained from an early age to put the welfare of the state ahead of their own interests, to protect it from dangers internal and external. Plato requires that they live a frugal life and have an unquestioning acceptance of the structure and the ideology of the Republic, preventing the possibility of surrender to corruption or power seeking. They are composed of two groups, the philosophic Rulers who wield supreme authority, and the Auxiliaries, who undertake military, police and executive functions as determined by the Rulers. The selection itself requires a rigorous monitoring system that weeds out the deficient, Socrates proposing that,

> we must look for the Guardians who stick most firmly to the principle that they must always do what they think best for the community. We must watch them closely from their earliest years, and set them tasks in doing which they are most likely to forget or to be led astray from this principle; and we must choose only those who don't forget and are not easily misled. (180)

The Guardians in turn watch over a society whose hierarchical structure is based on a myth that they were created with specific qualities ranging from those designated gold at the top (the Guardians), through silver (the Auxiliaries), to iron and bronze (farmers and others). Intriguingly, given the importance of genetic surveillance in utopian texts produced in the contemporary world, Plato sketches in a form of selective breeding, so that people mate in 'statutory festivals' in which 'the number of unions we will leave to the Rulers to decide' (240). They are permitted to mate only between certain ages, and if they transgress 'we shall regard it as a sin and a crime', while to mate without the 'Rulers' sanction' will be regarded as 'putting upon the state a bastard on both civil and religious grounds' (242). These distinctions are not rigid: it is possible for children of one class to be born with qualities associated with a higher class, so that if a child of 'the industrial and agricultural class . . . is born with gold or silver in its nature, [the Guardians] will promote it appropriately to be a Guardian or an Auxiliary' (182). So, while from Oscar Gandy's perspective the four-tier division of society might appear a rigid and determining form of social sorting, Plato requires that individual qualities be rewarded, institutionalising an important form of flexibility.

The *Republic* is a major source of utopian thinking, partly because, as Danielle Lecoq and Roland Schaer declare, 'it poses in the most radical terms the question of the constitution of the city as a coherent totality, as a single multiplicity' (Lecoq and Schaer 2003: 67). Plato proposes that coherent totality or single multiplicity need to be maintained and, if necessary, enforced, for the Republic to function successfully. His Guardians provide models for much later utopian works, whether as benign overseers, as in the Samurai class of Wells's *A Modern Utopia*, who approximate the philosophical Rulers, or in the repressive mode more associated with the Auxiliaries.

Examples of the latter, such as the Thought Police of *Nineteen Eighty-Four*, or the more ambiguous Precrime unit of *Minority Report*, whose task is to prevent crime by stopping it before it happens, seem responsive to the question attributed to the Roman satirist Juvenal, 'Who will guard the guardians?' Although that question was not asked in relation to *The Republic*, its biting scepticism reflects one challenge to the perfect society Plato formulates, against the 'imperfect societies' such as democracies, tyrannies and oligarchies considered in Part Nine (356–420). Glaucon admits that he doubts the imagined Republic 'will ever exist on earth', to which Socrates replies that 'it doesn't matter whether it exists or will ever exist', for only in the ideal society described here can the citizen fully take part in the public affairs so vital to society. Anti-utopianists such as John Gray condemn this model of a perfect, static world as inherently and irredeemably oppressive. For them, the necessity for Guardians exposes the masked but ever-present force watching restlessly to ensure against deviance from within and threats from without.

While *The Republic* can be read as a proto-utopia, the genre proper begins with Thomas More. One of the compelling facets of *Utopia* is that this scholarly text depicting a fictional world initially published in Latin half a millennium ago and intended for a small, learned audience still informs thinking on surveillance in the twenty-first century. As utopian scholars know, the name 'Utopia' blends the prefixes 'eu' (meaning 'good') and 'ou' (meaning 'no') with 'topos' (meaning 'place') to create a neologism that plays on the paradox of the good place that is no place. And to add to that playful and provocative ambiguity, the text's narrator, a European traveller who visits the island of Utopia and returns to trumpet its virtues, is named Raphael Hythloday, his surname meaning 'purveyor of nonsense'. This word play reflects how the text presents us with stimulating puzzles, open-ended questions and inventive scenarios. George M. Logan comments that More's

> decision to present his imaginary society in the form of a long speech by a fictional personage is responsible for much of the book's interest and for much of its enigmatic quality. Fictions are attractive, but in their very nature they are not apt to resolve into unambiguous meanings. (Logan 2002: xviii)

That rich and productive ambiguity runs through many later generic examples. Logan's term 'fictional personage' states an important truth – that the inaugural utopian text, published before the appearance of what would later be recognised as novels, does not have what we might consider a list of characters as such beyond Hythloday and fictional representations of real people such as Thomas More and his friend Peter Giles, who supposedly listen to Hythloday's account and quiz him on it. Hythloday, as an unabashed booster for Utopia the place, offers a highly subjective assessment, one that 'More' and 'Giles' query, but *Utopia* the text itself never aspires to any detailed exploration of the subjectivity of the island's inhabitants; their thoughts remain unimportant to More and therefore go unexpressed in the text. Later utopian works would deal more intensively with subjectivity, and chapters in this book relate it to surveillance.

*Utopia*'s title foregrounds the importance of place, emphasising how physical setting and the arrangement of spaces are important. Being an island, in part explains its distinctiveness, the result of its founder, King Utopus, digging a trench to separate it from the mainland. Utopia interacts with the outside world, nonetheless, trading with and fighting against other nations. It also accepts ambassadors, as well as visitors such as Hythloday. He reveals the centrality of the design and control of space for the ideal community, noting 'there are fifty-four cities on the island, all spacious and magnificent, entirely identical in language, customs, institutions and laws'. Importantly, these towns are placed at regular intervals over the island, and are, as far as location permits, 'built on the same plan and have the same appearance' (43). Hythloday later reiterates the point, saying that 'If you know one of their cities, you know them all' (44). The standardisation of design, though in one way a reflection of the egalitarian ideals that permeate Utopia, also eliminates some degree of individuality and freedom. From the perspective of monitoring its inhabitants, this formation potentially enhances scrutiny, if their rough whereabouts can be known. The potential for surveillance, then, is built into the urban design of Utopia, although this aspect is not dealt with overtly in the text itself. Freedom does get restricted by other features, so that, as the epigraph at the opening of this chapter reveals, doors open and shut automatically and nothing is private. A note in the margins on this point declares that 'This smacks of Plato's community' (46), where the Guardians live in communal dwellings. The text that names the genre, then, itself points back to antecedents. For Hythloday, the absence of privacy premeditated in the design of houses remains unproblematic, but we can assume that many sixteenth-century readers felt, and were meant to feel, anxious about his blithely expressed statement that nothing is 'private'.

From the outset, then, utopias question whether privacy is necessary for a good society. And that envisaged lack of seclusion, perhaps not surprisingly, extends from the domestic to the public realm. The spaces and places in Utopia are arranged so

> that nowhere is there any chance to loaf or any pretext for evading work: there are no wine-bars, or ale-houses, or brothels; no chances for corruption; no hiding places; no spots for secret meetings. Because they live in the full view of all, they are bound to be either working at their usual trades or enjoying their leisure in a respectable way. (59)

The easy conflation of wine-bars with corruption and ale-houses with loafing, presumes a relationship between particular spaces and suspect activity, between secrecy and duplicity, or worse. Part of the remedy on Utopia comes from eliminating these problematic spaces and places, with the expectation that doing this will eliminate the corresponding action. For Ruth Eaton, an emphasis on the built environment coincides with a Renaissance sense that the city and society were 'objects that could be invented intellectually', so that,

> Running parallel to the utopian genre is that of the ideal city. In the former, the social arrangement appears to be the primary concern and the urban the secondary; in the latter, this is usually reversed . . . In the ideal city tradition,

criticism of the existing urban situation is expressed explicitly on occasion but often merely implied. (Eaton 2000: 121)

The potentially transformative impact of private and public spaces designed and constructed specifically for a preferred social outcome gets associated on Utopia with the eradication of privacy. Making citizens more visible to each other, or perhaps less invisible, promotes community, equality and good behaviour. Eaton comments that these intellectual exercises in their early instantiations 'employed the classical vocabulary of the Renaissance whereby space was rationally organized, mirroring the arrangement of the universe' (124). She makes the point that early North American cities like Boston contain small areas that follow an organic pattern, but that the grid quickly came to dominate the urban and regional planning in the United States. The Land Ordinance of 1785 split territories into townships, each six miles square and subdivided in turn, a pre-urban cadastre resembling that suggested by Thomas More in Utopia (130). These proposed (and in the case of the developing United States) occasionally realized arrangements expressed aesthetic and political ideals: 'For More, the checkerboard land division represented equality. For Thomas Jefferson, it was the concretization of a democratic ideal' (130). Washington DC's design partly embodies that ideal, with its grid system of street and avenues supplemented by transverse diagonals, although the most sustained and famous imposition of a grid design in the United States was that on Manhattan.

Making work and leisure activities visible to all so that citizens are 'bound' to be working or playing in a respectable way fuses compulsion and restraint. Built into the prohibition on Utopia is a realisation that citizens might want to hide, or to meet for secret meetings. For all the conditioning that takes place on the island, along with construction to spaces to eradicate privacy, the desire for secrecy retains enough attraction to require the threat of punishment. The process of monitoring entails making citizens visible to each other in order to ensure compliance. While there is no mention of official monitors, the act of making actions publically visible is interpersonal, so that Utopia's citizens observe each other. Almost paradoxically, given the intention to make every person visible, Utopia has a uniform dress code, another element retained in many later examples of the genre. The uniform distinguishes 'between the sexes and between married and unmarried persons' – a simple, if blunt, form of social sorting – 'and is the same throughout the whole island and throughout one's lifetime' (49). One wonders whether this sartorial austerity would appeal to the more fashion conscious first readers of Utopia, even given Hythloday's positive if qualified declaration that such clothing 'is by no means unattractive'.

His obvious confidence that the arrangements he describes will be attractive also feeds into the section 'The Travels of the Utopians', which presents several challenges to freedom of movement. Mobility is a primary element in modern utopias. In More's time very few people travelled long distances, and many spent most of their lives close to the environment where they were born. That was not true, though, for the educated, relatively prosperous men likely to read Utopia initially. The restrictions to them might seem needlessly constricting. Hythloday explains that:

Anyone who wants to visit friends in another city, or simply to see the country, can easily obtain permission from [officials], unless for some reason he is needed at home. They travel together in groups, taking a letter from the prince granting them leave to travel and fixing a day of return. (58)

Despite his casual tone, we might hear the background murmur of regimentation and constraint in this account. Travel has often activated surveillance protocols, Peter Adey observing that 'Borders are key sites in the distinction of territories. As places of sorting and effective differentiation of the (global) mobilities of people and things, borders are married to the practice and evolution of surveillance' (Adey 2012: 193). Adey adds that borders can be internal as well. The travel restrictions in Utopia could be said to be internal and restrictive, imposed at the borders of the island's fifty-four individual cities, and requiring approved documentation as well as fixed travel dates. Presumably, some form of recording system helps track errant travellers. The sanctions for not gaining the necessary permissions would, to many readers, be severe: a person 'caught without the governor's letter, is treated with contempt, brought back as a runaway, and severely punished'. Worse still, if the person 'is bold enough to try it a second time, he is made a slave' (58). No matter the ideal setting and the forceful socialising processes at work, illegal behaviour such as travelling without permission still, it seems, takes place. Monitoring strives to discourage, modulate or suppress that behaviour, but clearly has not eliminated it over the centuries Utopia is supposed to have existed. Because the scrutiny needs to take place at all, monitoring can never be done away with. While the people on Utopia are not individualised, as are characters in novels, the need for surveillance and punishment implies a level of resistant agency beyond that of simple compliant ciphers. That agency reflects the power dynamic Thomas More understands as inherent in such practices. He tests the assumptions of his readers by creating a scenario where infractions of tough rules trigger excessive sanctions, a situation related by a narrator who unthinkingly lauds the society in which this state of affairs prevails. Hythloday's sanguine reading of Utopia adds further argumentative torque to the text, inducing readers to review their preconceptions and to respond to the provocations. Individual responses are unlikely to be uniform, a product of the inventive provocation the genre inspires. Critically, despite constructing a fictional world, Utopia throws a piercing searchlight onto the actual societies in which it is read, both at the time of its publication and later. As these societies themselves are likely to have distinctive qualities, that light will hit different facets from new angles. The questions Utopia asks, along with the problems it raises, then, are not circumscribed by the text's historical moment.

For brevity's sake, we now speed forward several centuries. More's Utopia is a richly imagined place. Surveillance, it needs saying, is not his primary concern, even if different forms of monitoring are important to the island's makeup and operation. Jeremy Bentham's late-eighteenth century Panopticon scheme, by contrast, deals overtly with surveillance. Because it proposes both a real world solution to the rising prison population in Britain at the time and a more general argument for social reform if the Panopticon principle is adopted, it projects into an actual future.

The architectural drawings for the Panopticon, showing a circular structure with a central tower from which an unseen Inspector could at all times 'see' occupants who came to internalise the idea that they were being monitored, are now among the most famous images in surveillance studies. Ultimately, despite Bentham's efforts and arguments, the scheme failed to gain sufficient government acceptance to be implemented in his lifetime. Michel's Foucault's reinterpretation of it two centuries later gave the Panopticon immense new recognition. Foucault's 'dystopian' reading of Bentham has been astoundingly influential, so that Kevin Haggerty can find the Panopticon conceptually oppressive, while admitting that it still retains pride of place in surveillance studies. Foucault is partly to blame and to praise for these consequences, and Bentham scholars such as Anne Brunon-Ernst have made a point of distinguishing Bentham's Panopticon from Foucault's panopticism (Brunon-Ernst 2012: 1–13). In passing, she also observes that Foucault's interpretation of the Panopticon, while making Bentham's work available to a wider audience, turned its author 'into a forerunner of Big Brother' (3). I want to focus here not on Foucault, who is dealt with in dozens of surveillance texts, but on Bentham's proposal relative to other utopian works. There is also the question of whether Bentham's Panopticon is utopian. But understanding utopianism as social dreaming that can include intentional communities as well as fantastic imagined worlds allows an inclusiveness that can incorporate Bentham.

Whether the Panopticon is treated as a utopian plan is itself complicated, for as Janet Semple admits, 'Bentham is not generally seen as a utopian thinker'. She adds that he 'rejected the possibility of a golden age . . . [and] stigmatized Thomas More's "Romance", itself as an 'anti-rational fallacy, for its whole concept ignores causes and effects' (Semple 1993: 297). Despite this, Semple quotes J. R. Poynter, who reads Bentham's *Pauper Management Improved* work as 'a Utopia, and . . . not the least interesting of that species'. Poynter declares that 'Enough systematic regimentation was involved to make the plan horrible to modern minds: Bentham the Big Brother was no doubt benevolent in intent, but as dogmatically authoritarian as most of the kind' (299). The reference to Orwell underlines the generic interconnections this chapter investigates, while the sense that Bentham's management scheme might seem dystopian to modern minds emphasises how utopian works are open to divergent interpretations in different contexts, or by different readers in the same context. Interestingly, Foucault contended that, for Bentham, 'the Panopticon was at once a programme and a utopia', adding that 'Bentham describes, in the *utopian* form, a general system, particular mechanisms which really *exist*' (Foucault 1980: 164, original emphasis; Cited in de Champs 2012: 63). As Emmanuelle de Champs cautions, while Bentham 'referred to his Panopticon plans as "Utopia" in several instances, it was to insist on the fact that they had not yet been implemented'. She adds that whether 'the Panopticon was destined to remain an *ou-topos*, a place which existed nowhere but in the imagination of its author' or 'was also a *eu-topos* . . . has fuelled debates for nearly two centuries' (de Champs 2012: 65). Despite de Champs' sensible caution, Bentham's claim for the Panopticon certainly sounds eutopian:

Morals reformed – health preserved – industry invigorated – instruction diffused – public burthens lightened – Economy seated as it were on a rock – the Gordian knot of the Poor-Laws not cut, but untied – all by a simple idea in Architecture. (Bentham 1995: 31)

And the argument he makes proposes a future better than the present in which Bentham finds himself. Bentham's criticism that utopias were wish fulfilments fails to distinguish between potentially realisable projects created by humans, and perfect places deriving from the efforts of gods or supernatural forces.

The surveillance implications of the Panopticon are far less contentious, especially in light of Foucault's energetic if contentious interpretation of Bentham's plan. Foucault would give surveillance studies its most durable and productive metaphor from the 1980s and on at least into the first decade of the twenty-first century. We need to see Bentham's Panopticon in its own terms, though, rather than simply as the source of Foucault's interpretation. Briefly stated, a central aspect of the Panopticon, both literally and theoretically, is the presence of an Inspector who is invisible to the inmates of whatever specific institution employs Bentham's simple architectural idea. In this, a central tower allows the Inspector to observe at all times the inmates of cells organised in circular tiers around the tower. The key to the Panopticon's effectiveness, however, is less its design than what it promotes over time in the minds of the inmates. Although they cannot literally see the Inspector, they come to internalise the idea that they are seen at all times by that Inspector, even when, logically, that might be impossible. The Panopticon's brilliant and devastatingly effective psychological insight is that those within the cells eventually internalise the scrutiny they feel themselves to be under, and are told that they are under. In doing so they put themselves under permanent surveillance, acting according to socially accepted norms so as to avoid punishment. Bentham, as a utilitarian, cares less that the inmates actually are morally improved than that they perform as though they are so improved. Their motives are unimportant relative to their behaviour, a potent notion that will feed forward more than two centuries into B. F. Skinner's eutopian *Walden Two* and the dystopian *A Clockwork Orange*. Bentham focuses on the practical application of the Panopticon principle, his list of projected improvements in health, industry, education and economics an impressive measure of real world utility. Practical application is critical to the case Bentham puts forward for the Panopticon, which in part was conceived to alleviate Britain's overcrowded prisons. Yet Bentham recognised that the same structure could be modified for use in workshops and schools to improve diligence, or in hospitals to monitor patients.

Practical though Bentham thought the Panopticon to be, and although he put enormous effort into getting it approved by agencies of the British government, the design failed to achieve the success he expected and thought it deserved. Had he been successful, the practise of sending convicts to the British colonies might not have developed so extensively in the late eighteenth and early nineteenth century. As a consequence, the history of Australia, a nation that started as a British penal colony, might have been very different. But the vital link between the most advanced form of the Panopticon, the prison and utopian thinking, generally deserves brief consideration. Semple, in *Bentham's Prison: A Study of the Panopticon Penitentiary*, writes that 'There is no necessary contradiction in perceiving the panopticon both as a utopia and as an instrument of oppression.' She adds that '[C.F] Bahmueller implies that utopia should be equated with heaven, but it can mean many things, "nowhere", an unreal or impractical world, or an absurd speculation as to the future' (300). It might also mean a piece of inspirational and aspirational social dreaming. Semple observes that:

> The panopticon shares in the characteristics of other Enlightenment utopias, of which Krishan Kumar writes: 'Their overriding aim is the elimination of social discord and individual unhappiness caused by unrestrained desires and strivings' [Kumar 1987: 37]. This is a central element in Thomas More's Utopia (sic) and the similarities between it and the panopticon are so striking that it is difficult to believe that Bentham was not deeply influenced by More's work. (300)

Kumar points to generic connections prevalent in utopian works, even if some might not fully grant Bentham the status of utopianist. The real world quality of his proposal in itself does not exclude it from the list of utopian works, because a distinction between fiction and fact ignores how utopian writers generally construct fictional worlds in order to make positive or negative comparisons with the actual world inhabited by the reader or viewer. Utopian works take their cue from the reality in which they are produced, even when they propose options that seem fantastic in relation to that reality. The generative quality of these texts only increases as readers and (more recently) viewers from different contexts, sometimes centuries later, make their own interpretations and integrate those of others. Literary and social history makes plain that works such as *Utopia* or Bentham's Panopticon trigger responses well after their moment of creation, adding to the sum of inventive thinking about social organisation, personal agency, power and freedom, all of which have surveillance aspects. The obvious and illuminating differences between even these two early texts advertise how the utopian genre is both wide-ranging and peculiarly interactive.

We now fast forward again, this time to 'modernity'. Anthony Giddens and Manuel Castells separately argue that surveillance as we understand it is fundamental to the structures and processes of modernity. In *The Nation State and Violence* (1985) Giddens notes how Max Weber's incisive account of bureaucracy registers the increase of surveillance in the workplace, arguing that surveillance underpins the success of modern capitalism and is intricately linked with the state control of the means of violence. Manuel Castells in *The Rise of Network Society* (1996) brilliantly explains the centrality of information technology to modern life, technology whose reach and power continues to extend astonishingly. Works such as *Utopia* illustrate that the sorts of questions surveillance raises about, say, privacy, or the scenarios to which it applies, are not restricted to the modern age. These works can provide useful historical yardsticks by which to measure the differences between earlier and later assessments, or to note similarities. The great majority of utopian novels and (more obviously) films considered in these chapters belong to the modern period, many projecting beyond the contemporary world. Indeed, almost all those considered from this point on are twentieth- and twenty-first century creations. An example of what Howard Segal labels the 'technological utopia' (Segal 2012: 29–32) warrants space, though, for what it tells us about nineteenth-century speculation about the sort of highly organised world Weber saw as indicative of modernity. Edward Bellamy's *Looking Backward* would prove one of the most influential utopias of the century often understood as the great century of utopian texts. *Looking Backward* also proved a spur for other authors to fashion their own projections. Krishan Kumar judges that Bellamy's work 'created an appetite and a vogue for utopias that did not subside for a dozen years'. He estimates that 'Between 1889 and 1900 at least 62 utopias and novels influenced by Bellamy were published – most in the United States, but several also in Britain and Germany' (Kumar 1987: 135).

*Looking Backward*'s protagonist, Julian West, falls asleep in the grim Boston of 1887, a city exemplary of destructive and acquisitive capitalism, and wakes more than a century later to find exploitation and class tensions eradicated. In its place, twenty-first century Boston, and indeed the United States as a whole, is a technically advanced, harmonious society, rationally organised and prosperous. The centralisation of manufacturing and administration enabled this transformation, so that the nation is structured as a single industrial unit. The prevailing principle, West is told by his guide, Dr Leete, is that of 'military service', while a new social spirit based on 'the solidarity of the race and the brotherhood of man' has been realised. Order takes precedence, but the profit motive that determined both the structure and the outcomes of nineteenth century Boston has been abolished, replaced by a credit system that distributes the annual product of the nation, and that is given 'to every citizen on the public books at the beginning of the year'. To facilitate this system, 'a credit card is issued him with which he procures at the public warehouses, found in every community, whatever he desires whenever he wants it' (94), an interesting forerunner of the disembodied transactions common to contemporary society. But whereas twenty-first century credit cards are intimately linked to consumer capitalism, those in *Looking Backward* are part of a form of consumer socialism. There, the credit card system 'totally obviates the necessity for business transactions of any sort' (198). In both cases, the cards are linked to individual identities, but tellingly in the case of Bellamy's eutopia, they help to promote equity. And the nation's wealth is distributed among men and woman, something that surprises West, whose concept of gender difference initially is firmly fixed in that of his own century. Assuming that men would be given a greater credit than women, he finds that:

The maintenance of all people is the same. There are no exceptions to that rule, but if a difference were made . . . it would be by making the women's credit larger, not smaller. Can you think of any service constituting a stronger claim on the nation's gratitude than bearing and nursing the nation's children? (198)

From the perspective of Bellamy's own time, such a progressive system would have seemed revolutionary; indeed it would seem so for many countries in the twenty-first century. While there is no discrimination on gender lines, the use of all credit cards is monitored to keep track of spent credit, so that any unused credit at year's end gets incorporated into the 'general surplus'. Again, West finds it difficult initially to comprehend this radical change, worrying that such a system must discourage saving. Dr Leete must instruct him that in the America of 2000 the accumulation of personal wealth is unnecessary because 'the nation guarantees the nurture, education and comfortable maintenance of every citizen from the cradle to the grave'. While West never finds out the full workings of the credit card system, it seems clear that it would require a centralised database of some description, and would function as a de facto identity card. West is told that the doctor's fees are collected via credit cards (114), and the reader assumes that other social services are organized in the same way. Given that Dr Leete offers nothing but a positive reading of this arrangement, it seems reasonable to accept that Bellamy himself sees nothing worrying here.

Nor does Bellamy find anything problematic about the organisation of manufacturing and construction along the line of an 'industrial army', in which all men serve until the age of 45. This army is made up of ten departments, each representing a specific industry, related to a 'subordinate bureau, which has a complete record of the plant and force under its control, of the present product, and means of increasing it' (152). West is told that:

> Each bureau is responsible for the task given it, and this responsibility is enforced by departmental oversight and that of the administration; nor does the distributive department accept the product without its own inspection; while even if in the hands of the consumer an article turns out unfit, the system enables the fault to be traced back to the original worker. (152)

The centrality of monitoring to this vast national enterprise is embodied in the person of the President, whom West hears likened to a 'general up in a balloon, with perfect survey of the field, [making it easier for him] to manoeuvre a million men to victory than for a sergeant to manage a platoon in a thicket' (154). To enhance his supervisory capacity, the President is assisted by,

> an inspectorate, a highly important department in our system; to the inspectorate come all complaints or information as to defects in goods, insolence or inefficiency of officials, or dereliction of any sort in the public service. The inspectorate, however, does not wait for complaints. Not only is it on the alert to catch and sift every rumour of a fault in the service, but it is its business, by systematic and constant oversight and inspection of every branch of the army, to find out what is going wrong before anybody else does. (157)

Bentham had argued the use of the Panopticon in the late eighteenth-century workplace, but Bellamy's late nineteenth-century depiction of monitoring systems in emerging mass production speaks to the rise of scientific management in that

era. Bellamy treats this organisational strategy as the most efficient way of producing the nation's wealth as the basis for distributing it equitably. Later representations of mass production in films such as Fritz Lang's *Metropolis* (1927) or Charlie
Chaplin's *Modern Times* (1936) would offer more critical takes on the application
of scientific management to the workplace. In its own time, though, Bellamy's centralised eutopia, with its alluring mix of welfare state and material prosperity, proved
immensely popular and influential.

The greatest utopian writer of the last hundred years, H. G. Wells, also promoted
the type of rational, technology-driven eutopias favoured by Bellamy. Even so, in *A
Modern Utopia*, Wells includes Bellamy among the writers he feels produces dull and
static worlds. Wells tries consciously to move outside the established pattern on aesthetic and on polemical grounds, wanting to engage and to persuade. 'Our business
here', he writes, in a passage that deftly describes the aims of many a utopian writer,

> is to be Utopian, to make vivid and credible, if we can, first this facet and then
> that, of an imaginary whole and happy world. Our deliberate intention is to be,
> not, indeed, impossible, but most distinctly impracticable, by every scale that
> reaches only between today and tomorrow. We are to turn our backs for a space
> upon the insistent examination of the thing that is, and face towards the freer
> air, the ampler spaces of the thing that might be. (Wells 1994: 11–12)

He also aims to complicate the situation for the reader by stating that he, H. G.
Wells, (an already famous speculator about the future), is *not* the narrator of the
book. A figure called The Owner of the Voice conveys information about the
modern utopia to which he ventures, accompanied by a companion referred to only
as The Botanist. The latter regularly irritates the former, especially as he seems
less concerned with the wonders they encounter than with his own unrequited
love back on Earth. These textual manoeuvres are only some of the various formal
innovations that Wells attempts, and in many cases achieves, creating what Károly
Pintér (developing the ideas of Darko Suvin) labels 'narrative estrangement' (Pintér
2010: 135). These manoevures enable Wells to 'envision and justify in detail a
twentieth century utopia while commenting on his own utopian ideas ironically and
satirically'. Simon James suggests that the utopian tradition activates 'a Bakhtinian
dialogue of argument between positions' and that 'Wells's utopias are not only in
dialogue with each other, but also with previous literary utopias: Plato in particular, is a constant point of reference, especially throughout the highly meta-textual
*A Modern Utopia*' (James 2012: 127). *A Modern Utopia*, then, actively probes the
limitations of the established form. Rather than have his utopian travellers move
to another part of the current world, for example, or to come back from the past or
the future, as was more the norm at the time Wells wrote the book, they travel to a
planet identical to Earth, except that it has developed along utopian lines. Having
two travellers, who are relatively realistic and distinct, and more importantly, with
different judgements on the world they have left and the world they arrive in, adds
to the dialogic quality of the text. The variety of voices heard gets enhanced by the
addition of an opinionated 'Voice of Nature' on the utopian planet, a character

himself at odds with that world, and who disputes the predominantly positive reading of the planet given by the Owner of the Voice.

In the preface, Wells justifies this complex and consciously unsettling approach as a necessary advance on what he terms pre-Darwinian utopias, those without an understanding of the determining force of evolution on ideas and cultures. Previous utopian works are 'perfect and static States, a balance of happiness won for ever against the forces of unrest and disorder that inhere in things'. For Wells, though, any utopian novel with pretensions to be modern 'must not be static but kinetic, must shape not as a permanent state but as a hopeful stage, leading to a long ascent of stages' (50). This requires freethinking that for Wells equates to freedom of movement in a world where national boundaries do not exist. The 'modern view', The Owner of the Voice announces, 'steadily intensifies the value of freedom, until we at least see liberty as the very substance of life, that it is life itself, and that only the dead things, the choiceless things, live in absolute obedience to the law' (20). One manifestation of this freedom is territorial, the dynamism of modern utopia naturally creating a 'migratory population', one 'as fluid and tidal as the sea' (20). In a typically imaginative forerunner of Zygmunt Bauman's sense of 'liquid modernity', and Bauman and David Lyon's notion of 'liquid surveillance', we are told that 'all local establishments, all definitions of place are even now melting under our eyes. Presently all the world will be awash with anonymous stranger men' (95). It is crucial to grasp that for Wells a world awash with anonymous stranger men is an inherently desirable, creative force.

There are limits to freedom, though: 'since man is a social animal, the play of will must fall short of absolute freedom' (20). Indeed, it might appear that freedom needs to be administered if all are to enjoy it. A Modern Utopia has a Paris-based bureau recording and transmitting information on the identities and movement of all the world's citizens. The French base can be seen as a welcome sign of international fellowship in the World State he envisions. Choosing Paris also reflects the highly bureaucratised nature of French society at the turn of the century, as well as advances made by figures such as the Frenchman Alphonse Bertillon, whose anthropomorphic system that used measurements and photographs for criminal identification had been in use for nearly two decades. This eutopia requires all inhabitants to have an identity card that they need to show when travelling. The narrator explains that these 'index cards' 'might conceivably be transparent and so contrived as to give a photographic copy promptly whenever it was needed, and they could have an attachment into which would slip a ticket bearing the name of the locality in which the individual was last reported' (96). They function differently from the credit cards Bellamy imagines.

It is worth remembering that when Wells wrote these words, international travel was possible with relatively little fuss, let alone documentation. John Torpey comments that the economic liberalism of the time 'undergirded an unprecedented trend toward the relaxation of passport controls on the movement of late nineteenth century Western Europe, a period that has been called "the closest approximation to an open world in modern times"' (Torpey 2002: 54). World War I would reverse that relaxation, but Wells is writing nearly a decade before its outbreak, seeing the documents as crucial to the efficient tracking of large movements of individuals around the globe. The description of the workings of the Paris bureau deserves lengthy quotation:

> A little army of attendants would be at work upon this index day and night. From sub-stations constantly engaged in checking back thumb-marks and numbers, an incessant stream of information would come, of births, of deaths, of arrivals at inns, of applications to post-offices for letters, of tickets taken for long journeys, of criminal convictions, marriages, applications for public doles and the like. A filter of offices would sort the stream, and all day and all night for ever a swarm of clerks would go to and fro correcting this central register, and photographing copies of its entries for transmission to the subordinate local stations, in response to their inquiries. So the inventory of the State would watch its every man and the wide world write its history as the fabric of its destiny flowed on. At last, when the citizen died, would come the last entry of all, his age and the cause of his death and the date and place of his cremation, and his card would be taken out and passed on to the universal pedigree, to a place of greater quiet, to the ever-growing galleries of the records of the dead.
> Such a record is inevitable if a Modern Utopia is to be achieved. (967)

In A Modern Utopia, the identity card outlasts the actual person whose details it contains and whose life it records. The Owner of the Voice does acknowledge that some readers might 'rebel' at the idea of being tracked, believing that they have a 'right . . . of going unrecognized and secret whither one will'. He counters that this will still be possible in terms of 'one's fellow wayfarers', and that only the State 'would share the secret of one's little concealment'. He admits that many a Liberal would find what he labels in an evocative phrase 'this organized clairvoyance' as 'the most hateful of dreams', but he responds that the suspicion of government stems from 'mental habits acquired in an evil time' (114). A modern reader, however, versed in the ways in which categories such as race, religion, sexual orientation or mental capacity were used later in the twentieth century as the basis for various forms of crimes against humanity, might look suspiciously at the seemingly benign phrase, 'and the like' in the formulation above. What might be included under this loose category, and to what purpose?

The assurance about the necessity of the identity card and the bureau that administers it, as well as the confidence in the State as responsible and benevolent might appear dangerously innocent, but this forgets that utopian texts regularly force readers to make difficult choices or face problematic scenarios; we are prodded to think and to argue with the fictive world placed before us. In A Modern Utopia, Wells's tactic of claiming that the Owner of the Voice is not him adds a further distancing effect, so that we might interpret the Owner's enthusiasm as akin to that of Raphael Hythloday, something itself to be critically assessed. (We might also deny Wells his anonymity, and read the text as though the Owner of the Voice essentially is Wells; no doubt many readers do just that.) Incorporating other perspectives, such as those of the Botanist and the Voice of Nature, Wells builds in dynamic complexity that many previous utopian works lack, being solely the account of one positively-, or negatively-inclined narrator. As the previous chapter noted, Wells was already an established novelist capable of creating more fleshed out characters than were usual in utopian writing, and he lamented the 'generalised people' who inhabited those other texts. Wells is interested in the different motivations and perspectives of characters, and though clearly the Owner of the Voice takes precedence, his views need not be accepted. This flexibility, however, is limited by *A Modern Utopia*'s decidedly masculine orientation. Wells can imagine a world in which women are liberated relative to the world of 1905 – they are allowed to be divorced, are paid full wages if they choose to have children and can fashion a career for themselves if they choose that course – but the key reference points are those of the men who engage in debate about what constitutes a modern eutopia.

Charlotte Perkins Gilman's *Herland* (1915) presents an alternative perspective. As its title implies, women are Herland's only inhabitants. Cut off for several thousand years from the rest of the world, and after a period of turmoil in which the few remaining men, after failing to take control by force, are themselves killed, Herland develops along matriarchal and matrilineal lines. Through the 'miracle' of parthenogensis, or asexual reproduction, women begin to give birth to female children without the necessity of men. Utopian texts often propose inventive solutions to various problems regarding reproduction (such as Plato's statutory festivals or Huxley's bottled cloning), and Gilman's radical response to the problem of how a land made up solely of women could survive allows her to contemplate a world in which patriarchal ideas and structures have long been rejected and forgotten. The 'discovery' of Herland by three American males (Van, who narrates, and his companions Jeff and Terry) provides the narrative and conceptual dynamic that creates an outsider's depiction of eutopia, very much in keeping with standard generic tropes. All three men initially are bound to the patriarchal mores of their times, and find it difficult to believe that a well-built, organised and successful society could be created by women – 'This is a *civilised* country . . . there must be men' (Gilman 1999: 159; original emphasis) Van protests. He and Jeff, especially, ultimately come to understand and praise the superiority of the discovered world. Before they do, the relentlessly macho Terry insists that in a land without men there will be 'no inventions or progress; it'll be awfully primitive' (156), while the more enlightened Jeff still declares patronisingly that 'It will be like a nunnery under an abbess – a peaceful, harmonious sisterhood' (156). Both are proved wrong, for Herland is vibrant and sophisticated, based on a broad power structure itself founded on the notion of Maternal Pantheism. Van and Jeff come to recognise that the inhabitants are highly skilled, intelligent, physically powerful and that 'Everything was beauty, order, perfect cleanness' (165). Rather than a divisive, competitive world, one Terry takes to be the only type capable of development and survival, Herland's concentration on Human Motherhood ensures that all children are cared for by the society at large: 'we each have a million children to have and to serve,' the men are informed, '– our children' (207).

The surveillance implications partly derive from the monitoring of the female children born in Herland that underpins Human Motherhood. One of the women tells the men that 'The children in this country are the one centre and focus of all our thoughts. Every step of our advance is always considered in its effect upon them' (204). Jeff likens this sense of community to a colony of ants, and while the sexist Terry claims that 'Women cannot cooperate – it's against nature' (204), the more philosophical Van acclaims 'the fullest and subtlest coordination' (204) that has taken place. Motherhood for those in Herland is a religion that involves, Van accepts, 'that limitless feeling of sisterhood, that wide unity of service which was so difficult for us to grasp' (205). That sense of unity, community and sisterhood feeds in to the education system, in which,

> The Herland child was born not only into a world carefully prepared, full of the most fascinating materials and opportunities to learn, but into a society of plentiful numbers of teachers, teachers born and trained, whose business it was to accompany the children along that, to us, impossible thing – the royal road to learning. (238)

Surveillance of children in Herland primarily involves benevolent supervision in order to promote individual development and communal interests. Yet the finite spaces and resources require the management of fertility, so that most women only are allowed one child. And in order to maintain the quality of the children, they practice a form of eugenics, having 'made it our first business to train out, to breed out, when possible, the lowest types' (217). As with elements from other utopian texts, this genetic culling has a certain cold rationality that shocks modern readers with knowledge of various genetic atrocities, most obviously those of the Nazis. As with Aldous Huxley's *Brave New World*, before these were revealed, eugenics often was interpreted positively, its linguistic connection to eutopia an active sign of positivity.

An important consequence of the absence of men in Herland for thousands of years before Terry, Van and Jeff arrive is that these new men, who initially understand themselves as active explorers come to discover a lost and fantastic world, find that they are under different types of visual scrutiny. Surveillance in this instance has the usual gender bias inverted, so that the men (first spotted from trees high above them by female scouts) are captured and 'exhibited'. Van comments that 'They studied us, analysed us, prepared reports about us, and this information was widely disseminated all about the land' (222). When they are anaesthetised at the end of Chapter 2, Van expects to be 'studied as curiosities', and he notes with a little concern that 'one or another pair of eyes is on us every minute except at night' (178). The men try to escape, but the overwhelming number of women quickly cuts off their exit. They are kept in a fortress for six months and in another city for three months, Van reporting that 'we were under surveillance for three more, always with a tutor or guard or both' (193). Essentially, the men are studied for any insights and advances they might provide Herland, it being a eutopia whose inhabitants 'recognised the need for improvement as well as of mere repetition' (198). This imperfect but inquisitive place overturns the men's preconceptions of 'a dull submissive monotony', where instead they find 'a daring social inventiveness far beyond our own' (216). Van and Jeff do reject their prejudices, although Terry tries to impose his masculinist notions, leading him to attempt rape. For this he is expelled from Herland. Human Motherhood and Herland survive his attack, the 'motherliness which dominated society' (209) continuing as before, ensuring that all children are protected and nurtured, monitored to ensure their proper development.

Herland joins Looking Backwards and A Modern Utopia in presenting surveillance in positive forms that are critical to the eutopian projects they all envision. Without the monitoring of (among other things) children, industry and travel respectively, the worlds imagined by Perkins, Bellamy and Wells would not flourish, nor possibly even exist. The diversity of the surveillance systems depicted, even in this small sample, and their applicability to specific forms of social organisation, indicate the range of surveillance modes recognised more than a century ago, and the heterogeneity of eutopias themselves. The twentieth century as a whole, however, was more the realm of the dystopia, particularly after the social and cultural haemorrhages of a first and then a second world war. Baccolini and Moylan note the influence of 'H. G. Wells's science fiction visions of modernity' on 'E. M. Forster's "The Machine Stops", and more famously, works such as Yevgeny Zamyatin's We, Aldous Huxley's Brave New World and George Orwell's Nineteen Eighty-Four', which, they observe, 'came to represent the classical, or canonical, form of dystopia (original emphasis; Baccolini and Moylan 2003: 1). The following chapter deals in detail with Orwell's novel, while the rest of this chapter briefly considers We and Brave New World. It also examines two films where surveillance infiltrates the workplace in negative ways – Fritz Lang's Metropolis and Charlie Chaplin's Modern Times – and one in which monitoring underpins B. F. Skinner's positive behaviourist eutopia, Walden Two.

Although written by a Russian and completed in 1921, We was first published in English in New York in 1924, acquiring a cult status that two decades later would attract Orwell. There are overlaps between We and Nineteen Eighty-Four, Zamyatin positing a dystopian world under a strict ideology and ruled over by a figure called the Great Benefactor. Zamyatin also includes ideas found in later dystopias: problems authorities have in controlling sexual desire; the craving for privacy; the distinction between the performance of orthodox action when being monitored and secret, unorthodox views; standardised identity; porous boundaries between eutopian and dystopian worlds. Set in the twenty-sixth century, We imagines OneState, a unified and uniform hyper-rational place, surrounded by a Green Wall, whose people are designated by alphanumerics – the protagonist is D-503, his female lover O-90 – and called Numbers. Their lives are organised along the lines of scientific management pioneered by the nineteenth-century American mechanical engineer Frederick Taylor:

Every morning, with six-wheeled precision, at the very same hour and very same minute, we get up, millions of us, as though we were one. At the very same hour, millions of us as one, we start work. Later, millions as one, we stop . . . And at one and the same second we leave for a stroll and go to the auditorium, to the hall for the Taylor exercises, and then to bed. (13)

D-503, as a loyal Number, initially finds nothing wrong with this, and believes the orthodox view that 'the greatest of all monuments of ancient literature that has come down to us' is 'the Railroad Timetable' (12). As well as rigid uniformity, which the Numbers cherish, OneState is a world of almost total transparency: buildings are made of glass so that Numbers are almost constantly visible to each other, except for state-approved Sex Days, when they can pull blinds down for 15 minutes. Otherwise, D-503 explains in his journal:

> we live in broad daylight inside these walls that seem to have been fashioned out of bright air, always on view. We have nothing to hide from one another. Besides, this makes it easier for the Guardians to carry out their burdensome, noble task. No telling what might go on otherwise. Maybe it was the strange opaque dwellings of the ancients that gave rise to their pitiful cellular psychology. 'My [sic] home with my castle!' Brilliant, right? (19; original emphasis)

His cynical dismissal of 'ancient' senses of privacy and ready acceptance of constant surveillance by the Guardians, coupled with the Taylorisation of action and thought signal the eradication of individual identity.

D-503 declares contentedly to the mysterious female I-330: 'Because no one is *one* but only *one of*. We're so identical...' (8; original emphasis). Her startling reply 'Are you sure?' (8), begins a process whereby D-503's identity increasingly is destabilised to the point that when he looks in the mirror he notes, 'I see myself and am astonished, like I'm looking at some "him"', adding almost immediately 'I AM NOT HIM' (59; original emphasis). A little earlier he writes arrestingly, 'I became glass. I saw into myself, inside. There were two me's. One me was the old one, D-503, Number D-503, and the other . . . The other used to just stick his hairy paws out of his shell, but now all of him came out, the shell burst open, and the pieces were just about to fly in all directions . . . and then what?' (56). Yet if D-503 has seen inside his 'glass' self, he must hide it, or risk having his imagination removed in the 'Great Operation'. His rebellious thoughts, first activated and encouraged by I-330, prompt him to link up with her and the revolutionary group, the MEPHI, who plan to overthrow OneState. The MEPHI aim to destroy the Green Wall, uniting eutopian and dystopian spaces, and integrating the humans who live on the outside. Those outsiders are distinguished by being covered in fur, something that links them to D-503, who has what he thinks are worryingly hairy hands. While the outward signs of difference are only too apparent, D-503 struggles to hide his new self from the Guardians.

He has previously been happy to be totally unfree, seeing freedom as 'disorganised wildness' (13). This is the sanctioned stance, his friend R-13 mocking Adam and Eve, who,

> were offered a choice: happiness without freedom, or freedom without happiness, nothing else. Those idiots chose freedom. And then what? Then for centuries they were homesick for the chains. (61)

The novel vividly and unsparingly exposes the motivations and justifications of complicity and orthodoxy, the reality that the majority might prefer chains over freedom, group identity over individuality, all guaranteed by the constant surveillance of their peers, the Guardians and the Great Benefactor. Ultimately, D-503 suffers the Great Operation and returns to his orthodox self, though with the fate of OneState still in the balance. As Winston will do in *Nineteen Eighty-Four*, D-503 proclaims his allegiance to authority, although in the latter's case not to the Great Benefactor, but to reason, 'Because reason has to win' (225). The reader is not expected to agree.

*We* exemplifies a pattern in twentieth and twenty-first century dystopias, of an individual rebelling against an oppressive and intrusive power, some successfully (as in *The Handmaid's Tale* or *The Truman Show*), others not (*Nineteen Eighty-Four* or *Brazil*). It also examines the tension between adjacent eutopian and dystopian spaces. Fritz Lang's germinal film *Metropolis* does this as well, presenting a starkly stratified world in which the wealthy play in eutopian gardens amidst the trappings of modernity and modernism, while below ground, uniformed and standardised workers perform the enervating industrial tasks that maintain the luxurious lives of those above. H. G. Wells's *The Time Machine* (1895) presents a version of this division with his Eloi and Morlocks, but where with Wells the subterranean Morlocks prey upon the effete Eloi, in *Metropolis* those above are oblivious to the enslaved workers beneath whose robotic movements are geared to Taylorised rhythms. The link between these worlds appears in the form of the pure young woman from below, Maria, whose visits the eutopian world and captivates Freder, the son of Joh Fredersen, the tough-minded Master of Metropolis. Freder will descend to the world of the workers below, and in the film's finale will act as mediator (the 'heart') between his father ('the brain') and the leader of the workers, Grot ('the hands'). The complex plot involves intrigue and deception, but in surveillance terms a key element of Fredersen's control is the prototype of an Orwellian telescreen, which he uses to observe the workers from his palatial office, and from which he issues instructions to his foreman so that the workers can be exploited to maximum effect.

The scientific management that powers the eutopian world constitutes a form of monitored arrangement that, unlike Bellamy's projection, reduces individuals to machine parts and ruthlessly pushes them to the edge of endurance and beyond. In a key scene Freder sees the excessive demand made on workers who overload a massive machine so that it explodes, killing and injuring workers. Disoriented by the chaos, he imagines the huge device as an ancient temple that devours workers, crying out 'Moloch', a deity to whom children were sacrificed. Eventually, and somewhat reluctantly, the competing interests of Fredersen and Grot are reconciled, partly by Maria, partly by Fredersen, the implication being that the heartless industrial system, built on the sort of managerial and organisational principles lauded by D-503, will be dismantled. Lang exploits cinema's visual possibilities in showing the Taylorised movements of the monitored workers as mechanised ballet, and in Freder's crazed vision of the transformed machine as Moloch. In one of early cinema's most iconic scenes he also explores the scopophilia inherent in film viewing, depicting the lascivious dance performed by a robot Maria created by an archetypal mad scientist, Rotwang. This robot version of Maria will be used by Fredersen to deceive the workers, but she also performs an erotic dance for the male elite that reduces them to mesmerised voyeurs. The stylised shots of the watching men, their faces aghast with passion, are interspersed with the disturbingly compelling image of the screen full of eyeballs, testament to the homogeneity of the men's lust and the centrality of vision to gratification. Simultaneously, the sequence alerts the audience to their own voyeuristic tendencies, the power of the image, and the problematic pleasure surveillance can galvanise. *Metropolis* examines links between pleasure, vision and eutopia as well as control, monitoring and dystopia.

Only a few years later, Aldous Huxley's *Brave New World* also distinguishes eutopian and dystopian spaces, in this case the superficial, materialistic, pleasure-seeking World State, and desolate desert landscapes like that of Malpais (which translates as 'badland'). Huxley's vision of the future, set in the year 632 AF – 'AF' standing for After [Henry] Ford' – begins provocatively in the Central London Hatchery and Conditioning Centre. New citizens are created using artificial breeding techniques that produce a hierarchy of five classes from Alpha down to Epsilon, who are then conditioned to reinforce the attributes pertinent to their class. Huxley describes the final stages of the process in detail:

> And already the bottle had passed, and it was the turn of the labellers. Heredity, date of fertilization, membership of the Bokanovsky Group – all details were transferred from test tube to bottle. No longer anonymous, but named, identified, the procession marched slowly on; on through an opening in the wall, slowly into the Social Predestination Room.
> 'Eighty-eight cubic metres of card-index,' said Mr Foster with relish, as they entered.
> 'Containing all the relevant information,' added the Director.
> 'Brought up to date every morning.'
> 'And co-ordinated every afternoon.'
> 'On the basis of which we make our calculations.'
> 'So many individuals, of such and such quality,' said Mr Foster.
> 'The optimum Decanting Rate at any given moment.' (7)

The novel radically updates the selective breeding that takes place in Plato's *Republic*, through a scientific process that requires constant surveillance to ensure the production of different classes of citizens custom-made for specific roles. When Huxley wrote the novel in the early 1930s such genetic manipulation was fantastic, but as someone who had planned to be a scientist before a bout of blindness in his teens, and whose brother became an eminent evolutionary biologist, Huxley's projection was not entirely fanciful.

*Brave New World* rejects Wells's optimism, Huxley writing to a friend that *Brave New World* was 'a novel about the future', one that dealt with 'the horror of the Wellsian Utopia and a revolt against it' (Huxley 1969: 348). Huxley includes an epigraph in the novel from the Russian thinker Nikolai Berdiaeff that asks whether, in an age when eutopias seem possible, people might want something non-utopian, less perfect, but more free. Genetic surveillance and the scientifically stratified society deriving from it, as well as postnatal conditioning, remain foundational to the structure and cultural texture of World State, ensuring the stability yearned for by citizens after years of wars and other forms of chaos and deprivation, a desire distilled in the state motto COMMUNITY IDENTITY STABILITY. This is Huxley's satirical reworking of the Declaration of Independence's 'Life, Liberty and the pursuit of Happiness' or the French Revolution's 'Liberté, Egalité, Fraternité'. The biological process is not foolproof, and very occasional errors such as Bernard Marx, an Alpha who has been decanted incorrectly before birth, refuse to fit into the heavily conformist world that employs sex, drugs and mass consumption to pacify its citizens. Where dystopias often oppress their citizens with restrictions and scarcity, *Brave New World* sedates them with abundance. That strategy also has its surveillance component, for the sexual orgies, sports, drugs and other pleasures are required to be enjoyed communally, with those unwilling to participate (such as Bernard) or experiencing them in an unsanctioned manner, quickly exposed as nonconformist. As one slogan has it: 'When the individual feels, the community reels' (84). Peer surveillance ensures the endless and excessive consumption necessary to maintain the economy, reinforced by sayings such as 'ending is better than mending' that encourage the purchase of the new rather than the repair of the old; 'old' itself is a pejorative term.

Surveillance in *Brave New World* operates in different modes and encompasses biology, economics, personal relations and social structure. It also involves monitoring spaces so that degraded places such as Malpais are kept separate from eutopian zones. Predictably, the most subversive character comes from Malpais: the independent-minded, natural born John Savage, who has learned morality from Shakespeare's works. While initially enchanted when brought to World State – he cries out, 'Oh brave new world' in adoration, a reference to the innocent Miranda's similarly naïve declaration in *The Tempest* – he eventually comes to reject all that he sees, opting to commit suicide rather than continue to lead what he takes to be the immoral life in eutopia. Before this despairing final act, though, he has become a celebrity in a world obsessed with appearances. As with *Metropolis*, *Brave New World* explores the problematic allure of voyeurism on characters. David Rosen and Aaron Santesso observe that Huxley is interested in 'subtler, noncoercive, multidirectional forms that surveillance can take', and is 'deeply invested in the more pleasurable or participatory forms of social watching'. They read Lenina Crowe, for example, as a character who seems to 'derive her very being from the social gaze – and is nothing without it' (Rosen and Santesso 2013: 183). Bernard Marx's association with John Savage even turns him into a minor celebrity, tempting him to conform.

The dangers of conformity are explored in Charlie Chaplin's 1936 classic, *Modern Times*, which, as with *We*, *Metropolis* and *Brave New World*, considers connections between the standardisation of identity, their links to modern forms of industrial production, and the role of surveillance in maintaining inhumane order. Chaplin deals with these weighty subjects comically, using his character the Little Tramp as an Everyman trapped with others on a production line. The film opens with the image of a clock, governing symbol of modern rationality, that quickly dissolves into a flock of sheep entering a chute, a solitary black sheep amid the white mob symbolic of the non-conformist. This in turn dissolves into a flock of workers leaving the subway on their way to work – with obvious inferences – and then entering a massive factory in which, as relatively miniscule figures, they are looked down upon from on high by foremen. The scene then changes to the President of the Electro Steel Corp in his office, one wall of which has a large screen by which he can, like the Master of Metropolis, communicate orders to his foremen and observe his workers. He first commands the foreman to speed up Section 5, where Chaplin works as a nut tightener, to '4.1', the number itself a form of arbitrary and oppressive precision. On the shop floor Chaplin and his fellow workers on the production line struggle to perform menial tasks at a steadily increasing pace. Where *Looking Backward*'s bureaucratised industrial army produces efficiently for the common good, the mindless and dehumanising work in *Modern Times* reduces the workers to standardised and disposable units of Taylorist management. Where the President of the United States watches benevolently and authoritatively over Bellamy's Boston of the future, the President of the Electro Steel Corp utilises televisual monitoring to extract greater productivity from exhausted workers. This is played out comically, with brilliantly choreographed gags that show Chaplin and his two co-workers locked together in frantic ritual. The reality of surveillance in the workplace gets reinforced when Chaplin tries to have a cigarette in the factory washroom he presumes to be 'private' space. This room has its own television screen, however, which the President activates; seeing Chaplin, he orders him back to work. In another scene that erupts into brilliant slapstick, an automatic feeding machine, designed so that employees can be fed while still working, repeatedly malfunctions, attacking the traumatised Chaplin who is trapped within it.

Lang's grimly orchestrated workplace in *Metropolis* is transformed in *Modern Times* into an automated anarchy for comic effect, but both films record the imposition of principles drawn from scientific management on hapless workers, caught in a monitored world of robotic action and inhumane expectations. In *Metropolis* workers are killed when the massive machine they tend explodes, while in *Modern Times*, after the President twice gives instruction via the television screen for the production line speed to be increased, Chaplin's character is driven crazy. Unable to keep pace with the line speed, he literally is drawn into the inner workings of the machinery, sliding between the cogs while continuing to tighten nuts. When hauled from the machine his madness continues as he flits around the factory, chaotically spraying co-workers with oil or chasing women, the hexagonal buttons on their dresses reminding him of the nuts he compulsively tightens. As a result of his various transgressions and distressed mental state an ambulance rushes him to an asylum. While dazzlingly comic, Chaplin's satire on the modern production line makes a serious and compelling critique of the vigorously scrutinised workplace that reduces workers to monitored automata while not allowing zones where they might escape the boss's profit-focused gaze. *Modern Times* deftly and engagingly accounts for the intimate relationship between modern capitalism and surveillance, with the integral and inevitable deterioration of workers' rights, agency and privacy.

Not all utopian texts of the period presented surveillance negatively. B. F.

Skinner's *Walden Two* offers up a behaviourist eutopia that rebuts *Brave New World*'s ridiculing of hypnopedia and conditioning. Huxley's point is not that these and other methods are ineffective so much as that they produce creatures unable to think and feel for themselves, programmed instead to accept the pre-ordained and monitored life of World State. That this might be achieved without the biological technology required in *Brave New World* suggested that the eutopia of compliant, happy individuals was far nearer than Huxley might have expected or wished. *Walden Two*, its title registering the influence of Henry David Thoreau's eutopian *Walden* (1854) published nearly a century earlier, would itself become a model for intentional communities in the 1960s (see Kuhlmann 2005). The novel adheres to the general principle of behavioural engineering, and focuses not on the global eutopias usually proposed in the twentieth century, but on a small community of roughly 1,000 people. The community depicted in *Walden Two* represents a pro-totype that might if successful be applied to larger communities. Skinner, looking back from the mid-1970s, stated that an 'important theme' was that 'political action was to be avoided' and that what was needed was not new kinds of leaders or government 'but further knowledge about human behaviour and new ways of applying that knowledge to cultural practice' (Skinner 1976: xvi). While organised rationally and dedicated to the idea that science holds the key to understanding and improving human behaviour, the fictional community established in *Walden Two* by T. E. Frazier (whose name suggests B. F. Skinner, of course) has, according to Frazier, 'a roundness, a flexibility, a flow' (39). The effect, he assures the group who visits Walden Two, is 'psychological. We're utterly free of that institutional atmosphere which is inevitable when everyone is doing the same thing at the same time' (39). This vision is entirely at odds with the dystopian arrangement of time and space in *We*, or *Metropolis*, or *Modern Times*, where psychological damage is almost inevitable under the crude scientific management theories of industrial production.

*Walden Two* was first published only a year before *Nineteen Eighty-Four*, and it says much for the booming post-war economy in the United States that much of the novel's focus and criticism is directed not at austerity as at crass materialism. The community aims to do away with this by dispensing with money and having labour-credits. This arrangement consciously updates the scheme in *Looking Backward* (Frazier refers to it on page 46), but the far smaller scale here means that rather than sprawling bureaucracies, the records of worker credit expenditure can be monitored from 'just entries in a ledger' (45). There is a form of government, though, with 'Managers of Food, Health, Play, Arts, Dentistry, Dairy' as well as 'dozens of others'. A Board of Planners 'make policies, review the work of the Managers, keep an eye on the state of the nation in general' (48). The crucial element of Walden Two, though, the factor that Frazier feels underpins its harmony, is the behavioural engi-neering of children from infants upwards. In *Brave New World* children are crudely manipulated in post-natal experiments that fit them to their place in the genetic hierarchy. Walden Two requires setting 'up certain behavioural processes which will lead the individual to design his own "good" conduct when the time comes. We call that a sort of "self-control"' (96). The community inculcates self-control using scientific experiments that entail 'shaping human behaviour'. Where benevolent maternal surveillance determines the eutopian world of *Herland*, in *Walden Two* benevolent behaviourist surveillance ensures that all its 'ethical training is complete by the age of four' (98). A range of 'safely administered' lessons and experiments carried out by the social engineers during a person's childhood work towards not a docile conformity, in Frazier's eyes, but to generalised goodness. He acknowledges the possibility of failures, but comments that 'We watch for undesired consequences just as a scientist watches for disturbing factors in his experiments' (101). The language suggests the far more manipulative and determining *Brave New World*, but Frazier states that apart from 'discouraging childbearing by the unfit' (a category he does not define), the community does not engage in genetic engineering (126). In *Walden*, Thoreau famously states that 'The mass of men live lives of quiet desperation' (Thoreau 2008: 8). In *Walden Two*, Frazier remains confident that properly monitored social engineering will lead to individual flourishing, social harmony and far more complete and well-lived lives.

This sweep over eutopias and dystopias before *Nineteen Eighty-Four* leaves out far more than it includes, but it does hint at the myriad ways in which utopian novels and films represent and assess aspects of surveillance in advance of Orwell's now-classic vision. Especially in twentieth-century works, where multidimensional characters begin to replace the lifeless creatures Wells complains of, these writers and filmmakers explore how surveillance might influence or challenge what it means to be human. Especially from Bellamy on, they start to comprehend some of the ways in which modern society has surveillance built into its metaphorical foundations, how various forms of scrutiny are integral to processes and structures that impinge upon the present and promise to model or direct the future. These visions are anything but uniform, even when they depict potential worlds where uniformity is ensured and required by surveillance. Utopian texts are sometimes criticised for being programmatic or overly-determined, populated by two-dimensional characters whose purpose remains limited to embodying and enacting an 'author's message'. No doubt this can be the case with individual novels or films, but the same dismissal can also be made of all genres. Understood collectively, though, utopian works supply amazingly variegated and imaginative examples. They call readers and viewers to evaluate not only what is presented to them on screen or the page, but to reflect on how those visions relate to and critically assess the societies in which they live, and to project those in which they might live. This open-ended, speculative function remains fundamental to the genre even when specific texts appear to foreclose possibilities and options. From Thomas More's *Utopia* onwards, they have actively provoked thinking on innumerable topics and proposed as many brave new worlds for us to contemplate. Understanding the generic network constructed by eutopias and dystopias over the centuries, we better understand their individual worth. As critical as *Nineteen Eighty-Four* was to the early stages of surveillance studies, it was never the first utopian work to consider surveillance, nor would it be the last. That said, it still warrants attention.

# 3   Nineteen Eighty-Four

Whatever sociologists have to say, it would be foolish to ignore the one name that is always invoked in surveillance studies: George Orwell. His novel, *Nineteen Eighty-Four*, and its monstrous anti-hero, Big Brother, have become bywords within the surveillance genre. (Lyon 2003: 9)

I do not believe that the kind of society I have described necessarily *will* arrive, but I believe . . . that something resembling it *could* arrive . . . (Orwell 1998g: 135; original emphasis).

She would not accept as a law of nature that the individual is always defeated. (Orwell 1997b: 142)

David Lyon's qualified and slightly defensive 2003 validation of *Nineteen Eighty-Four* above foreshadows Benjamin's Goold's somewhat reluctant acceptance in 2004, quoted in the introduction to this study, about the novel's undeniable impact on half a century of popular and academic imagination. A decade after Lyon's observation, John Gilliom and Torin Monahan are more openly dismissive in their comment that:

Big Brother, from George Orwell's novel *Nineteen Eighty-Four*, is probably the most famous bogeyman and symbol of surveillance society . . . [but] doesn't really make sense of *our* world. . . . Much of the surveillance in our lives is non-threatening – hardly the sense we get from Orwell's classic dystopia. (Gilliom and Monahan 2013: 20–1)

They have good reason to be sceptical: Facebook did not even exist when Lyon wrote his assessment, nor Google Maps, Twitter, Instagram or the game-changing iPhone, along with other technical inventions and social innovations that have transformed how an exponentially increasing number of Internet users communicate, find information, organise their finances, connect with and perform themselves to their real and virtual 'friends'. The new reality – that all these activities leave digital traces that are collected, sorted and utilised by countless public and private agencies and corporations – reconfigures notions of identity, privacy, society, threats real and potential in ways that would probably surprise the David Lyon of 2003, let alone the George Orwell of 1949. Certainly they mark out a world very different from that imagined in *Nineteen Eighty-Four*.

Instances such as the Edward Snowden revelations or WikiLeaks disclosures play to more traditional 'Orwellian' fears about despotic totalitarian forces at work within and between Western states. Gilliom and Monahan, however (and they are not alone), simply make the reasonable observation that *Nineteen Eighty-Four* does not really make sense of our world in all its digitised novelty. They comment that:

> For most of us, the government is not a despotic totalitarian force watching our every move at the slightest sign of deviation. For most of us, surveillance comes not from a unitary state bent only on domination and control, but from a chaotic blend of government, media, work, friends, family, insurance companies, bankers, and automated processing systems. (20–1)

They are correct, and this book argues that Orwell's novel cannot and indeed should not be freighted with the importance it retains in the press and in public discourse. We need to go beyond *Nineteen Eighty-Four* in order to understand and respond rationally to the challenges good and ill that surveillance presents to us. That said, its continuing and compelling ubiquity warrants attention, for if nothing else that pervasiveness confirms how creative texts collectively can inform our awareness of surveillance. Orwell's own statement above, the italics emphasising that his book proposes a potential rather than an inevitable future, insists that we must be active agents in constructing better tomorrows, or in staving off worse tomorrows. That statement, as his biographer Bernard Crick notes, is a conflated and corrected version of a letter Orwell wrote to F. A. Henson, an official of the United Automobile Workers in the United States. Orwell responds to Henson's query about the novel's political position. Orwell had been told that the *New York Daily News* 'wrote up "1984" as an attack upon the Labour Government', something he emphatically and publically denied. This confusion or contestation over the 'meaning' of *Nineteen Eighty-Four* within months of it appearing speaks to the subjective quality of literary interpretation generally, a quality enhanced perhaps by the conscious provocation the novel engages in. This chapter interprets the novel as presenting less of a totalised surveillance world than is often assumed, one in which there are gaps and spaces where Big Brother does not or cannot watch you.

Orwell's double quotation marks around the date 1984 highlight a particular and peculiar element of the novel's approach. While completing *Animal Farm* in 1943, he had begun sketching ideas in a notebook for two much longer novels, one titled *The Quick and The Dead*, the other provisionally titled *The Last Man in Europe*. On page 2 of notes for the latter (Orwell: 1998b: 367–70), he sets down things to 'be brought in', the first item of which is the now iconic word 'Newspeak'. We now know that Newspeak, along with other elements from that notebook examined later in this chapter, would be integral to *Nineteen Eighty-Four*, but Orwell did not begin to develop his ideas fully until 1945, and would not complete the novel until December 1948. For much of that time the working title remained *The Last Man in Europe*, and as late as October 1948 Orwell still had not decided on that title or his alternative, *Nineteen Eighty-Four* (Orwell 1998f: 457). His publisher in the United States, (Harcourt, Brace) was unhappy with *Nineteen Eighty-Four*, and Orwell, surprisingly for a writer who often fought aggressively against the whims of publishers, agreed that it might appear there with the other title, writing to his literary agent, Leonard Moore: 'I doubt whether it hurts a book to be published under different names in Britain and the USA' (Orwell 1998f: 456). The eventual selection of *Nineteen Eighty-Four* on both sides of the Atlantic would have important effects on the novel's significance, creating an association with the future that would not have been the case with *The Last Man in Europe*. Additionally, the chosen title generalised the situation of Winston Smith well beyond Airstrip One or Europe itself, so that readers around the globe could and would incorporate the scenario into their own situation, their own thinking. By decoupling it from a geographical zone, Orwell broadened its applicability.

For all that, the title he settled on was a phrase, not a year. A persistent myth is that the year 1984 was chosen because it reversed the last two numbers of the year 1948, when Orwell was completing the novel. But the typescript clearly shows that Orwell originally had Winston Smith write '1980' in his diary; Orwell later changed that to '1982' and later again to '1984' (Orwell 1984: 23). While the year appears in Winston's diary, as we would expect of such a document, a novel called *1984* would inevitably have suggested a prophecy, something to be checked against the actual year for accuracy. Anthony Burgess, author of *A Clockwork Orange*, falls into this trap with his *1985*, which projects a future Britain from the year 1976, when Burgess's novel was published. Burgess's work is his rebuttal of *Nineteen Eighty-Four* as prophecy, but the utopian texts Orwell read and drew from or reacted against predominantly had titles that indicated broad applicability: *News from Nowhere*; *A Modern Utopia*; *The Iron Heel*; *Brave New World*; *We*; *The Sleeper Wakes*. The title *Nineteen Eighty-Four* denotes a concept rather than a year, similar to what Joseph Heller would later achieve with *Catch-22*. It evokes an atmosphere more encompassing and open-ended and therefore more menacing than would have been the case with *1984*, which perhaps accounts for Orwell's indicative quotation marks in his response to the *New York Daily News*. The title as a phrase helped keep the novel 'fresh' in readers' minds even after the use by date had been reached, an effect that would not have kicked in had Orwell called it *The Last Man in Europe*. Orwell means the novel to continue provoking beyond a single moment, something emphasised in his advice noted in Chapter 1: 'The moral to be drawn . . . is a simple one: *Don't let it happen. It depends on you*' (Orwell 1998g: 134). Rather than a pessimistic or even a despairing text for a man who knew he was terminally ill, *Nineteen Eighty-Four*, like many a dystopia, was written to warn readers, to stimulate them, not to stifle their thoughts and actions. Time has shown that, more than any other text on surveillance, the novel has done just that.

Within six months of Orwell's death, however, and only a year after the first hardback publication in Britain, the American publisher Signet produced a paper-back edition with the title rendered as *1984*, establishing a pattern in that country only reinforced by a 1953 CBS television adaption starring Eddie Albert as Winston Smith, and Michael Anderson's 1956 film adaptation, starring a transatlantic cast featuring Americans Edmond O'Brien and Jan Sterling as Winston and Julia. The BBC's 1953 adaptation, which generated a parliamentary debate of over what was seen as its excessive violence, retained *Nineteen Eighty-Four* as its title. Many translations of the novel (including into Japanese, Norwegian, Italian, Dutch and French) used *1984* as a title (see Fenwick 1998: 147–53). One of the most culturally significant examples that specifically tied the novel to the year came in 1984 itself, occurred when the Apple Macintosh desktop computer was launched as the inno-vative alternative to IBM. Apple employed director Ridley Scott, who had recently completed *Blade Runner*, to produce an advertisement portraying Apple as a subver-sive individual destroying a totalitarian power that viewers might have interpreted as IBM. Shown only once nationally on American television, during the 1983 Super Bowl, the one minute ad, replete with imagery that evoked the 'Two Minutes Hate' from the novel, finished with the caption: 'On January 24th, Apple will introduce the Macintosh. And you'll see why 1984 will not be like "1984".' The associations were so powerful that the company was requested to 'cease and desist' showing the ad, which it did, but by then the ad had done its public work. It has since been recognised as a classic ad, even though, as William Coulson observes, it also 'was considered a flagrant infringement of copyright and trademark laws' (Coulson 2009: 106).

We might treat the ad differently by understanding how it connects into and deftly employs an important generic precursor, riffing on established connotations while taking them in new directions. The same could be said of *Nineteen Eighty-Four* itself, which consciously takes on established tropes, sometimes questions them, and speaks to concerns and themes, character types and narratives already raised by the utopian genre. We profit from understanding *Nineteen Eighty-Four* within a network extending back at least to Thomas More. The chapters that follow illustrate how Orwell productively triggers some later novels and films, while other utopian texts create scenarios distinct from those he did or even could imagine, offering readers and viewers an ever-increasing catalogue of possibilities. This chapter offers a sustained interpretation that challenges readings of *Nineteen Eighty-Four* that deal superficially with the novel's treatment and assessment of surveillance. Familiarity can breed neglect as well as contempt, the connections between the text and the topic seeming so self-evident and well-established that some general readers and scholars miss complexities and nuances. Those readings often downplay or fail to recognise critical factors, such as the monitoring of written and spoken language, the varied levels or zones of surveillance that operate within Oceania, the subver-sive energy of Julia – exemplified in the quotation at the start of the chapter – the complicity on the part of the many that remains crucial to the maintenance of the Party, and what might be seen as the failure of that Party really to monitor inside the head of Winston Smith. In addressing these and other aspects, this chapter re-presents *Nineteen Eighty-Four* as an important text on the topic not because its depiction of surveillance provides a comprehensive reading of our time – it does not – but because it still has things to teach attentive readers about certain aspects of contemporary surveillance, and because it prepares the way for inventive texts that open up new surveillance prospects.

Orwell's interest in utopias derives much of its energy from his lifelong reading of H. G. Wells. In his essay 'Wells, Hitler and the World State' (1941) he writes 'that I doubt whether anyone who was writing between 1920 and 1940 . . . influenced the young so much. The minds of all of us, and therefore of the physical world, would be perceptibly different if Wells had never existed' (Orwell 1998a: 539). As a boy he expressed the desire to produce something along the lines of *A Modern Utopia* (Orwell and US), and Crick relates that he borrowed the copy of a family friend 'so often and admired it so much that eventually it was given to him' (Crick 1992: 93). By 1937, though, Orwell's admiration had curdled, so that in *The Road to Wigan Pier* he characterises Wells as ' "the arch-priest of 'progress'"', and as someone who 'cannot write with any conviction *against* "progress" . . . The thought that he cannot face is that the machine itself might be the enemy' (1997a: 188). By this stage, Orwell finds Wells's thinking blinkered and potentially repellent to the potential socialists Orwell was trying to encourage in *Wigan Pier*. 'In his more characteristic Utopias (*The Dream, Men Like Gods*, etc.)', Orwell writes,

> he returns to optimism and to a vision of humanity, 'liberated' by the machine, as a race of enlightened sunbathers whose sole topic of conversation is their own superiority to their ancestors. *Brave New World* belongs to a later time and to a generation which has seen through the swindle of 'progress'. It contains its own contradictions . . . but it is at least a memorable assault on the more fat-bellied type of perfectionism. Allowing for the exaggerations of caricature, it probably expresses what a majority of thinking people feel about machine-civilization. (Orwell 1997a: 189)

Elsewhere, he compares Wells and Huxley from different angles, writing in 1940, for example, that *Brave New World* is 'a sort of post-war parody of the Wellsian utopia' in which the hedonistic tendencies 'are immensely exaggerated'. While he grants that Huxley's work is a brilliant caricature of the 1930s, he argues that it probably casts 'no light on the future. No society of that kind last more than a couple of generations, because a ruling class which thought principally of a "good time" would soon lose its vitality. A ruling class has got to have a strict morality, a quasi-religious belief in itself, a *mystique*' (Orwell 1998a: 211; original emphasis). He makes this judgement in a review of the 1940 reprinting of Jack London's *The Iron Heel*, comparing that work with Wells's *The Sleeper Wakes* and Huxley's *Brave New World*. *The Iron Heel* gets assessed as 'hugely inferior' to *The Sleeper Wakes*, but for Orwell it has the advantage that 'London could grasp something that Wells apparently could not, and that is that hedonistic societies do not endure' (211). Orwell contends that London's love of violence lets him comprehend how 'the possessing class would behave when once they were seriously menaced', justifying his view that London had 'what one might fairly call a Fascist strain' (212). During World War II, unsurprisingly, London's crude but perceptive representation of the state dominated by power and by pain, as opposed to one founded on hedonism, seems to Orwell the more appropriate reading of the moment, a more convincing projection of possible futures.

On Christmas Eve 1943 Orwell proposes a different argument in one of his short 'As I Please' articles for *Tribune*, where he distinguishes between neo-reactionary or neo-pessimist writers – who believe that 'Man is non-perfectable, merely political changes can affect nothing, progress is an illusion' – and Socialists. He acknowledges that the neo-pessimists are more likely to be proved right in many instances, but indicates that 'The real answer is to dissociate Socialism from Utopianism. Nearly all neo-pessimist apologetic consists in putting up a man of straw and knocking down again. The man of straw is called Human Perfectibility' (Orwell 1998c: 35). We can hear in this position a forerunner of the argument seven decades later, touched on the introduction to this book, where Lucy Sargisson criticises John Gray for conflating utopianism and perfectionism. Orwell adopts a similar tactic in defending socialism: 'Socialism is not perfectionist, perhaps not even hedonistic. Socialists don't claim to be able to make the world perfect: they claim to be able to make it better' (35). The same *Tribune* issue also carried an article by 'John Freeman', which Peter Davison attributes to Orwell (see 37–8), titled 'Can Socialists be Happy?' Here, Orwell notes that 'by far the best known Utopias are those of H.G. Wells', and though he accepts that readers would like to abolish the things that Wells abolishes in works such as *A Modern Utopia* – 'Ignorance, war, poverty, dirt, disease' – he asks 'is there anyone who actually wants to live in a Wellsian Utopia?' He calls *Brave New World* 'an expression of the actual fear that modern man feels of the rationalised hedonistic society which it is within his power to create' (Orwell 1998c: 39–40). Nor are Wells's utopian visions the only one deserving critique, Orwell calling William Morris's *News From Nowhere* 'a sort of goody-goody version of the Wellsian Utopia. Everyone is kindly and reasonable ... but the impression left behind is that of a sort of watery melancholy' (40). What is clear is that eutopian examples fail to provide anything other than points of harsh contrast to the world he later envisions in *Nineteen Eighty-Four*.

The more obvious generic connections are dystopian works such as Jack London's *The Iron Heel* and Yevgeny Zamyatin's *We*. Orwell reviewed *We* for *Tribune* in January 1946, labelling it 'not a book of the first order, but ... certainly an unusual one' (Orwell 1998e: 13). He makes the claim that 'Aldous Huxley's *Brave New World* must be partly derived from it' (something Huxley would deny). Orwell suggests that Zamyatin's book 'has a political point which the other lacks', for while with Huxley 'the problem of "human nature" is in a sense solved, because it assumes that by prenatal treatment, drugs and hypnotic suggestion that the human organism can be specialised anyway that is designed', in *We* 'many of the ancient instincts are still there' (14). For Orwell, Huxley's failure to understand the role of political power means that 'though everyone [in *Brave New World*] is happy in a vacuous way, life has become so pointless that it is difficult to believe that such a society could endure'. He also judges that Zamyatin's 'intuitive grasp of the rational side of totalitarianism – human sacrifice, cruelty as an end in itself, the worship of a leader who is credited with divine attributes – makes Zamyatin's book superior to Huxley's' (15). Much of the *We* review is a summary of the novel's plot and themes, elements that many critics have seen in *Nineteen Eighty-Four* itself. Certainly, *We* captured Orwell's imagination, when he read about it in *25 Years of Soviet Russian Literature*, a study by the American scholar Gleb Struve. Orwell reviewed Struve's book positively in 1944, writing to him that it has 'roused my interest in Zamyatin's "We", which I had not heard of before. I am interested in that kind of book, and even keep making notes for one myself that may get written soon or later' (Orwell 1998c: 99). He would later try with Struve to get Fredric Warburg to bring out an edition, describing it to Warburg in March 1949 as:

> an interesting link on the chain of Utopia books. On the one hand it debunks the super-rational, hedonistic type of Utopia (I think Aldous Huxley's 'Brave New World' must be plagiarised from it to some extent), but on the other hand it takes account of the diabolism & (sic) the tendency to return to an earlier form of civilization which seems to be part of totalitarianism. It seems to me a good book in the same way as 'The Iron Heel', but better written. (Orwell 1998g: 72)

We see in this small sampling of responses to utopian writings generally (for an extended treatment see Steinhoff: 3–54) Orwell's awareness of the illuminating and sometimes perplexing variety of projections. What is also clear is his attempt to relate them both to his contemporary world and to imagined futures. He had already created a form of critical dystopia in *Animal Farm*, his self-described 'fairy story' depicting the betrayal of the successful revolution by animals against their human masters. While the animals at the end recognise that the intellectual pigs have deceived them, that very recognition suggests a political consciousness they did not have at the beginning of the tale. Such consciousness is manifested in the revolutionary song of solidarity, 'Beasts of England', taught to them by Old Major at the beginning of the narrative and still taught to the younger animals 'years later' by the maternal horse, Clover. In terms of genre and approach, the animal fable was an anomaly, given Orwell's previous work, and the same can be said of *Nineteen Eighty-Four*.

As already noted, his notebook for *The Last Man in Europe* includes the word Newspeak, a key term that would contribute forcefully to *Nineteen Eighty-Four* and eventually enter the lexicon. The manipulation of language had been a concern from at least the time of *Homage to Catalonia* in 1937, as it was in *Animal Farm* where the pigs' control is advanced through the adulteration of the seven commandments, eventually distilled in the cynical slogan 'All Animals Are Equal But Some Animals are More Equal than Others'. In addition to Newspeak, the notebook also mentions such things as the 'Position of the proles', the 'Dual standard of thought', 'The party slogans (War is peace. Ignorance is strength. Freedom slavery [sic]), 'The Two Minutes Hate', 'Leader-worship, etc' and 'Were we at war with Eastasia' (Orwell 1998b: 367–70). There is, however, no reference to specific characters (some are rendered as 'A, B and C'). Other elements in the notebook did not make it into the eventual novel, something quite normal in the transition from a writer's preliminary ideas to a completed text. One thing that strikes the reader versed in the novel Orwell did complete, though, is that, the reference to Newspeak apart, there is no mention of surveillance: no Big Brother, or 'Big Brother is Watching You' posters; no telescreens; no spies or Thought Police; no Ministry of Truth or Ministry of Love. Indeed, one phrase, 'Impossibility of detecting similar memories in anyone else', exposes a barrier to effective monitoring, especially of the large scale and systematic kind that find their way into *Nineteen Eighty-Four*.

For some commentators, *We* functions as the catalyst for the eventual novel. Peter Davison suggests, for example, that one source for the Golden Country in Orwell's novel is 'the habitat beyond the Green Wall that bounds the totalitarian regime' in *We* (Davison 1996: 96), and elements such as The Benefactor, mass gatherings affirming the power of OneState, uniforms or yunis, D-503's subversive journal, his sexual rebellion with I-330, and his eventual mental pacification via the Great Operation show up as traces in *Nineteen Eighty-Four*. Orwell began serious work on what would become *Nineteen Eighty-Four* in 1945, and in that same year the journalist Alan Moray Williams lent him a copy of the French translation of *We*, titled *Nous Autres*. Orwell's *Tribune* review confirms his interest in and qualified approval of the novel. Given the interactivity inherent in utopian works these connections are unsurprising, although ironically, in his review, Orwell proposes a clearer generic link between *We* and *Brave New World*:

> Both books deal with the rebellion of the primitive human spirit against a rationalized, mechanized, painless world, and both stories are supposed to take place six hundred years hence. The atmosphere of the two books is similar, and it is roughly speaking the same type of society that is being described, though Huxley's book shows less political awareness and is more influenced by recent biological and psychological theories. (Orwell 1998e: 14)

Orwell's summary of parallels between *We* and *Brave New World* highlights how the rationalised, mechanical and painless worlds they depict differ fundamentally from the distressed and malevolent austerity that pervades *Nineteen Eighty-Four*. Oceania is not a shiny futuristic fantasy, but is threateningly possible, something that could result from the sort of rapid political decline all too readily exemplified in the twentieth century Orwell had experienced.

*We*, *Brave New World* and *Nineteen Eighty-Four* share a concern with surveillance and its relationship to power, although only Orwell links power to a central factor of modern political life, the political party. Or Party with a capital, since the one party superstate of Oceania approximates actual totalitarian states in Europe in the 1920s, 1930s and 1940s. Zamyatin, writing before the dictatorships of Stalin, Mussolini or Hitler, imagined OneState as a totalitarian world in which all inhabitants are loyal to that state and to the Great Benefactor. Huxley's projection contains the relatively benign and unvenerated Mustapha Mond and an essentially apolitical world of hedonism. Oceania, though, is populated by members of the Party and by the 'proles', who make up 85% of the population. The Party itself comprises the Inner Party, with members such as O'Brien, and the Outer Party, to which most other named characters belong, including the protagonist, Winston Smith, his lover Julia, as well as neighbours and colleagues such as the moronically subservient Parsons, the cynical intellectual, Syme, and the insipid poet, Ampleforth. Even so, the Party as a whole makes up only 15% of the population, if we believe Emmanuel Goldstein's subversive account, with only 2% in the Inner Party, surprisingly small percentages given the prevailing sense of paranoia and oppression. That oppression is magnified, though, precisely because Winston is an Outer Party member subject to the highest and most insistent level of surveillance; had he been a prole, he might have experienced the world of Oceania as tawdry, but not totalitarian. This might seem a banal or trivial point, but it discloses the distinct scope of surveillance in specific zones of Oceania where the different subgroups live, and the different intensity with which they are monitored. When Winston wanders in the prole section of the city, for example, he fears being spotted by the Thought Police, because the blue overalls of the Outer Party (those in the Inner Party wear black overalls) 'could not be a common sight' in the area and 'it was unwise to be seen in such places, unless you had definite business there'. There is not 'any rule against walking home by such a route', we are told, 'but it was enough to draw attention to you if the Thought Police heard about it' (86–7). Compared with OneState, where there is no differentiation between numbers, where all are equally under surveillance everywhere, the degree of monitoring in the prole section is surprisingly lax. Winston knows that he is doing something risky in walking through there, but with no official barriers or checkpoints, arrest remains only a possibility: 'The patrols might stop you if you happened to run into them' (86). When Winston enters a prole pub there is no mention of telescreens, nor posters of Big Brother, and this is the case elsewhere in the prole sector. His questioning of an old man in that pub about conditions before the Party took control, though fruitless, appears to go unscrutinised.

It might be thought that Winston is being monitored secretly in order to draw out his hidden, unorthodox behaviour. When he first views the room he will rent from Mr Charrington for secret liaisons with Julia, for example, he notes: 'There's no telescreen!' Charrington replies, 'I never had one of those things. Too expensive' (101). Because Charrington eventually reveals himself as a member of the Thought Police, his response can be treated as a lie to put Winston at his ease. If so, it still represents a different sense of surveillance power than that of Bentham's Panopticon or Zamyatin's We, both of which impose orthodoxy by maintaining the impression that the inmates or citizens are always being watched. Winston might be being duped by Charrington, but he is not being oppressed. Similarly, when he and Julia meet in the countryside for illicit sex, we read:

> In general you could not assume that you were much safer in the country than in London. There were no telescreens, of course, but there was always the danger your voice might be picked up and recognised; besides, it was not easy to make a journey by yourself without attracting attention. (123)

The blunt statement that there are no telescreens is revealing. Even if Julia and Winston are being monitored, they do not feel that they are being monitored. They can be judged naïve, but the supposed absence does allow them freedom from the dominant assumption felt by those in the Panopticon, who act in accordance with the belief that they are constantly scrutinised. The pair have lusty and rebellious sex in the country and in their 'secret' room because they do not feel monitored. Winston experiences the most intense form of surveillance in his home, revealed in an early passage that remains one of the most referenced in all surveillance literature:

> Any sound that Winston made, above the level of a very low whisper, would be picked up by [the telescreen]; moreover, so long as he remained within the field of vision which the metal plaque commanded, he could be seen as well as heard. There was of course no way of knowing whether you were being watched at any given moment. How often, or on what system, the Thought Police plugged in on any individual wire was guesswork. It was even conceivable that they watched everybody all the time. But at any rate they could plug in your wire whenever they wanted to. You had to live – did live, from habit that became instinct – in the assumption that every sound you made was overheard, and, except in darkness, every movement scrutinised. (5)

Again, the qualifications convey a situation something less than that of total surveillance – sounds below a very low whisper are not picked up; Winston might not be seen if he steps outside the field of vision of the telescreen; there is a chance he might not be being watched at a given moment; darkness provides some form of cover. Certainly by the normal standards of Western modernity this is extreme and repressive, and is meant to be read as such. Yet Winston can subvert this domestic monitoring in small ways, so that when he turns towards the telescreen in his flat, he makes sure to 'set his features into the expression of faint optimism which it was advisable to wear when facing the telescreen' (6). Those watching him seem deceived. His flat also has the telescreen in 'an unusual position', so that he can hide from scrutiny in a 'shallow alcove' if he keeps 'well back': 'He could be heard, of course, but so long as he stayed in his present position he could not be seen' (7). In this hidden space he can write his diary, his counter history and testament to independent thought. Winston eventually finds out in the Ministry of Love that 'for seven years the Thought Police had watched him like a beetle under a magnifying glass', that 'There was no physical act, no word spoken aloud, that they had not noticed, no train of thought that they had not been able to infer' (289). Still, there is a fundamental difference between knowing oneself to be under constant surveillance and believing, however erroneously, that one has moments of free thought and action. Small but significant acts of rebellion distinguish Winston and Julia from those under the total surveillance environment of the Panopticon.

The closest approximations to the Panopticon are the Thought Police. As early as the second page we read that while a police helicopter patrol was 'snooping into people's windows', it 'did not matter, however. Only the Thought Police mattered' (4). For all that menace, only when Mr Charrington reveals himself at the end of Part Two does it occur to Winston 'that for the first time in his life he was looking, with knowledge, at a member of the Thought Police' (234). The more obvious evidence of the surveillance regime is the telescreen, one of the novel's most emblematic features, and for many readers the visual embodiment in several senses of the Party's intrusiveness, the loss of privacy, the crushing of any systemic subversion. Orwell introduces it on the opening page, Winston Smith entering his flat where there was 'an oblong metal plaque like a dulled mirror which formed part of the surface of the right-hand wall' (3). In this first instance, the telescreen functions not visually, but aurally. And rather than oppressively monitoring Winston's movements, it transmits in 'a fruity voice . . . a list of figures which had something to do with the production of pig-iron (3). The more sinister aspects of the telescreen's power quickly emerge, but initially we might understand the fruity voice and pig-iron figures as a satirical stab at self-important, boring bureaucrats. Given how large the telescreen looms in subsequent interpretations of the novel, this first description produces another surprise: 'The instrument (the telescreen, it was called) could be dimmed, but there was no way of shutting it off completely' (3). It is somewhat deflating that an instrument later to become synonymous with the adjective 'Orwellian' can be dimmed, or that two chapters later it gets used for compulsory Outer Party exercises, mockingly called 'The Physical Jerks' (33–4). This is dark satire, perhaps, but definitely an attack upon mandated exercise. When Winston and Julia visit O'Brien's flat they find that Inner Party members have the 'privilege' of switching off the telescreen entirely (176). Given the other instances where the telescreens are absent or not fully functioning, their coverage of activities, even those of Party members, is anything but homogenous or complete.

Admittedly, the reach and influence telescreens do have is impressive and repressive, and not only for the novel's original readers. Telescreens spew out Party propaganda as well as monitor Party members, part of overlapping surveillance networks that include the Thought Police, normal police patrols, family, friends and colleagues. Telescreens scrutinise private and public spaces, and enforce aural and particularly visual surveillance. Their effect on behaviour, particularly Party members, is massive and undeniable:

> It was terribly dangerous to let your thoughts wander when you were in any public place or within range of a telescreen. The smallest thing could give you away. A nervous tic, an unconscious look of anxiety, a habit of muttering to yourself – anything that carried with it the suggestion of abnormality, of having something to hide. In any case, to wear an improper expression on your face (to look incredulous when a victory was announced, for example) was itself a punishable offence. There was even a word for it in Newspeak: *facecrime*, it was called. (65)

Yet this example reveals that visual surveillance of itself is insufficient to control thoughts as opposed to actions. The true meaning of actions can also be concealed, and is concealed by those who wish to game the system. Perhaps the most extreme instance of this occurs when Julia falls over, and an innocent Winston helps her up, 'standing straight in front of a telescreen' (112). She uses this ruse to slip him the incendiary and highly dangerous handwritten note that he surreptitiously reads later on, and that says: '*I love you*' (113; original emphasis). This daring and, for Winston, completely unexpected act, constitutes a small but massively symbolic blow against a Party that wants to crush the sex drive and manipulate emotions so as to control desire. It also marks Julia down as a highly subversive character, one capable of exploiting failings in the surveillance system for her own benefit.

Julia has often been written off in analyses of *Nineteen Eighty-Four* as a two-dimensional fantasy figure for Winston and his creator, perhaps most devastatingly by Daphne Patai in a key feminist study, *The Orwell Mystique: A Study in Male Ideology* (2004: 238–51; see also Patai 2004: 200–14). Rather than defend the novel against valid criticism of its misogynist excesses, we might productively consider Julia in terms of the surveillance setting of Oceania in which she finds herself. Given that she has grown up under the sign of the Party and is to Winston's jaundiced eyes the epitome of a faithful member, Julia later reveals herself in the supposed privacy of Mr Charrington's as taking it for 'granted that everyone, or nearly everyone, secretly hated the Party and would break the rules if he thought it safe to do so. But she refused to believe that widespread, organized opposition existed or could exist' (159). Her own rebellion, then, like Winston's, is self-motivated, but unlike his does not depend on the dangerous and misplaced fantasy that O'Brien might be in collusion with the Brotherhood. She takes a far tougher and more dismissive view of Party propaganda, assuming correctly that 'The details about Goldstein and his underground army . . . were simply a lot of rubbish which the Party had invented for its own purposes and which you had to pretend to believe.' She discloses that 'Times beyond number, at Party rallies and spontaneous demonstrations, she had shouted at the top of her voice for the execution of people whose names she had never heard and in whose crimes she had not the faintest belief' (159). Julia's rebellion is anarchic, hedonistic and egotistical in many ways, but it entails a sound comprehension of how various forms of surveillance work in Oceania and how they might be undermined or otherwise deceived. The novel credits her with being in some ways,

> far more acute than Winston, and far less susceptible to Party propaganda. Once when he happened in some connection to mention the war against Eurasia, she startled him by saying casually that in her opinion the war was not happening. The rocket bombs which fell daily on London were probably fired by the Government of Oceania itself, 'just to keep people frightened'. This was an idea that had literally never occurred to him. She also stirred a sort of envy in him by telling him that during the Two Minutes Hate her great difficulty was to avoid bursting out laughing. (160)

This disregard or contempt for Party propaganda does not manifest itself in acts of organised resistance, but in everyday defiance on a personal level. Julia's victories over the surveillance regime are limited but tangible, and at least as efficacious as those of Winston. Unlike him, she refuses to, accept as a law of nature that the individual is always defeated. In a way she realised that she herself was doomed, that sooner or later the Thought Police would catch her and kill her, but with another part of her mind she believed that it was somehow possible to construct a secret world in which you could live as you chose. All you needed was luck and cunning and boldness. (142)

Julia's belief in a secret life almost immediately is undermined by her arrest along with Winston, but that belief is preferable to Winston's combination of misplaced faith in O'Brien and underlying fatalism.

Her palmed note to him also gestures to one of *Nineteen Eighty-Four*'s most salient pieces of surveillance, that of language, and of ideas. In *We*, the validation of the train timetable as the highest form of literature constitutes Zamyatin's barb at attempts to control or standardise creativity, but Orwell makes the manipulation of language, and with it of facts and of history, far further. Newspeak, remember, was the first thing Orwell wrote down in his notes for *The Last Man in Europe* in 1943, and the articulation of the rationale in the Newspeak Appendix constitutes one of the most powerful elements in the novel as a whole, even though it appears after the narrative proper. The early appearance of Newspeak speaks to Orwell's abiding concerns with the control of language and ideas gained through dealings with his own publisher, Victor Gollancz. Gollancz, an active and unabashed promoter of socialism on the Soviet model, wrote a foreword to Orwell's documentary on working-class life in the north of England, *The Road to Wigan Pier* (1936), that criticised many of the key arguments in that book, on the grounds that Orwell's case for socialism was 'emotional' rather than the 'scientific' type of which Gollancz approved (Orwell 1997a: 225). Gollancz also refused to publish Orwell's projected eye-witness account of what he had seen while fighting in the Spanish Civil War, presuming that Orwell would write from an unorthodox left-wing perspective. Orwell was forced to find an alternative publisher, the far smaller firm of Secker and Warburg, for what became *Homage to Catalonia*. To reinforce how acceptable political views were promoted, *The Road to Wigan Pier*, published by Gollancz's influential Left Book Club, sold more than 40,000 copies, while *Homage to Catalonia* sold 683 copies in its first six months (Marks 2011: 52). Gollancz later refused to publish *Animal Farm* on the grounds that its criticism of the Soviet Union in 1944, when that country was an ally, was politically inappropriate. Orwell would again turn to Secker and Warburg, and ended his contract with Gollancz, who consequently also missed out on publishing *Nineteen Eighty-Four*. The reality that Orwell's words and ideas would be monitored and if necessary blocked or distorted even by those with similar views was already embedded in his thinking when he came to write *Nineteen Eighty-Four*.

In a variety of earlier essays Orwell sketched assessments and ideas that found their way into *Nineteen Eighty-Four*. 'Inside the Whale' (1940), for example, asks 'why should *writers* be attracted to a form of socialism that makes mental honesty impossible?' (Orwell 1998a: 102). Orwell asserts that 'Almost certainly we are moving into an age of totalitarian dictatorships – an age in which freedom of thought will be at first a deadly sin and later on a meaningless abstraction. The autonomous individual is going to be stamped out of existence' (110). Given O'Brien's sadistic image of the future as 'a boot stamping on a human face – for ever' (280), the metaphor is arresting. A year later in 'Literature and Totalitarianism' (1941) Orwell claims that totalitarian states have 'abolished freedom of thought to an extent unheard-of in any previous age' (Orwell 1998a: 503). He continues that totalitarianism,

> though it controls thought . . . does not fix it. It sets up questionable dogmas, and it alters them from day to day. It needs the dogmas, because it needs abso-lute obedience from its subjects, but it cannot avoid the changes, which are dictated by the needs of power politics. It declares itself infallible, and at the same time it attacks the very concept of objective truth. (504)

And in 'Wells, Hitler and the World State' (1941) he criticises Wells for failing to understand that the 'energy that actually shapes the world springs from the emotions – racial pride, leader worship, religious belief, love of war – which liberal intellec-tuals mechanically write off as an anachronisms' (Orwell 1998a: 538). 'Notes on Nationalism' (1945) carries the provocative charge that nationalists believe 'the past can be altered', as well as the larger and more troubling claim that 'much of the propagandist writing about time amounts to plain forgery. Material facts are suppressed, dates altered, quotations moved from their contexts and doctored so as to change their meaning. Events which, it is felt, ought not to have happened are left unmentioned or utterly denied' (Orwell 1998d: 148). 'Politics and the English Language' (1946), possibly his greatest essay on the topic, argues that political orthodoxy, which Orwell sees as increasingly prevalent in his contemporary world, turns the speaker into 'some kind of dummy' or

> machine. The appropriate noises are coming out of his larynx, but his brain is not involved as it would be if he were choosing the words for himself . . . [H]e may be almost unconscious of what he is saying . . . And this reduced state of consciousness, if not indispensable, is at any rate favourable to political ortho-doxy. (Orwell 1998d: 427)

While not quite the state of unquestioning orthodoxy the Party aspires to in *Nineteen Eighty-Four*, 'Politics and the English Language' shows Orwell addressing the poverty of political language in the world around him, criticising real people for lapses into mechanistic orthodoxy, and cautioning actual readers to be alert to, or dismissive of, such language. His novel transforms those concerns into thought-provoking narrative, as when Winston overhears a man from the Fiction Department whose language is 'pure orthodoxy, pure Ingsoc'. Seeing him, Winston has

> a curious feeling that this was not a real human being but some kind of dummy. It was not the man's brain speaking, it was his larynx. The stuff coming out of him consisted of words, but it was not speech in the true sense: it was a noise uttered in unconsciousness, like the quacking of a duck. (57)

The link between Orwell's lived reality and his dystopian vision could scarcely be closer.

In *Nineteen Eighty-Four* itself the Party routinely monitors language, and through the introduction of Newspeak aims in time to eradicate unorthodox speech and thought. In a more literal way, language in the form of the iconic slogan BIG BROTHER IS WATCHING YOU drives home the ubiquity of surveillance, while the Ministry of Truth's slogans

WAR IS PEACE

FREEDOM IS SLAVERY

IGNORANCE IS STRENGTH

hint at those in *Brave New World*. Here, they command the eye and attempt to impose Ingsoc beliefs within the minds of Party members; ideology metaphorically watches over them. Winston's own work at the Ministry is part of the larger adulteration of facts and history in the Ministry of Truth, Winston himself being compliant, the reader told that his 'greatest pleasure in life was in his work' (46). Similarly, Syme, Winston's almost-friend from the Research Department, enjoys being 'one of the enormous team of experts' who are 'engaged in compiling the Eleventh Edition of the Newspeak Dictionary' (51). Syme tells Winston the 'destruction of words' being carried out is 'a beautiful thing' (54), elaborating that 'the whole aim of Newspeak is to narrow the range of thought. In the end we shall make thoughtcrime literally impossible, because there will be no words in which to express it' (55). Scrutinising language, then, has an overt and consequential political function, Syme proudly adding that 'The Revolution will be complete when the language is perfect' (55). This stark correlation between the control of language and power gets repeated treatment in the novel, but while a range of Newspeak words and names – facecrime, thoughtcrime, duckspeak, unperson, speakwrite, Pornosec, Minitru – is employed, the actual use of Newspeak by characters is rare. Tellingly, Newspeak exists more substantially in 1984 through documents or in the abbreviated jargon that Winston deals with, such as 'times 17.3.84 bb speech malreported Africa rectify' (40), a set of instructions he receives to correct a report in *The Times*. The infrequency with which Newspeak appears in the narrative points to the world of Oceania as a work in progress, one in which, Syme tells Winston, 'By 2050 – earlier, probably – all real knowledge of Oldspeak will have disappeared' (56). Given the cultural resonance attending the telescreen since the novel's publication, it unsettles expectations to find parts of Oceania are telescreen-free. Similarly, the regular use of the term 'Newspeak' in the real world of the twenty-first century makes it surprising to find that the projected triumph of Newspeak in the novel would still be decades away.

Syme's linguistic speculation gets reiterated in the *Appendix: The Principles of Newspeak* that follows the narrative proper. This attachment gives a detailed rationale for Newspeak relative to the aims of the Party and Ingsoc philosophy, substantially extending the explanation given by Syme. Such an appendix is an unusual literary device, but a textual footnote early in *Nineteen Eighty-Four* (5) alerts the reader to Newspeak, something Orwell clearly thought vital. The Appendix opens by mapping the position of Newspeak in 1984 itself, explaining that 'there was not as yet anyone who used Newspeak as his sole means of communication, either in speech or writing'. It is, however, gaining 'ground steadily, all Party members tending to use Newspeak words and grammatical constructions more and more in their everyday speech' (312). Even so, the version of Newspeak used is 'a provisional one', to be replaced by the 'final perfected version', the one worked on by Syme and others. 'The purpose of Newspeak', as Syme tells Winston, is 'not only to provide a medium of expression for the world-view and mental habits proper to the devotees of Ingsoc, but to make all other modes of thoughts impossible' (312). The control of language entails an intrinsic surveillance element, the use or non-use of approved phrases and formulations making it possible to monitor Party allegiance while simultaneously embedding Party ideology. Accepting the causal relationship between words and thoughts (a highly contestable notion, it needs be said), Newspeak makes orthodoxy as well as heterodoxy visible through texts and audible through speech. Clearly this is an ongoing process, rather than one that can be, or has been, instituted at one moment. Syme chides Winston for writing in Newspeak while 'still thinking in Oldspeak' (54–5), exposing the level of thought that cannot be as easily monitored or modified even by those whose job it is to use Newspeak. Winston's ability to perform Newspeak while thinking Oldspeak allows him a small, if diminishing freedom from surveillance.

Winston's diary represents an important manifestation of that freedom, a textual space in which he can construct his personalised counter-history and work through suppressed memories and thoughts. D-502's journal in *We* is an obvious precursor, and Margaret Atwood would later incorporate a modified oral version in *The Handmaid's Tale*. In *Nineteen Eighty-Four*, the diary supplies Winston with a much-needed opportunity to record his thoughts, vent his anger and attempt to contemplate and connect to a future he accepts he will never experience:

> *To a time when thought is free, when men are different from one another and do not live alone – to a time when truth exists and what is done cannot be undone: From the age of uniformity, from the age of solitude, from the age of Big Brother, from the age of doublethink – greetings!* (30; original emphasis)

Language that goes unmonitored (or that seems to go unmonitored), as with the diary, offers the opportunity for free and potentially resistant thought, at least until it is detected. Although Winston acknowledges that, even before writing his diary, he has committed 'the essential crime that contained all others in itself. Thoughtcrime' (21), he continues to write subversive, self-damning thoughts, such as '*Freedom is the freedom to say that two plus two makes four. If that is granted, all else follows*' (84; original emphasis) and 'If there is hope, it lies in the proles.' That secret and extremely dangerous thought keeps 'coming back to him, statement of a mystical truth and a palpable absurdity' (85). For as long as he writes in his diary, notions of freedom and hope – impossible to articulate and barely able to be thought in other circumstances – sustain him. The Thought Police might read the diary's content, but in so far as Winston does not know for certain that his words are under surveillance, he can write with a measure of desperate independence.

The diary gives Winston's thoughts textual form that can be scrutinised, putting him in jeopardy. Julia boldly declares, though, that the mind remains inviolate, famously stating, 'They can make you say anything – *anything* – but they can't make you believe it. They can't get inside you' (174; original emphasis). After writing '2+2=5' on the table in the Chestnut Tree Café Winston thinks, 'But they could get inside you' (303), through torture and various sadistic forms of mind control, all carried out in one of literature's most infamous surveillance spaces, Room 101. Is he correct? Or, rather, in what way is he correct? O'Brien's efforts before and after Room 101 reduce Winston to an essentially passive and tear-filled lover of Big Brother in the last lines of the narrative. By that final paragraph, Winston is broken, hollowed out. Two paragraphs before this, however, we read that 'Much had changed in him since that first day in the Ministry of Love, but the final, indispensable, healing change had never happened, until this moment' (310–11). The Party does manage to 'get inside' Winston, but from a surveillance perspective, a telling point remains that while the psychological and physical torture carried out obliterates his thoughts and replaces them with Party orthodoxy, those effects are not achieved by surveillance. For all the telescreens, spies, public demonstrations of allegiance and Thought Police in Oceania, constant monitoring has not got inside Winston by the time he enters the Ministry of Love. Replacing unorthodox thoughts with orthodox thoughts, to the point that 'He loved Big Brother', is not necessarily to 'know' those errant thoughts in any meaningful sense.

The scenes in the Ministry of Love are some of modern literature's most harrowing. But it is worth recalling that Winston and Julia are not lone prisoners there. Among others, surprisingly, are two of the more complicit Party members, the poet Ampleforth and Winston's repulsive neighbour, Parsons. Where Winston and Julia have been snared by the Thought Police, Ampleforth and Parsons fall victim to other forms of surveillance. Ampleforth, so he believes, fails to find an appropriate Newspeak equivalent for 'God' while translating a Kipling poem (242), a bleakly comic literary joke given Orwell's championing of Kipling (Marks 2011: 124–5). Parson's daughter betrays her father, supposedly for repeatedly saying 'Down With Big Brother!' in his sleep (245). Ampleforth goes to Room 101 before Winston, as do other prisoners, registering again that despite the extent of surveillance in myriad forms and the immense Party pressure to comply, even those most obviously invested in Ingsoc and Big Brother have the potential to lapse or fall short. We might read these instances as examples through which the Party maintains control by sacrificing the faithful to encourage the others, but if it has to do this with its own members (leaving aside the proles), Oceania hardly approximates the total surveillance society of popular thought.

For all that, the scenes in the Ministry of Love emphasise the brutality at the heart of the Party. After several chapters of intellectual sparring, interspersed by torture and physical degradation, Winston has been reduced to a physical wreck, O'Brien contemptuously telling him that he is 'rotting away', that he is '[a] bag of filth. Now turn and look at the mirror again. Do you see that thing facing you?

That is the last man. If you are human, that is humanity' (285). Despite Winston's acknowledgement of his feeble body, he still manages 'a feeling of pity' for himself. And beyond the self-awareness he responds to O'Brien that for all he had confessed about Julia, he had not betrayed her, in the sense that he 'had not stopped loving her' (287). Even at this stage, when O'Brien asks Winston his ' "true feelings towards Big Brother"', Winston immediately replies:

'I hate him.'
'You hate him. Good. Then the time has come for you to take the last step. You must love Big Brother. It is not enough to obey him: You must love him.'
He released Winston with a little push towards the guards.
'Room 101,' he said. (295)

The process of getting Winston to this last step has taken four sections and nearly sixty pages; that in Room 101 takes less than five pages. The weighting reinforces the effectiveness of what takes place in Room 101, which as O'Brien tells Winston, contains 'the worst thing in the world' (296). For Winston, this is rats. But it also exposes how long Winston has held out against the full force of Party interrogation. He finds out that he has been under surveillance secretly for seven years, a revelation that makes him understand that he cannot fight against the Party, and that temporarily prods him to believe that he can and should surrender to the Party's logic. But he remains unable to completely believe what the Party requires, that 'whatever happens in all minds, truly happens'. Knowing that 'the mind should develop a blind spot whenever a dangerous thought presented itself . . . [that] the process should be automatic', he sets to work 'to exercise himself in crimestop' (291), the Newspeak word for employing the blindspot. Despite his efforts, he fails, a failure exposed in a 'strange, blissful reverie' of the eutopian 'Golden Country' (292–3) that he has dreamt about and that he finds recreated when he and Julia escape to the country for illicit sex. The reverie ends with him crying out his love for Julia. Horrified by the revelatory act that will have been monitored, he appreciates that the Party will,

know now, if they had not known before, that he was breaking the agreement he had made with them . . . In the old days he had hidden a heretical mind beneath an appearance of conformity. Now he had retreated a step further: in the mind he had surrendered, but he had hoped to keep his inner heart inviolate. He knew that he was in the wrong, but he preferred to be in the wrong. (293)

What is striking here is that these rebellious thoughts and deeds take place after months in the Ministry of Love, after routine physical and mental humiliation and manipulation, and with someone who knows himself to be powerless and who is making a conscious effort to overcome his unorthodox tendencies. The awareness of having been under surveillance for seven years has had little impact on his sense of self, nor on his willingness 'to be in the wrong'. If anything, it creates or reveals to him a distinction between outer appearance (the face), thought (the mind) and a metaphorical and potentially inviolate 'inner heart', a distinction he had hoped to employ against intrusion.

Winston's imprisonment requires him to think more deeply on the nature of his rebellion, about his relationship to the Party, above all his feelings for Julia. Until just before he is taken to Room 101, though, he remains remarkably self-aware and relatively non-compliant. Having had a new set of teeth put in to replace those torn from his ravaged body, for example, but not having seen what his face now looks like, he comes to understand that '[i]t was not easy to preserve inscrutability when you did not know what your face looked like' (293–4). This odd thought leads to something more profound in terms of resistance to surveillance, because

> mere control of the features was not enough. For the first time he perceived that if you want to keep a secret you must also hide it from yourself. You must know all the while that it is there, but until it was needed you must never let it emerge into your consciousness . . . From now on he must not only think right; he must feel right, dream right. And all the while he must keep his hatred locked up inside him like a ball of matter which was part of himself and yet unconnected with the rest of him, a kind of cyst. (294)

This strategy marks a significant advance in awareness from the fairly obvious understanding of facecrime that he had earlier displayed, an advance that occurs not despite his time in the Ministry of Love, but because of it. And it gives Winston a defiant reassurance that while he might be shot at any time, the Thought Police will 'have blown his brains to pieces before they could reclaim it. The heretical thought would be unpunished, unrepented, out of their reach forever. They would have blown a hole in their own perfection. To die hating them, that was freedom' (294). Within a page Winston is sent to Room 101, and ultimately he will come to love Big Brother, but the defiant thought that to die hating the Party was freedom serves as a powerful counterblast that can still echo beyond the end of Winston's narrative. We make an interpretive error if we allow all the weight of the novel to fall on the final words of that narrative: 'He loved Big Brother'; Winston's resistance deserves our attention as well. He is only broken by means of the gothic cage of the rats placed over his head, the fear of having his face eaten by rats causing him to 'betray' Julia. The horror of this scene, dramatically effective to the point of excess, reveals that although O'Brien can successfully tap into Winston's deep fears and his willingness eventually to sacrifice Julia so as to save himself, the use of caged rats is an extraordinarily crude method of gaining compliance from a rebellious Party member. He betrays Julia only because he is terrified, not because he divulges her thoughts or secrets. Winston's 'victory over himself' is achieved by overwhelming and disabling terror. He is no longer a threat at the end of the narrative, but the pathetic figure with gin-scented tears trickling down his face is compliant only as an automaton is compliant. The Party rewires his consciousness for its benefit, but never truly or fully knows his thoughts, the essentially Pyrrhic victory marking a failure of the surveillance state.

*Nineteen Eighty-Four* the text does not end, however, when Winston's narrative ends. The words 'THE END' (311) that complete the story of Winston Smith form a bridge to the Newspeak appendix beyond. Margaret Atwood argues convincingly that the appendix speaks to (and from) a post-Ingsoc world, its language and historical perspective indicating that the world of the Party has been superseded, is now itself an historical relic (Atwood 2012: 145–6): 'Newspeak was', the appendix begins, 'the official language of Oceania and had been devised to meet the ideological needs of Ingsoc' (312). For Atwood, the past tense signals that Oceania is no more. While the Appendix explains the logic and proposed effect of Newspeak, it also admits that moving Party members to adopt the approved language was still an incomplete process in 1984. O'Brien himself speaks almost entirely in standard English throughout, as do the Party faithful such as Syme, Parson and Ampleforth. The translation into Newspeak of writers 'such as Shakespeare, Milton, Swift, Byron, Dickens' (most of whom Orwell wrote essays on; see Marks 2011) was proving a 'slow and difficult business'. The capacity to monitor written and spoken language in 1984, then, falls well short of the ideal, the projected Newspeak completion date of 2050 an index of difficulty. That date itself only applies to Party members, which leaves the 85 per cent of Oceania's population who are proles still beyond the Party's surveillance reach. The relative absence from prole areas of telescreens and Thought Police underlines the limits of surveillance in Oceania, especially if we conditionally accept Winston's thought and words: 'If there is any hope it lies in the proles.' Looking for a real life analogue to this fictional wish, we might recall how the Berlin Wall fell in 1989 not because of meticulously organised political action, or a triumphantly emerging Brotherhood, but because normal people gathered en masse and defied the East German surveillance state, with unimagined consequences.

Yet the continuing power of *Nineteen Eighty-Four* to inform public, media and (less influentially) academic thinking and action on surveillance is remarkable. Often, however, the subtleties, gaps and conundrums in the novel's depiction of Oceania are ignored for a more mythical, totalising account of surveillance. We need to attend to what Orwell actually wrote in the novel, rather than the distilled version that has entered the public consciousness. Surveillance scholars sometimes vent their frustrations at the hold the novel has on our imaginations, especially given that the contemporary world of surveillance is far more variegated than Orwell proposes, with computers, the Internet, mobile phones and social media only part of a vastly more sophisticated and nuanced world than Orwell imagines. Such scholars have reasons to be frustrated. In the twenty-first century, the age of Big Data is transforming the way surveillance functions, and although the term obviously echoes Big Brother, it produces resonances Orwell did not hear. Some contemporary citizens are just as likely to feel safe as feel scared when monitored by government and private agencies, while modern consumer capitalism and social welfare require the aggregation and transmission of personal information and the construction of 'digital doubles' to track our movements and provide information and services. For all this, *Nineteen Eighty-Four*'s enduring cultural place suggests that it still has something to tell readers about the complexities of surveillance: about what is; about what can be seen, or kept invisible; about the monitoring of spaces and status of privacy; about the reach and limitations of technology, and about the many ways in which surveillance complicates concepts of identity. This chapter has provided ways of interpreting Orwell's particular portrait of surveillance, in part by connecting it back to the creative utopian genre that it draws from and develops. The following chapters project forward, examining how writers and filmmakers variously have imagined surveillance in the decades since *Nineteen Eighty-Four*.

# 4  Visibility

Surveillance is about seeing things and, more particularly, about seeing people. (Lyon 2007: 1)

For simplicity I have arranged this [classification of surveillance] largely in a series of discrete either/or possibilities (e.g. visible or invisible, gathered by a human or a machine). But there may be continuous gradations between the extreme values (e.g. between the visible and invisible). (Marx 2002: 14)

If someone needed to go to a house physically next door to their own but in the neighbouring city, it was a different road in an unfriendly power. That is what foreigners rarely understand. A Besź dweller cannot walk a few paces next door to an alter house without breach.

But pass through Copula Hall and she or he might leave Besź, and at the end of the hall come back exactly (corporally) to where they had just been, but in another country, a tourist, a marvelling visitor, to a street that shared the latitude-longitude of their own address, a street they had never visited before, whose architecture they had always unseen, to the Ul Qoman house sitting next to and a whole city away from their own building, unvisible there now they had come through, all the way across the Breach, back home. (Miéville 2009: 86)

Visibility is a central concept in surveillance studies, built into the very roots of the defining term that fuses the French 'sur' ('over') and 'veiller' ('to watch'). The opening sentence of David Lyon's *Surveillance Studies: An Overview*, cited above, states this with definitional clarity, and the three parts of his synoptic account – 'Viewpoints', 'Vision' and 'Visibility' – underscore the significance of vision and visibility to surveillance scholars. Utopian works from *Utopia* to *Nineteen Eighty-Four* depict scenarios where diverse forms of vision and visibility enable distinct types of monitoring, whether the absence of private meeting places in More's text, Bentham's Panopticon, the identity cards in *A Modern Utopia*, maternal oversight in *Herland*, worksite screens in *Modern Times*, genetic and peer monitoring in *Brave New World* or behaviourist scrutiny in *Walden Two*. These forms can be malignant or benign, either in intent or operation, and individuals, groups and societies accept or reject (successfully and otherwise) the control they exercise. This chapter initiates the approach adopted in subsequent chapters by opening up texts and territories produced after Orwell, exploring how more recent utopian novels and films represent and critically engage with the actualities and possibilities new and enduring modes of surveillance create.

It is worth re-emphasising that genres other than the utopian have produced incisive accounts of surveillance in the modern world (see Nellis and Kammerer). The most obvious of these, perhaps, is spy fiction, literary and cinematic, where the playful excesses of Ian Fleming or the dour but more realistic work of John Le Carré and many others have illuminated parts of the dark arts of espionage. These revealing and compelling works, though, only peripherally touch upon the everyday life of their readers or viewers. Surveillance is something carried on at the national or international level in secret by state operatives in spy fiction and films, and though police procedural or forensic pathology fictions also supply thought-provoking and popular accounts of surveillance elements for mass consumption (see Andrejevic 2007), these tend to focus on the sorts of extreme crimes such as murder that have little to do with the lived reality of readers and viewers. Thrillers such as Francis Ford Coppola's brilliant *The Conversation* or Tony Scott's pacy *Enemy of the State* are undeniably inventive and informative as well as provocative. Television's *24* offers an almost fevered take on surveillance methods that nullify a regular sequence of national threats; indeed it might be argued that *24* functions to terrify viewers rather than to comfort them about those threats (see Monahan 2010). *The Wire* supplied a sophisticated take on the surveillance of a relatively circumscribed community. For all this, these treatments of surveillance tend to focus on particular aspects (crime or terrorism) without venturing into broader and deeper examinations of the personal and social effects, beneficial and detrimental, of monitoring. And while characters within them employ technology that is cutting edge, or slightly beyond the current technical threshold, they rarely venture far into the future. Utopian texts, by contrast, energetically investigate that wider domain, merging past, present and imagined future in any number of ways, from gendered monitoring in *The Handmaid's Tale* that invokes Christian fundamentalism, to crime prevention in *Minority Report* and genetic apartheid in *Gattaca*. *The Truman Show* assesses surveillance as entertainment, while Dave Eggers looks at rapidly morphing forms of social media in *The Circle*, and Spike Jonze's *Her* links artificial intelligence to real and artificial emotions and interactions. This preliminary selection of examples hint at the explosion of imaginative and exploratory works post-Orwell that deal with monitoring in different forms and contexts. The abundance of works means that, as with the chapter on surveillance in utopian works before *Nineteen Eighty-Four*, what follows remains highly selective. A full-length study could be made, for example, of Philip K. Dick's novels and their ingenious depictions of surveillance.

Accepting that surveillance is about seeing things and seeing people, the question of what is seen, and what is not seen, is crucial to the sweep and depth of that surveillance, and to its effectiveness. Lyon is alert to this, as is Gary T. Marx, who in the quotation above proposes continuous gradations between the visible and invisible. *Nineteen Eighty-Four* presents one illustration of those gradations with its differential monitoring of Inner and Outer Party members and the proles. Other fictions suggest different gradations, while China Miéville's challenging novel *The City & The City* invents a category beyond the visible, what Miéville terms the 'unvisible'. The ramifications of that perplexing concept, captured in the quotation above from the novel, include the action of 'unseeing', whereby citizens of two states (Besź and Ul Qoma) whose geographical coordinates are identical are required consciously to 'unsee' each other or face arrest. Miéville also envisions a process through which citizens of one state who need to cross over into the other state are taught to see what they had previously unseen. *The City & The City* extends the limits of what might constitute visibility. Marx makes the critical observation that in any case 'most surveillance systems have inherent contradictions, ambiguities, gaps, and blindspots' (Marx 2003: 372), a statement that counters the paranoid view that surveillance systems are monolithic or foolproof. Bob Arctor in Philip K. Dick's *A Scanner Darkly*, a character who is both an undercover surveillance agent and a subject of surveillance, muses on the limitations of monitoring technology: 'What does a scanner see? he asked himself. I mean, really see? Into the head?' (Dick 2006: 146). His questions recall Julia's statement about the state not being able to get inside the head.

Elsewhere, Marx comments that, even if someone is visible, there 'is frequently a gap between visible conforming behaviour and less visible attitudes, emotions and fantasies' (Marx 2003: 372), something central to the behaviour of key characters in *We* and *Nineteen Eighty-Four*. Surveillance 'targets', Marx argues, 'often have space to manoeuvre and can use counter-technologies' (372); he lists and dissects an array of these. He distinguishes 'moves' that subjects can and do use to neutralise or subvert surveillance, all of which entail some subverting of visibility. These moves include 'discovery' (finding out if surveillance is taking place, and then evading it); 'switching' strategies, in which an authentic surveillance result is transferred to an inauthentic subject, and 'piggybacking', where an illegitimate individual uses a legitimate individual to infiltrate spaces or systems from which they are excluded. Subjects under surveillance might also seek 'to physically block access to the [surveillance] communication or to render it (or aspects of it such as the identity, appearance or location of the communicator) unusable' (Marx 2003: 379). A subject might adopt 'masking', which goes beyond 'blocking' 'to involve deception in respect to the identity, status, and/or location of the person or material of surveillance interest' (380). Here 'the surveillance mechanism operates as intended but the information collected is misleading and useless' (360). Agencies doing the monitoring successfully obtain visual information, but not about the intended subject. The subject supposedly under scrutiny retains a degree of invisibility in this instance, in the sense of not being watched as him- or herself. Marx's informative set of surveillance counter-moves exposes the limitations of a simple visible/invisible binary for both surveillants and subjects. Interactions between targets and surveillance systems increase the gradations between the visible and the invisible, Marx contending that

'The strategic actions of both watchers and the watched can be thought of as moves in a game, although unlike traditional games, the rules may not be equally binding on all players' (374). Visibility, as central as it is to surveillance and to surveillance studies, is nuanced and interactive, allowing or even encouraging those in the game occasionally to cheat.

Utopian texts do not have subjects so much as characters, and though the degree to which readers and viewers are privy to the consciousness of these characters varies, characters do provide ways of understanding how surveillance systems and regimes operate on individuals, and how those individuals respond to surveillance. By extension, these responses can be applied to other characters, or used as a point of contrast to the different responses of those other characters. So, for example, Winston's thoughts and actions provide a point of reference, a means of assessing to some degree the thoughts and actions of Julia and O'Brien, Parsons and Syme, and any number of characters beyond, even those whose compliance functions to maintain the system. Responses are various both within individual works and across the network of utopian texts, allowing the possibility of an increasingly sophisticated awareness by readers and viewers of surveillance's impact and ramifications. This is increasingly the case in utopias over the last century in which more individualised characters are prominent and where those characters are fully immersed in the projected world. The traditional journey by an outsider to a eutopian or dystopian place, who then returns and recounts what was seen, makes visible what we might understand as the external world, while much of the total experience of living in the eutopia or dystopia remains largely invisible. This does not disregard the importance of 'externals', but indicates the value of integrating them with 'internal' consciousness that remains invisible but potent. Modern dystopias, especially, register the assault on that consciousness by surveillance, as well as the sorts of counter-manoeuvres Gary T. Marx distinguishes. The ensuing struggles mark the gradations between visibility and invisibility, and perhaps beyond to unvisibility, as contested social ground.

Feminism has been a powerful and transformative force in modern and contemporary society, so not surprisingly utopian texts have depicted and examined the gendering of visibility and of surveillance more generally. Women particularly are put under intense and sometimes oppressive scrutiny by conservative surveillance regimes, and though *Herland* presents a eutopian portrait of maternal supervision, *Brave New World* fashions a more conventional vision of objectification, while decoupling women from the monitored reproduction that underpins its genetic hierarchy. In distinct ways Marge Piercy's 1976 novel *Woman on the Edge of Time* and Margaret Atwood's *The Handmaid's Tale* (1985) incorporate both motherhood and objectification, exposing how women are particularly vulnerable to surveillance powers, especially those enforced in male-dominated societies. It is not simply the fact that they are women that exposes the respective central characters, Connie Ramos and Offred, to antagonistic observation: Connie is a working class Chicano with an established though misleading criminal record, while Offred is sexually fertile in a near future where fertility is problematic. Their individual circumstances are substantially different, as are the societies they inhabit, and so the forms of surveillance they suffer, and their reactions to them, are distinct. In both cases, though, their dystopian worlds are offset by other places that are, if not eutopian, then are better than those in which they live. These projected futures exist when the tyrannical surveillance regimes of the present have passed away.

Connie Ramos lives in a New York contemporary with the age in which the novel was published in the 1970s. She gets institutionalised early on for violently defending her niece, Dolly, from Dolly's pimp, Geraldo. He manipulates Connie's existing record of violence, which includes violence against her daughter Angelina, from whom she is now separated, to have Connie incarcerated. At the police station front desk her

> counters of identity had been taken: welfare ID, Medicaid, old library card, photos of Dolly with Nita [her daughter], of Angelina as a baby, at one held by the father, Eddie, at two with herself, at three holding [her partner] Claud's hand with that grin like a canoe – the way she had drawn mouths. There were no pictures of Angelina at four, or afterwards. (18)

These counters, bureaucratic and personal, reflect discrete forms of identity, though only the former are visible to the government agencies with power over Connie. Arrest brings her into institutions where police and hospital records, coupled with the visible signs of her class, ethnicity and gender, function to discriminate against her along the lines Oscar Gandy elaborated in *The Panoptic Sort*. The medical and mental institutions into which she is thrown threaten and in some ways consciously work to dissolve her autonomy and sense of self. The text ends beyond Connie's own narrative with what are labelled 'Excerpts From the Official History of Consuelo Camacho Ramos'. The first report, from the 'Department of Mental Hygiene at Bellevue Hospital' (377–8), details her bringing Angelina to the hospital, and admitting 'beating her daughter, while drunk or drugged' (377). Her genuine remorse is registered as 'bizarre behaviour' (377). The Clinical Summary, which has a standardised set of capitalised rubrics that include IDENTIFICATION, PAST HISTORY, MENTAL STATUS, EMOTIONAL REACTIONS, and SENSORIUM, MENTAL GRASP AND CAPACITY, ends in the DIAGNOSIS: 'Schizophrenia, undiff. type 295.90' (378). The second report, from the Department of Mental Hygiene Rockover State Psychiatric Hospital, has a slightly different standardised list that includes the medication administered to Connie: Thorazine, Prolixin and Artane. There follows the DIAGNOSIS: 'Paranoid Schizophrenia, type 295.3'. These diagnoses are part of the classificatory system of codes in the authoritative Diagnostic and Statistical Manual of Mental Disorders, the numbers an outward sign of what purports to be a precise form of social sorting. The powerful symbolism of numbers, which suggest rationality, recall the production line speed in *Modern Times*. There follow official reports about various incidents in Connie's life, as well as the more ambiguous 'After the implantation patient was markedly better with no episodes two months. Symptoms then recurred. Amygdalotomy indicated but not carried out because of incident . . . .' The ellipsis suggests something ominous has occurred. The implication is that brain surgery has pacified her, while the novel ends with more matter-of-fact sentences: 'There were one hundred thirteen more pages. They all followed Connie back to Rockover' (381).

The Official History of Consuelo Camacho Ramos, all 113-plus pages, produces an institutionalised version of a life monitored by authorities, an account that sanctions the horrendous treatment she endures over years. Readers, though, gain access to her thoughts, and are given the backstory explaining the circumstances that determine her actions, actions that several authorities deem dangerous or psychotic, and punishable or treatable with medication and surgery. Connie is no saint – the 'incident' above is her attempt to kill the doctors who are treating her – but she is far more sinned against by institutions than she is sinning, and readers understand the 'invisible' Connie that goes unseen. Her ethnicity and class activate prejudices within bureaucracies that Gandy would appreciate, prejudices that work to keep her powerless; in one report she is identified as a 'Mexican-American Catholic', in another as an 'obese Puerto Rican'. Her admitted failings as a mother in extraordinarily trying conditions are skewed vindictively against her, as in this interchange with a social worker who begins by stating:

> 'You were then hospitalised at Rockover State for eight months.'
> 'They said I was sick and I agreed. Someone close to me [Claud] had died, and I didn't want to live.'
> 'You have a history of child abuse – '
> 'Once! I was sick!'
> 'Your parental rights were terminated.' (25–6)

Stigmatised as a bad mother, and as a violent and psychotic woman by the male neuroscientists who want to neutralise her surgically, Connie understands the gender bias at work with such experiments. She has overheard the chief surgeon, Dr Redding, comment that while 'three little psychosurgical procedures' on male prisoners led to a public outcry, the 'San Francisco Children's Hospital does hundreds with sound and thermal probes – mostly on neurotic women and intractable children – and no one says boo' (221). Connie recognises the sort of mental experiments being carried out (a radical and literal example of 'getting inside the head' of an individual) as existential threats. And while the surgeons do not have the overtly political motivation to make Connie and her fellow inmates adore their leaders, as is the case in *We* and *Nineteen Eighty-Four*, they are intent on transforming their patients into socially compliant individuals. Connie's attempts to escape, along with those of her best friend, Sybil, an ardent feminist, constitute a repudiation of the norms of their monitored environment. As in other acts of rebellion depicted in novels and films, their success or failure is less important than that they try, although if we accept that Connie is returned to Rockover State Psychiatric Hospital, it appears that the authorities have triumphed in a way comparable to those in the novels by Zamyatin and Orwell.

In this instance, though, there is an alternative reading of Connie's fate. Although the novel's contemporary world is relentlessly dystopian, *Woman on The Edge of Time*'s title gestures to Connie's capacity to interact with another time and place, specifically the imagined Massachusetts village of Mattapoisett in 2137. Much of the explicitly eutopian nature of that village lies outside the concerns of this book, but there are important surveillance elements worth foregrounding. Connie, not surprisingly, is disoriented in finding out that she has a receptive mind, is a 'catcher' able to communicate across time and space. Initially, too, she finds many of the aspects of Mattapoisett repugnant, or simply odd. The breakdown of gender distinctions is an important example, made manifest in the use of the pronoun 'per' for both males and females, while the eradication of the traditional family (the result of machines called 'brooders' that produce new offspring) means that there are no surnames. Connie's reaction to the brooders underlines the world from which she comes: 'I suppose you have numbers', she comments, 'I guess you're only called by first names because your real name – your identification – is the number you get at birth' (77). She is surprised to find that there are no identifying numbers: 'But the government', she asks, 'How are you identified?' (77) There is no government in the form she knows it, and no universal identification system. The brooders also break down the gender hierarchy, Connie being told by Luciente, her main contact at Mattapoisett, that 'as long as we were biologically enchained, we'd never be equal. And males would never be humanized to be loving and tender. So we all became mothers' (105). This extreme or enlightened move ties in with other insights into questions of power that relate to the threat Connie faces from psychosurgery. 'It's that race between technology', Luciente tells her,

> and insurgency – those who want to change the society in our direction. In your time the physical sciences had delivered the weapons technology. But the crux, we think, is in the biological sciences. Control of genetics. Technology of brain control. Birth-to-death surveillance. Chemical control through psychoactive drugs and neurotransmitters. (223)

Connie's institutional insurgency involves drastic, violent action in order both to save herself and to destroy the experimenting doctors, while her life generally has been a struggle to extricate herself from bureaucratic protocols and punishments based on powerful though fatally flawed surveillance systems. While the Official History might suggest that she fails to overcome the powers engaged in birth-to-death surveillance, the existence of Mattapoisett in the imagined future, and the possibility that Connie escapes to there, intimates that, ultimately, the insurgency validated in that eutopian alternative might succeed.

The main action of another illuminating novel dealing with gendered surveillance, Atwood's *The Handmaid's Tale*, takes place in a near future dystopia, a refashioned United States that employs the Old Testament as its foundational text. Established in reaction to a failed coup by radical Muslims (a possibly confected excuse for the Christian takeover), the renamed state of Gilead is ruled by elite male Commanders, who oversee a staunchly patriarchal regime. The inability of these men and their wives to have children initiates a form of sexual surrogacy in which fertile young 'handmaids' substitute for those wives. The Old Testament again provides the justification, for in Genesis the infertile Rachel offers her handmaid to her husband Jacob, 'that I may have children of her' (Genesis, 30.3). Beyond this biological control, Gilead functions as a fundamentalist Christian state that uses adulterated passages from the Bible to subjugate women, and to create a totalitarian nation with the attendant surveillance mechanisms: secret police (called The Eyes of God); heavily patrolled borders; intense peer surveillance; social sorting visually enforced by uniforms, as well as group activities and rituals (including public hangings) designed to expose and crush dissidents. A repressive gender imbalance applies, for although men are restricted in some ways by the prevailing ideology, women are its primary victims, and are consciously the target of much of the overt surveillance that takes place. This gender-oriented bias, the novel reveals, is at least partly a backlash against the third wave feminism of the late twentieth century, but it adopts notions from older social codes of order and propriety, the handmaids being warned that ' "Modesty is invisibility . . . Never forget it. To be seen – to be *seen* – is to be – her voice trembled – penetrated. What you must be, girls, is impenetrable"' (39; original emphasis).

The most visible expressions of Gilead's social organisation and a surveillance mentality that strives to keep women invisible and impenetrable are the full length uniforms women wear, which designate their respective places in a rigidly hierarchical structure. Men wear different versions of military attire to signal the martial elements Gilead promotes, and traditional 'male' values. Women are differentiated by garments whose colours display their respective roles within the system: the Commanders' wives wear blue, perhaps in reference to the Virgin Mary, while their Daughters wear white to evoke purity; the red robes, gloves and shoes of the Handmaids symbolise fertility; the Aunts, who instruct and monitor the Handmaids' activities, wear a serviceable brown, while the older, infertile Marthas, who function as servants, are dressed in green. In all cases, the garments are full length to signal Gilead's conservative Christian values, the encompassing headgear worn by the Handmaids making it impossible for them to be seen except by those directly in front of them. And then there are the 'invisible' women. The most clearly at odds with the fundamentalist values of Gilead – including feminists, lesbians and political dissidents – are transported to the nuclear and ecological disaster zones known as Colonies. They are designated as Unwomen, a term with obvious Orwellian undertones. Other women are retained in Gilead, kept from the public eyes in brothels and clubs to satisfy the lust and egos of Commanders. Called Jezebels, they are dressed in the style of pre-Gileadean 'men's clubs'. In these places, men are afforded a communal privacy away from their wives and the other women under their putative command, a freedom that allows them illicit sexual pleasure.

This private and deceitful intimacy jars against the grimly public 'Ceremony' that brings surveillance vigorously into the bedroom. In this ritual, Commanders impregnate their respective handmaids while their wives (who will claim any subsequent baby as their own) oversee the act. Although the protagonist and narrator, Offred, closes her eyes, she describes such an event in harrowing detail (104–5), beginning with the presence of the Commander's wife, ironically named Serena Joy, who lies further up the bed, 'her pubic bone under the base of my skull'. Offred and Serena link hands, supposedly to 'signify that we are of one flesh, one being. What it really means is that she is in control, of the process and thus of the product' (104). Making the act visible also supposedly transforms it into a rite, though any pretence of dignity or reverence is obliterated as Offred describes how:

> My red skirt is hitched up to my waist, though no higher. Below it the Commander is fucking. What he is fucking is the lower part of my body. I do not say making love, because this is not what he's doing. Copulating too would be inaccurate, because it would imply two people and only one is involved. Nor does rape cover it: nothing is going on here that I haven't signed up for. There wasn't a lot of choice but there was some, and this is what I chose. (104–5)

The rampant hypocrisy of this debased ritual is clear to all three participants, the Commander quickly zipping up his pants and leaving, while Serena Joy tells Offred to 'Get up and get out' (106). As a consequence, Offred observes, 'the juice of the Commander runs down my legs' (106), lessening the chances of pregnancy. She returns to her room and applies butter to her face and hands as an alternative form of skin lotion, an act that signifies hope: 'As long as we [Handmaids] do this, butter our skin to keep it soft, we can believe that we will someday get out, that we will be touched again, in love or desire. We have ceremonies of our own, private ones' (107). These complicated distinctions between public and private, between acts visible to the fundamentalist regime and those invisible to it, and between the present dystopia and some anticipation for something better beyond it, all insinuate Offred's individual narrative, placing it at odds with the far larger social framework in which an adulterated Bible provides the historical and ideological basis (as well as the tropes, iconography and ceremonies) for male domination that rests on several types of surveillance.

Gilead has relatively primitive monitoring technology – there are no cctv cameras, for instance, and little overt use of computers, although passes are required. A telling exception occurs in the opening days of the new order when the credit cards of all women ('Any account with an F on it instead of an M', 187) are rendered inactive. This sweeping and unexpected piece of electronic social sorting instantly places women in economic servitude to men. A later sanctioned instance of credit cards that allows for a satirical take on piety occurs at a store called Soul Scrolls, from which Commanders' wives can show their religious devotion by ordering print-outs of prayers by 'Computerphone':

> There are five different prayers: for health, wealth, a death, a birth, a sin. You pick the one you want, punch in the number, then punch in your own number so that your account will be debited, and punch in the number of times you want the prayer repeated. (176)

Offred notes sardonically that this public signal of faithfulness to the regime 'helps their husbands' careers' (176). But much of the visual surveillance of the Handmaids entails simple person-to-person monitoring, whether by the 'Eyes', the male secret police, the more militaristic male order of Angels, or the Aunts, who acculturate the Handmaids to Gilead's laws and keep them under regular scrutiny. Women in Atwood's novel are both oppressed and oppressors. Or, rather, the hierarchy of Aunts, Marthas, Wives and Handmaids maintains an interactive regime of power that relies upon peer monitoring and differentiated benefits for different classes of women. The relatively high place of the Aunts in the strata of women, below the Wives and Daughters, but above the Marthas, Handmaids and Econowives (wives of low-ranked men), gets rewarded by them being allowed to read and write; the implications of this benefit are looked at below. Even so, the patriarchal hierarchy means that while the Aunts who patrol the young women selected to be Handmaids have 'cattle prods slung on thongs from their leather belts', they are not 'trusted with guns. Guns were for the guards, specially picked from the Angels' (14). Women are relegated even as monitors.

The world Atwood creates fuses Biblical sources with more modern forms of surveillance and social sorting, elements that combine to screen, control or if necessary expel ethnic, political or religious 'others'. African-Americans, for example, are labelled 'Children of Ham' (from a contentious reference in Genesis) and supposedly are resettled to National Homeland One in North Dakota (94), though their actual fate is left ambiguous. Jews, designated 'Sons of Jacob' (also referencing Genesis) are declared 'special', and are 'given a choice. They could convert, or emigrate to Israel.' Many have done so in the past, although a rumour spreads that non-Jews 'got out that way, by pretending to be Jewish, but it wasn't easy because of the tests they gave you and they have tightened up on that now'. Offred adds that 'You don't get hanged only for being a Jew though. You get hanged for being a noisy Jew who won't make the choice. Or for pretending to convert' (211). Hangings are the most visible, brutal, and perhaps the most effective visual exhibition of control. Gilead's inhabitants are required to view, or cannot ignore, the offenders hanged on the ceremonial Wall, as when Offred and her friend Ofglen walk past:

> We stop, together as if on signal, and stand and look at the bodies. It doesn't matter if we look. We're supposed to look: this is what they are there for, hanging on the Wall. Sometimes they'll be there for days, until there's a new batch, so as many people as possible will have a chance to see them.
> What they are hanging from is hooks. (42)

The undoubted power of watching can be double-edged, nevertheless, as when Offred, thinking about the Commander as he reads the Bible to a group of women, muses that 'to be a man, watched by women . . . must be entirely strange. To have them watching him all the time . . . To have them sizing him up' (98). The sexual innuendo coded into those last phrases recognises the relationship between watching and desire, and the likelihood that the scrutinising male Angels also might be prey to sexual yearnings. As Offred wonders before she becomes a Handmaid, before she is renamed Offred: '[The Angels] were objects of fear to us, but of something else as well. If only they would look. If only we could talk to them. Something could be exchanged, we thought, some deal made, some trade-off, we still had our bodies. That was our fantasy' (14). Later, when she is being looked at by two relatively lowly-ranked young Guardians, she moves her 'hips a little', and though initially slightly ashamed, immediately understands that:

> I enjoy the power; the power of a dog bone, passive but there. I hope they get hard at the sight of us and have to rub themselves against the painted barriers, surreptitiously. They will suffer, later that night, in their regimented beds. (32)

Even those made visible by surveillance personnel and protocol can retain a modicum of control, can subvert and manipulate the power dynamic for their own purposes and advantage. Nonetheless, women are for the most part miserably subservient, and though the hierarchy of Wives, Aunts, Handmaids and all allow for degrees of power among the women, their inferior place in relation to equivalent men is obvious and visibly enforced.

Not surprisingly, given Atwood's acknowledged debt to Orwell (see Atwood 2012: 141–9), a crucial determinant of the power imbalance derives from language and the way regimes use it to instil and maintain orthodoxy. Offred's name, as with those of the other Handmaids, functions as an intimate form of control, for it publically proclaims that she is the Handmaid 'of Fred', just as her friend Ofglen is the Handmaid of a Commander called Glen. Offred's real name is June, but her renaming robs her of that identity and some connections to her past (as it is designed to do) while establishing her Commander's power over her; there have been previous Offreds and there might be subsequent ones. More importantly, most women are not allowed to read texts, especially the all-powerful Bible, or to write. The exemption given the Aunts for their monitoring of the Handmaids acts as a powerful incentive for the Aunts to maintain control of their charges. Where in *Nineteen Eighty-Four* Newspeak was intended ultimately to limit thought and speech to Party ideology, in *The Handmaid's Tale* the restrictions on reading and writing are designed to keep women passive and ignorant, to dislocate them from problematic ideas contained in texts. These texts include the Bible, from which the women are forbidden access. Offred understands its power: 'The Bible is kept locked up . . . It is an incendiary device: who knows what we'd make of it, if we ever got our hands on it? We can be read to from it, by him [the Commander], but we cannot read' (98). That reading, though, distorts the Bible to suit the regime. At times, readers realise that the words of the Bible have been reworked consciously to suit Gilead's patriarchal doctrine: '*From each*, said the slogan, *according to her ability; to each according to his needs . . .* It was from the Bible, or so they said' (127; original emphasis). Offred's suspicion is well-founded, for the original quotation, in which both pronouns in the slogan are male, comes from Karl Marx's *Critique of the Gotha Program*. Even when she is certain that there has been a misquotation, the prohibition on her consulting a written text is crippling (as it is meant to be): '*Blessed are the merciful. Blessed are the meek. Blessed are the silent*,' she hears, and comments: '*I knew they made that up, I knew it was wrong, and they left things out too, but there was no way of checking*' (100). Denied access to the word made visible in texts by strict surveillance, Offred and the majority of Gilead's women can be disempowered and manipulated.

As with her capacity to turn the power of the surveillance gaze to her profit,

Offred and others utilise the 'invisibility' of spoken language as opposed to visible text to subvert the regime's monitoring of language. There is a sanctioned spoken language that emphasises the Christian basis of Gilead, so that the Handmaids say farewell to each other with the slogan 'Under His Eyes', or splice phrases such as 'Praise be' into their talk. Yet the trainee Handmaids also use the cover of darkness in their dormitories to bond and swap information and impressions, and throughout the novel intimate conversations between women allow them to assess and criticise the state of affairs and to maintain a form of collective counter-history to that promulgated by the regime. Gossip, for example, especially by the Marthas, who by dint of their servant status see the private failings of the elites, or who pass information between each other, undermines the pious ideology that the state tries to impose. Offred overhears two of them, Cora and Rita, discussing the shooting of a Martha who was shot while fumbling to get her pass out. Cora accepts this as the Guardians doing their job in keeping people safe, but Rita retorts 'angrily', 'Nothing safer than dead . . . She was minding her own business. No call to shoot her' (30). And Offred discovers while walking and talking with Ofglen, who tells her 'You're always safest out of doors, no mikes', that Ofglen is part of a network of dissenters. 'Keep your head down as we walk,' Ofglen advises, 'and just lean a little towards me. That way I can hear you better. Don't talk when there's someone coming' (177). By this simple act of 'masking' they evade scrutiny and expand the network of rebels.

Nor are those who use verbal language subversively only women. The young Guardian, Nick, illicitly speaks to Offred (55), initiating a relationship that eventually leads to her escape from Gilead. Far more dangerously, when Offred goes for her monthly checkup to see if she is pregnant, the doctor, who 'isn't supposed to talk to me except when it's absolutely necessary', inspects her and then offers to 'help' her by having sex with her on the grounds that

> 'Most of these old guys can't make it anymore . . . Or they're sterile.' I almost gasp: he's said a forbidden word. *Sterile*. There is no such thing as a sterile man anymore, not officially. There are only women who are fruitful and women who are barren, that's the law. (70–1)

The categories 'barren', 'fruitful' and 'sterile' foreground language's social sorting function, as clearly as do titles such as Handmaid and Martha, Commander and Guardian. In this case the use of a forbidden word signals the doctor's derision for Gilead's biological rationale. His motives are suspect and self-serving, and his position puts Offred in jeopardy if she refuses, for – 'he could report me for cancer, for infertility, have me shipped off to the Colonies, with the Unwomen' (71) – but the 'invisibility' of the spoken suggestion also protects him. Later, the Commander's request to play Scrabble in private with Offred provides a more ambiguous, though still illicit use of unmonitored language, the spelling of words such as '*Prolix, quartz, quandary, sylph rhythm*' carrying a perverse though comic sexual charge. 'My tongue', Offred recalls, 'felt thick with the effort of spelling. It was like using a language I had once known but had nearly forgotten, a language having to do with customs that had long before passed out of the world' (164). These instances, among others, mark language as a tool of subversion as well as oppression. In working to enable communication beyond the reach of surveillance systems it initiates interpersonal negotiations that challenge the extent and efficacy of control. Those within the supposedly dominant group at times employ language in ways that can erode that dominance. While technology, protocols and principles embed surveillance in the foundations of societies, human interaction can provide the means for small-scale resistance. The extent of that resistance is multifarious within and between distinct texts, so that the New York Connie Ramos inhabits in the contemporary timeframe of *Woman on The Edge of Time* is far more oppressive for her than the fictitious world of Gilead, with fewer characters able to fight against the entrenched and complicit forces of control. The links between surveillance and punishment are stronger and more efficacious there, too, so that Connie's dissent places her in a more precarious position than Offred endures. These instructive differences and variations are repli-cated throughout the utopian genre.

The repeated associations of women with enforced orality and relative powerless-ness, and men with textuality and authority, continues outside beyond the principal narrative. Atwood adapts the literary device of an appended text that Orwell had used to explain Newspeak, so that 'Historical Notes' appear after Offred seemingly signs off with the phrase 'and so I step up, into the darkness within; or else the light' (307). Readers then find that the text they have read as *The Handmaid's Tale* is in fact a transcription of Offred's verbal narrative that she has taped illicitly onto cassettes. Where *We* and *Nineteen Eighty-Four* explore the seditious possibilities of secret texts in surveillance states, *The Handmaid's Tale* highlights the historical use of orality by women as a successful weapon of insubordination against vigor-ously scrutinised lives. An important exception is the mock Latin phrase 'nolite te bastardes carborundorum' scratched on a wardrobe, which is translated as 'don't let the bastards grind you down'. That apart, orality allows Offred and others to operate within and against an oppressive system. The Historical Notes, presented at an academic conference in the year 2195, troublingly reveal that though Gilead is now a long forgotten exercise in fundamentalist Christianity, some of the sexism that underpinned it still exists in the secular world of the distant future. Recorded on multiple cassette tapes discovered in no discernable order, Offred's words are transcribed, edited and organised by two male academics. Not only has the invisible oral account been made visible textually, but the scholars also give those written words the title *The Handmaid's Tale*, fusing Geoffrey Chaucer's great narrative and the 'archaic vulgar signification of the world *tail*' (313). Repeatedly, the male aca-demic introducing this work at the conference, James Pieixoto, prizes the written over the oral, the male over the female, lamenting that only Offred's necessarily subjective verbal account has been discovered: 'What would we give, now, for even twenty pages or so of printout from [the Commander's] private computer!' (322). Unwittingly, Pieixoto reveals the nexus between visible text and control. The words that bring *The Handmaid's Tale* to an end, 'Are there any questions?', neatly marries an academic conference nicely with an invitation that readers engage in a probing investigation of their own world and the directions in which it might be heading.

The ending of Peter Weir's 1998 film, *The Truman Show*, is less unexpected than that of *The Handmaid's Tale*, while its focus is far closer to the here and now than Mattapoisset in 2137. (For the benefit of clarity, the movie's title is italicised while the show depicted in the film is not italicised). *The Truman Show* depicts and satirically comments on the televisual aspects of surveillance, exposing the interconnections between voyeurism and entertainment, surveillance and consumer capitalism. Unbeknownst to him, Truman Burbank's hometown island of Seahaven is an enormous set, its inhabitants all actors, and he himself the unknowing star of an immensely popular reality television show that has run since before his birth (ultrascans of him as a foetus announce his arrival). Over one and a half billion people tune in for that birth, and by the time the narrative begins, Truman has been under surveillance by thousands of cameras for thirty years. The Biblical associations are manifest: Seahaven is a Paradise, a eutopian monument to the United States of the 1950s confected by television, mainstream film and advertising. The show's director is named Christof, defined in an interview as 'Creator of "The Truman Show"', who sits in the studio above the world he has created directing actors, constructing the narrative, controlling the weather: famously, when Truman flees, he demands that, though ostensibly it is night, his crew 'Cue the sun'. Later, when Truman overcomes his conditioned fear of the sea and escapes by yacht in search of Fiji, Christof orders his increasingly unwilling technical assistant to upgrade the studio-produced storm to force Truman back home. By contrast to this wrathful God, at the climax of the film Christof speaks to Truman as a voice from sunlit clouds, attempting to coax Truman back to Seahaven, and a life that he argues is better than the dystopian real world beyond the set that Truman yearns to visit. He explains that he has monitored Truman all his life, and therefore knows his creation better than Truman knows himself. This elicits an immediate and forceful denial 'You never had a camera in my head' – a phrase that echoes Julia's 'They can't get inside you.' Truman knowingly expels himself from Paradise, escaping the show's totalising surveillance. But *The Truman Show* does not end there, because once Truman leaves, the show's television audience becomes the film viewer's focus. Sporadically through *The Truman Show*, that television audience has been softly mocked for its slavish adherence to the show, its emotional investment in a fictional character. Once Truman's escape has given them temporary exhilaration, they search for new thrills. Although a specific television show has ended, the appetite for voyeurism does not abate.

The film proposes tempting questions about the limits and levels of visual surveillance, about identity as performance, about the possibilities and strategies of resistance to surveillance regimes, about what surveillance 'sees' and fails to see, and about surveillance in different spaces, eutopian and dystopian. That final aspect will be looked at in the next chapter. For the moment, it is enough to understand that for the show's viewers, Seahaven accords with their sense of a eutopia. While there are activists who recognise the setup as equivalent to a prison, 'The Truman Show's' fans treat the island as a better world than the tame, conventional and emotionally neutered one they inhabit. Yet their naïve love of the show and its eponymous hero sustains the fictional world Truman himself comes to find hellish. By watching the show and its attendant advertising, as well as by purchasing products from the show, they perpetuate its success and Truman's continued incarceration within it. If they stopped watching, the show that is his manufactured life would end; Truman would be 'free'. Instead, they misinterpret their voyeurism as concern for and affective con- nection with him. Although they are not quite the Thought Police, their watching has a deleterious effect not only on Truman, but also on his 'wife', Meryl, who cracks under the strain as the pretence collapses, and his 'best friend', Marlon, whose need to confect false emotions and lies on cue (the latter fed through an earpiece from Christof) produces genuine moments of pathos as he struggles to reconcile true and false feelings. Meryl's and Marlon's respective names tap into the audience's sub- conscious desire for celebrities seen on the 'big screen'. If the studio and especially Christof are primarily responsible for keeping Truman under 24-hour surveillance, the television audience is also complicit and oppressive.

But Truman's passionate denial that the studio knows his thoughts calls into question what viewers and Christof had 'seen' over the thirty years of the show. There remains the equally complex question of what Truman has seen, and how that has been integrated into his own consciousness. Certainly for most of that time Truman has accepted outward appearances, and in the manufactured and monitored environment of Seahaven appearances are relatively easy to control. Yet while the world Truman inhabits is visible, as are his appearance and actions, his consciousness, he argues, remains invisible. In that sense Truman approximates Winston Smith. The clear difference is that Winston knows himself to be under surveillance, where Truman does not, or does not know the true circumstances in which he lives. And yet he does have a clear sense of the distinction between a 'real' self and a 'social' self. In an opening scene in front of his bathroom mirror he 'plays' the role of a climber wanting to reach the top of a mountain. While he has no awareness that a camera is relaying his performance to the show's audience, Meryl's call from the kitchen brings that performance to an end, and he takes on the acceptable persona of husband. We soon find out, though, that he is secretly collect- ing photographs from women's magazines in an attempt to piece together an image of his lost love, Lauren. The show's audience sees his 'secret', but Truman's need to hide the truth from his wife and work colleagues displays an awareness of and need for privacy in which his genuine emotions and desires can flourish. This concealed world begins increasingly to collide with the public world as Truman starts to see objects, people and situations that jar with the reality he has accepted: a falling light from the 'sky' that is the set; the exposure of the communication system that tracks his movements; his 'father' (who years before had been 'killed' on the show, but who has broken back onto the set); a lift revealed as fake; a photograph showing Meryl crossing her fingers in their wedding photo, cancelling her vows. Truman integrates these visual clues into a growing appreciation of the bizarre truth that he is being monitored. Even when he escapes from his basement by setting up an effigy to bluff those he suspects are scrutinising him he has no real knowledge of the show's reality, thinking merely that if he can escape Seahaven he might find Lauren in Fiji, where he thinks she lives – in fact, she lives in Los Angeles, and, ironically, is viewing his actions on television.

Truman's getaway by yacht exposes the surveillance system, which has presented itself as a benign and paternalistic part of a successful television show, as oppressive and consumer-driven, concerned primarily for the continuation of the show and for the revenue it generates. People as well as cameras and microphones are involved, for Truman has been under intense and highly personal peer surveillance throughout his life. Previously benevolent 'characters' reveal themselves as complicit self-serving actors keen to keep ongoing jobs, while the equally compromised crew that has become habituated to an unreflective monitoring routine are required to confront the murky morality of their actions. Directing their efforts is an increasingly frustrated and angry Christof, whose hubristic belief in his god-like powers faces a lethal threat. Informed by a lifetime of viewing Truman, Christof presumes that he 'knows' Truman. He does figure out how Truman has escaped the island by yacht, and while Truman is still within the massive set of the show, Christof believes that he can still dominate his creation, simultaneously employing cameras on the yacht to produce gripping drama for the viewing audience. But though he increasingly upgrades the manufactured storm to the point where Truman looks certain to die, Christof misjudges Truman's willingness to risk death rather than to continue his life as before. Studio pressure and the refusal of his crew to carry out Christof's orders force him to abandon that plan, but the Truman who survives the storm and sails triumphantly on still does not understand the false reality of the set he inhabits.

Only when his yacht literally crashes into the reality that is the edge of the set does Truman begin to comprehend the nature of his life to that point. At this outermost physical point of 'The Truman Show' he engages in philosophical and quasi-mystical discussion with Christof, the surveillance eye and voice from those sunlit clouds, who answers the question of who he, Christof, is with the vainglorious,

'I am the creator of a television show that gives hope and joy and inspiration to millions.'
    'Then who am I?'
    'You're the star.'

For Christof, the fake world of Seahaven is reality, Truman's constructed and scrutinised existence a real life. Meryl has foreshadowed this delusion in one of the staged interviews that opens the film: 'For me there is no difference between a private life and a public life. My life is my life is "The Truman Show". "The Truman Show" is a lifestyle. It is a noble life. It is [she pauses for dramatic effect] a truly blessed life.' Hers is more a professional self-justification than is Christof's, incidentally indicating how trapped he and others are within the confected surveillance world he oversees. His conversation with Truman reveals that he views his role in terms of a vicarious fatherhood: 'I was watching you when you were born. I watched your first step. I watched you on your first day of school. The episode when you lost your first tooth.' The unconscious slip into the television jargon of 'episode' makes known the artificial and perverse nature of his watching, while his response to Truman's subsequent silence – 'Say something god dammit. You're on television. You're live to the whole world' – betrays his televisual instincts and motivations. Truman, meanwhile, has turned away, his face invisible to viewers and to Christof. He turns and delivers a catchphrase he has given countless times to his observing neighbours: 'And in case I don't see ya – good afternoon, good evening and good night.' This act energetically rejects his manufactured identity, swapping his former, pliable innocence for candid experience. He leaves 'The Truman Show' with a theatrical bow, stepping from the artificial light and visibility of the set into the dark and invisible world beyond.

Were *The Truman Show* to finish there, the film's viewers might accept it encapsulating a typically 'Hollywood Ending', a tritely uplifting tale of one person's triumph over the system. Instead, after allowing the television show's audience a moment of individual or communal emotional uplift, the film cuts to two car park security guards who have cheered Truman's escape. Eating pizzas, they switch immediately from former aficionados of the now defunct show to bored television viewers, one asking 'What else is on?', the other replying 'Where's the tv guide?' What is in one sense a bathetic finale in fact throws a harsh satirical light on the audience whose lazy acceptance of the sinister aspects of the show has allowed it to continue, indeed have provided the economic energy for its success. But there are further implications, for 'The Truman Show' has brought surveillance into the living rooms of viewers, neutralising and naturalising the massive invasion of privacy it involves. When it was released in 1998 (a year before the first series of *Big Brother*, and six years before Facebook's chief Mark Zuckerberg's dismissal of privacy as no longer a social norm) *The Truman Show* presented a future in which commerce and surveillance would be merged for mutual benefit. It put that relationship under critical inspection, tellingly by placing the audience of television's 'The Truman Show' audience under temporary surveillance by the audience of cinema's *The Truman Show*. Part of the film's satirical bite came from the insinuation of a likely overlap between these audiences, that the somewhat pathetic and emotionally starved people watching 'The Truman Show' in living rooms, bars and (in one instance) a bath might be similar to those watching the film. The film implicates the wider public in the acceptance and proliferation of voyeuristic surveillance as entertainment, marking the eroding barriers between the public and the private and the morphing of surveillance into areas well beyond that controlled by the state. It also probes the extent to which what is visible and can be monitored by new technology is limited to externals, and so might not reveal the thoughts and defining qualities of an individual, especially when that individual resists scrutiny.

China Mieville's 2009 dystopian police procedural novel, *The City & The City*, adds a provocative complication to these concerns. Its near future world incorporates two mutually suspicious societies, Beszel and Ul Qoma, states that occupy the same space. These are, in Mieville's provocative terminology, 'topolgangers'. The relationships between surveillance and spaces gets considered in the next chapter, but *The City & The City* remains pertinent to questions of visibility in that the members of both societies are forbidden from seeing the members, buildings, signs and other cultural markers of the other. Those who fail to do so risk arrest by the mysterious and immensely powerful monitoring agency called 'Breach', which also happens to be the term for the crime of seeing citizens from the other state. The sanctioned approach requires both communities consciously to 'unsee' the other, an operation that sets up a crucial tension around visibility. Where Gary T. Marx allows for a gradation along the spectrum from visible to invisible, Miéville's novel extends the line to the 'unvisible' (86), that which is consciously unseen. Some examples from *The City & The City* suggest the implications of this disorienting situation. At one point the protagonist, Inspector Borlú, from Beszel, trying to discover the murderer of a student whose body is dumped in his home state, must undertake investigations in Ul Qoma. These states, remember, are situated on the same territory, but are inhabited by two societies. In order to function in Ul Qoma, Borlú must be trained to see things he had previously and actively unseen, requiring him being placed,

> in what they called an Ul Qoma simulator, a booth with screens for inside walls, on which they projected images and videos of Beszel with the Besz buildings highlighted and their Ul Qoman neighbours minimised with lighting and focus. Over long seconds, again and again, they would reverse the visual stress, so that for the same vista Bezel would recede and Ul Qoma shine. (160)

The formerly unvisible Ul Qoma becomes visible while his home state of Bezel recedes into unvisibility. The complexities of this situation are extended further by the necessity for others to see or unsee Borlú, as appropriate. So, having been allowed to move around Ul Qoma as a visitor, he gets noticed: 'I saw the groups of Ul Qomans unsee me because of my clothes and the way I held myself, double-take and see my visitors mark, then see me' (172). The confusion for the viewing Ul Qomans is only clarified by the signifying visitor's mark, but the interactive procedure of being 'unseen' and then being 'seen' by the same group creates a dynamic relationship that eradicates any simple binary of visible and invisible, seen and not seen, monitored and not monitored.

Later, the murderer exploits the ambiguities surrounding visibility in attempting to escape. He engages in sophisticated blocking and masking moves, using the peculiar elements of topolganger states and the need for citizens to unsee those in the overlapping state. The architecture and culture of Beszel and Ul Qoma are distinct, but tourists are also taught 'supposed differences in national physiognomies' (93). The murderer knowingly positions himself between the gestures associated with Besz and Ul Qoman citizens to take himself outside the normal range of intelligibility. Borlú realises that the killer is,

> instantly visible. That gait. Strange, impossible. Not properly describable, but to anyone used to the physical vernaculars of Beszel and Ul Qoma, it was rootless and untethered, purposeful and without a country. (353)

While visible, the killer is unclassifiable as either Besz or Ul Qoman. He exploits the threat that those who fail to unsee will invoke the all-powerful monitoring agency, Breach, and Borlú comprehends the paradox by stating that the killer 'walked with equipoise, possibly in either city. Schrödinger's pedestrian' (352), the final reference bringing to mind physicist Erwin Schrödinger's mental experiment, in which it could not be known whether a cat in a sealed box was alive or dead, or both, and where to open the box kills the cat. The murderer is not alone in utilising the peculiarities of the situation to escape authority, for a cluster of dissident groups from both states 'live between the cities, not exiles but insiles, evading justice and retribution by consummate ignorability' (161). These groups might be understood to inhabit gradations of unvisibility, and with distinct degrees of success; by the end of the novel, none has effected the political programme – union between the topol-gangers, or division – for which they have striven. Ultimately, Borlú can only catch the killer by violating the requirement that he unsees. He ends up becoming part of Breach, moving from investigating crime in Besźel to monitoring those who violate the rule to unsee. Doing so requires that he occupy a different space, not inside or outside Besźel and Ul Qoma, but as the novel's title foregrounds, 'between the city and the city'.

Another extension of vision takes it not beyond the visible but beyond the present and into the future. William Bogard's argument for the simulation of surveil-lance, touched on in Chapter 1, proposes that computer profiling 'is best understood not just as a technology of surveillance, but as a kind of *surveillance in advance of sur-veillance*, a technology of "observation before the fact"'. Bogard records that advertis-ers use profiling to target specific audiences, while police, among other things, use criminal profiling 'to spot potential drug traffickers' (Bogard 1996: 27). Philip K. Dick's 1956 short story 'Minority Report', from which the Steven Spielberg film was adapted, foreshadows some aspects of this argument by four decades, Dick imagining a Department of Precrime based on the predictive powers of three individuals, with pre-cognitive abilities that allow them to 'see' the future. The 'precogs' themselves are unaware of their talents; having enormous heads and emaciated bodies they are described dismissively as 'mutants'. Strapped in place and 'milked' for their visions, they speak gibberish that they do not themselves understand, which is then decoded by computers. Their value is that they are thought able to predict the future up to a fortnight in advance, and supposedly are monumentally successful: 'Precrime has cut down felonies by ninety-nine and decimal point eight percent' (Dick 2002: 4). Despite this apparent triumph, the story teases out several paradoxes and conun-drums, including the question of whether those who are arrested in advance of having committed a crime should be prosecuted, and the possibility that the precogs might be fallible. The story's title alludes to the rare occurrence in which one of the three precogs has a vision different from those the others see. This prompts ques-tions about the accuracy of the lauded system. Critically, the minority report exon-erates John Anderton, the protagonist and instigator of Precrime, of a murder seen by two of the precogs. A key consequence of two possible 'futures' being seen, one in which a murder is seen, one in which no murder takes place, is that the potential criminal, by an act of will, decides not to commit a crime they had pre-meditated. The thoughts the precogs have picked up are later rejected by their thinker, so that no crime is committed. 'Minority Report' asks what distinguishes prediction from mere probability? What are the limits and dangers of profiling? How might surveil-lance information be misused to satisfy particular political or social agendas?

Some of the questions are developed in Steven Spielberg's massively popular *Minority Report* (2002), which takes up many of the narrative and thematic concerns of the short story, placing the action in the Washington of 2054 and limiting the powers of the precogs to crimes of murder rather than to all felonies. The precogs in the film version are far more sympathetically portrayed than those in the story, their names – Agatha, Arthur and Dashiell – playfully referencing the murder mystery writers Agatha Christie, Arthur Conan Doyle and Dashiell Hammett. Agatha produces the crucial minority report that exonerates John Anderton and implicates Precrime Director Lamar Burgess, whose political ambitions are intertwined with the transposition of the Precrime experiment in Washington to the nation as a whole. The vital complication is that Burgess has manipulated the precog visions to cover up his own murderous past. As well as being central to the solving of the film's tangled and compelling thriller plot, the interaction of vision and surveillance operates in several guises. In a world in which retina scanning means that when John Anderton is on the run from his own Precrime team, who have been alerted by the precogs that he will kill a man he has never met in the next thirty-six hours, he is required to purchase a new set of eyeballs on the blackmarket that he then has attached (with the loss of his own eyeballs) by a sleazy struck-off doctor. Chapter 7, on 'Technologies', deals with the hi-tech surveillance systems that work to track Anderton and others, but at the human (or precog) level the effect of monitoring on the monitors themselves forms an intriguing subplot. Agatha, Arthur and Dashiell must regularly suffer the trauma of seeing premeditated murders being imagined by the perpetrators. Trapped in their communal pool and linked into the databases of the Precrime unit, the precogs essentially are exploited as fleshy utilities whose humanity is denied them. While the murder-free world of Washington predominantly (though not exclusively) is a glossy twenty-first century eutopia, the precogs essentially work as psychic slaves shackled to a hellish existence in the Precrime Department. Ultimately, once the Department and the system are dismantled, they are spirited away to a quiet haven, a eutopian place, where they can recover. Where the viewing audience in *The Truman Show* is criticised subtly for its mindless attachment to the show that perpetuates Truman's surveillance, the precogs are unshackled from their forced monitoring, enabling them to recover from the horrors they have been forced to see.

*Minority Report* powerfully exemplifies how the capacity to 'see' literally and figuratively can damage the viewer as well as the viewed. Accepting that visibility in many forms is central to how surveillance functions, what the texts looked at in this chapter show the differing impacts monitoring can have on particular characters and in specific circumstances. Not all are subject to the same levels of visual scrutiny and so not all respond similarly. Indeed the diversity of types of surveillance around the conceptual hub of visibility is multiplied in the reactions of those who come, deservedly or not, to be monitored. A recurrent argument in this book is that most characters accommodate themselves to the prevailing surveillance conditions, sometimes out of fear of punishment, as with *The City & The City*, or because of a false sense that the surveillance system is foolproof and protective, as in *Minority Report*, or again out of allegiance to a powerful ideological pull of the type we see in *The Handmaid's Tale*. The critical lesson from these texts is that there is no single completely validated response or programmed outcome for characters nor any automatic or guaranteed reactions from those imposing surveillance. Where visibility in

*Nineteen Eighty-Four* primarily was carried out by the state against the individuals, or by peer to peer monitoring encouraged by the state, contemporary novels and films have displayed more interactive and flexible relationships between those doing the surveillance and those subject to it, as well as a creative assortment of methods by which to avoid being seen or masking one's identity. These texts extend the definition of visibility to include not only the finely-graded scale from the visible to the invisible, but also potentially into new realms such as the unvisible. Whether or not we accept this final category, or are willing to extend the spectrum to include it fully, the concept itself is sufficiently imaginative and challenging to make us think anew about what we and others see or do not see, or think we see or do not see.

# 5   Spaces

The spirit of community has long been held as an antidote to threats of social disorder, class war and revolution violence ([Thomas] More pioneered such thinking). Well-founded communities often exclude, define themselves against others, erect all sorts of keep-out signs (if not tangible walls), internalise surveillance, social control, and repression. (Harvey 2000: 170)

Compound people didn't go to the cities unless they had to, and then never alone. They called the cities the pleeblands . . . it was best for everyone at OrganInc Farm to live all in one place, with foolproof procedures.
    Outside the OrganInc walls and gates and searchlights, things were unpredictable. (Atwood 2004: 33–4)

Cyberspace. A consensual hallucination experienced daily by billions of legitimate operators, in every nation, by children being taught mathematical concepts. (Gibson 1995: 67)

If surveillance involves the monitoring of people, it necessarily requires monitoring the spaces and places that people inhabit. Utopian texts have inherent spatial concerns, the root word 'topos' designating a 'place' to which might be attached prefixes with positive or negative connotations. This variety can extend across the many texts understood as utopian, but variations also can occur within individual works. For several centuries, utopian texts tended to depict relatively defined places, sometimes islands or hidden worlds. Especially over the last century, particularly in the shadow of works of H. G. Wells, such places are more likely to be global or planetary in extent. Within these capacious boundaries exist nations or superstates or enclaves, and at times, the explicit, hidden or developing tensions and divisions between these places require specific surveillance protocols and technologies. Boundaries are monitoring pinchpoints where designated groups and individuals can be included and excluded, although clearly surveillance can and does take place within those boundaries. At a more abstract level, comparisons between the world depicted within utopian texts and the worlds lived in by respective readers or viewers are built into the dynamic of any utopian work. Both the projected place of the text and the place occupied by readers and viewers are themselves open to multiple interpretations, reminding us that while some characters can find a space dystopic, others (sometimes the majority) within the same text will treat it as euto-pian, or as something less like hell.

I have used the terms space and place interchangeably, while understanding that, as Charles Crawford admits, 'space remains a contested issue among social scien-tists', especially in relation to place. Crawford notes that while some define space 'as abstract geometries, such as distance, direction, and shape', others understand it as 'what place become when things of meaning and value are removed' (Crawford 2010: 4). He classes David Harvey among the latter group, and yet Harvey's 2000 study of globalisation, which deals at length with the places people inhabit and with utopian works, is titled *Spaces of Hope*. Harvey's study provides the first epigraph for this chapter, sounding a warning about the intersections between utopian schemes, surveillance and oppression. He traces this back to Thomas More's *Utopia*. Given that the distinctions between place and space remained unresolved, this chapter employs 'spaces' as a capacious term that can integrate one or more places of human social interaction. Margaret Atwood's 2004 novel, *Oryx and Crake*, provides the second epigraph above, exemplifying the sometimes tense relationships between zones, in this instance so-called Compounds, whose privileged inhabitants live in fear of (and are screened from) the denizens of benighted 'pleebands'. Harvey has labelled real world equivalents of the Compounds as 'suburban "privatopias"' and 'ghettoes of affluence' (148), spaces in which the rich protect themselves from the rest. The model of utopian enclaves protected by monitoring from the dystopian worlds that abut or surround them has a clear environmental component, some-thing grounded literally in the state of the planet, and explored in films such as *Code 46* and *Children of Men*. But William Gibson's breakthrough novel, *Neuromancer*, quoted above, as well as incorporating dystopian megalopolises, also famously depicts intangible cyberspace.

Surveillance tends to be associated with metropolitan settings, understandably given the intricate relationship between monitoring and the fantastic expansion of cities that mark modernity. But as environmental crises increasingly get built into the concerns of utopian texts, these works evaluate ways of patrolling the 'natural world', and especially the borders between what are read as eutopian and dystopian spaces. The Green Wall in *We* stands as an earlier example of this environmental partition, locating an existential threat in the space beyond the Wall. Huxley's Malpais functions less ambiguously as a dystopian environment, certainly physically and perhaps culturally, although the novel's critique of those who inhabit the Brave New World complicates any sense of unproblematic division between the 'natural' world and the 'developed' spaces occupied by humans. Films such as *Code 46* and *Children of Men* offer separate treatments of near future worlds in which environ-mental degradation has created a geographical hierarchy, those within the respec-tive eutopian spaces shielded from those outside by guards, checkpoints, passes and penalties. In both cases, though, those living inside protective walls in relative ease and comfort are required to submit to monitoring processes that reinforce their status as surveillance subjects. While these processes entail the recognised loss of freedom, most characters are happy to accept such impositions as the price of security and a better material life, while those beyond the eutopian boundaries, for similar reasons, struggle and scheme to gain entry. Most characters, but not all, for in *Code 46* the protagonists Maria Gonzales and William Geld flee the environmentally superior world of Shanghai for the desert-like spaces of what is called El Fuera: 'The Outside'. Surveillance agents eventually track them down and repatriate Geld, but at irrevocable cost, in that he has his memories wiped. To live within the eutopian world means to exist within rigorously monitored comfort. Gonzales, by contrast, having committed several crimes that threaten surveillance protocols, gets permanently exiled to El Fuera, a space less subject to scrutiny, but substantially less inviting as habitat. In *Oryx and Crake* environmental meltdown accelerates the collapse of social divisions between the eutopian and the dystopian spaces. State and commercial surveillance does not exist, because there is no state, no commerce, and virtually no humans.

Walls and boundaries are key spatial indicators, establishing and preserving relationships both within and between spaces, and determining the movement of their inhabitants. In early utopian texts, including *Utopia*, the connection and subsequent comparison between spaces was activated by the traveller who journeys from one to the other and then returns home to report their findings. Utopia the island is, by definition, a separate space, but it can be reached by and does interact with other parts of the real world. Later utopian works that are global in scope can still have internal borders that distinguish different superstates, nations and zones. These partitions need not be inviolable, and sometimes the desire to escape from space that is oppressively monitored to one that is relatively free creates a narrative and thematic dynamic, as in Connie Ramos's attempts to flee from psychiatric institutions, or Truman's journey to the edges of the television set that has been his 'home', and then beyond the visual control of Christof to uncertain freedom in Los Angeles. The uncertainty about whether the space to which the character escapes is better than that from which they flee motivates Offred's final observation in *The Handmaid's Tale*:

> Whether this is my end or a new beginning I have no way of knowing: I have given myself over into the hands of strangers, because it can't be helped. And so I step up, into the darkness within; or else the light. (307)

Readers find that, in all likelihood, she does escape successfully, but her doubts reflect how utopian texts regularly conceive of situations or characters with sufficient complexity and ambiguity to generate multiple developments and outcomes. These possibilities require readers and viewers to contemplate an assortment of implications. Spaces, and the boundaries between them, can be provocatively indeterminate or contested. Ursula Le Guin's *The Dispossessed* (1974), for instance, introduces uncertainty on the opening page. Connections between two imagined planets, Annares and Urras, are made via 'ports' on each that are surrounded by walls. Le Guin describes the port on Annares as, 'like all walls', 'ambiguous, two-faced. What was inside it and what was outside it depended upon which side of it you were on' (1). *The Dispossessed*'s subtitle, *An Ambiguous Utopia*, advertises its sustained engagement with the enlightening challenges of ambiguity. Its protagonist, a physicist called Shevek, moves from Annares to Urras and back, declaring his antagonism to the political, intellectual and cultural divisions imposed by real and metaphorical walls: 'Those who build walls are their own prisoners. I'm going to go fulfil my proper function in the social organism. I'm going to go and unbuild walls' (332). The unbuilding of walls might bring to mind the unvisible zones of *The City & The City*. In a world of topolgangers, where different cities inhabit the same geographical space, any surety about spaces, and about how they might be surveilled, is provocatively unsettled.

While many utopian novels and films project forward to a future space, as has been noted the set of Seahaven in *The Truman Show* is rare in that it harks back to an earlier time and space, a romanticised 1950s. Seahaven stands as an example of New Urbanism; and literally stands, for the 'set' of 'The Truman Show' is the actual town of Seaside, Florida. New Urbanism, Amanda Rees explains, is one of a number of 'utopian visions' (Rees 2003: 93) that developed in part as a response to the earlier utopian movement of modernism, given ecstatic form in *Metropolis*. New Urbanism can be seen as a form of postmodernism, but one whose influences simultaneously stretch back to traditional senses of community that include neighbourhood interaction which puts people in physical and visual contact with each other. Rees argues that 'New Urbanism practitioners clearly connect the physical design and creation of community with the outcome of myriad benefits', adding that they believe 'environments can both support and constrain activities' and that 'the physical design can promote and discourage behaviours and attitudes' (97). This assessment affirms the longstanding interaction between architectural and urban design in utopian texts and surveillance that reaches back to *Utopia* and on through the Panopticon and the glass buildings in *We*. We can understand *The Truman Show* in similar terms, and Rees observes that the film employs Seaside to 'signify controlled perfection as part of a larger, damning critique of the vacuity of contemporary life' (Rees 104). Truman's engagement with his neighbours as he leaves for work provides a revealing example. Superficially a moment of interactive neighbourliness of a sort welcomed by New Urbanism, the contact depends on urban planning that pitches people into a regular and sometimes unwelcomed view of those around them. Truman's folksy response to the neighbouring family's 'Good morning!'—'Good morning! And if I don't see you, good afternoon, good evening and good night', is so ritualised as to have become a catchphrase. Truman uses it tellingly when he exits the set, signalling the words as a piece of sociability performed for those who 'see' him every workday morning. Other public interactions are equally forced or false. The daily meeting with his neighbour, Spencer, reinforces Truman's conditioned terror of dogs, his chat with a newspaper vendor involves his 'secret' buying of women's magazines in order secretly to construct an image of Lauren, while his regular if supposedly coincidental meeting with twins Don and Ron place him unknowingly in front of a billboard, in this instance as part of the show's underlying economics. At work he hides his attempts to find Lauren, but his dealings with colleagues register the workplace as pressured and invasive. Home provides an escape from the generally oppressive public spaces, although in a brief scene in the garden, the close shot of Truman's backside as he tends the lawn, while comic in itself, might serve as a sign of his attitude to his neighbours and his wife, Meryl.

His house provides some form of escape from this uncomfortable socialising, but even here there are distinct 'public' and 'private' spaces, the living room and kitchen being places in which Truman engages with his wife and mother in encounters that increasingly slide into uneasy confrontation. The bathroom and basement are rooms in which he feels his privacy protected. But even here his actions are subtly modulated. Before the mirror he performs various characters that allow him temporary alternative identities, before Meryl's inevitable call draws him back to the public world. In the basement, which Meryl regularly invades, he keeps a chest for his most private and secret mementos, including a composite photo of Lauren, reminders of his inner emotions and identity that must be submerged in the public domain. While all this 'privacy' is transmitted for the show's viewers, Truman actively maintains these hidden aspects of himself, speaking to his need for private spaces where he can fully be himself. Alone in his house, he finds evidence in a wedding photo that his marriage to Meryl has been faked, and, having pieced together at least some of the truth that he is under surveillance, he escapes from his basement and from the cameras he now assumes are watching him. He escapes by using his monitors' belief that they have him under constant scrutiny even in a private space, and that he is unaware of that scrutiny. His desire to flee Seahaven itself for the eutopia of Fiji and Lauren forces him to overcome his conditioned fear of the sea. Only at the limit of the space that is 'The Truman Show' set does he come to understand the extent to which he has lived under surveillance.

Truman's confrontation with Christof at the boundary between the manufactured and monitored space of the show and the world beyond (one that a sequel might reveal to be only slightly less surveilled) accentuates how borders differentiate spaces and act as critical pressure points for surveillance protocols. This is especially true in utopian novels and films that incorporate eutopian and dystopian realms, and in which characters struggle to enter particular spaces, or are denied access to those spaces. Andrew Niccol had written the original screenplay for The Truman Show (one considerably more dystopian than the film that eventuated) and he gives surveillance a darker treatment in his directorial debut, Gattaca (1997), for which he also wrote the script. (Because of delays in the production of The Truman Show, that film was released after Gattaca.) Gattaca examines genetic profiling as part of surveillance's role in 'digital discrimination', something considered in the following chapter. But the division of spaces into eutopian and dystopian zones constitutes a vital element in this discrimination, most forcefully realised in the eponymous Gattaca Aerospace Corporation, in which those designated as having superior genes, called 'Valids', are trained for space exploration. The film's protagonist, Vincent Freeman, dreams of such adventures, but the blood test given him immediately after birth, which has branded him genetically inferior – an 'Invalid' (pronounced 'In-Valid') – unconditionally denies him that opportunity. He can only work at Gattaca as a cleaner. Vincent's younger brother, Anton, by contrast, is the result of genetic selection his parents undertake with the help of a geneticist who removes supposed flaws, meaning that Anton is born with 'superior' genes, and so prospers in a world of genetic apartheid. With surveillance at the fertilisation stage, *Gattaca* enjoys obvious affiliations with *Brave New World*, although in 'the not-too-distant future' the film imagines the only major change needed is social acceptance of this contemporary form of eugenics. Niccol warns that shifting surveillance into the delivery ward and the geneticist's office, in the name of improving the gene pool, might produce a despotic society in which only certain genes are valued, while others deemed deficient are relegated or eliminated. Pre- and immediate postnatal spaces where embryos and newborns are rigorously scrutinised and evaluated become massively determining, enforcing dominant norms. In the case of the Gattaca Corporation these norms mesh scientific enquiry with commercial interests, although the company's director revels in the genetic superiority of Gattaca employees, and their manifest destiny. His name, Josef, recalls that of Nazi geneticist Josef Mengele.

While strict genetic requirements are required to enter the Gattaca space programme, within the Gattaca building itself there is repeated genetic testing of skin, hair and bodily fluids to guard against the possibility that Invalids might somehow infiltrate. Employees enter through turnstiles that automatically take blood samples, workspaces are constantly cleaned of skin and hair that is then scrutinised, and regular urine tests are imposed. These exams work to establish the identity of the employees, and, along with tests of athletic endurance, function to evaluate candidates for the space programme; only the elite performers among the Valids are chosen. *Gattaca* exemplifies a common feature of utopian novels and films, in that eutopian spaces are far more heavily monitored than the dystopian worlds outside or around them. Surveillance operates to establish and maintain the distinction between the ideal and the imperfect, between the desired and the dilapidated. Within the putatively ideal space, rigorous and oppressive monitoring ensures that Gattaca employees remain simultaneously aggressively competitive and ideologically docile, a de-individualised mass enjoying the benefits bestowed by the company while remaining outwardly accepting of their subjugation. Vincent Freeman is the exception, using the black market genetic material of a disabled Valid called Jerome Morrow to gain entry to Gattaca and thus move closer to fulfilling his lifelong dream. In order to accomplish his deceit he needs to remove any incriminating bodily detritus from this workspace, and supply false samples of blood and urine to the company medical technician, Lamar. He must also produce a false heart rate during the athletics examinations, but his ability to perform the necessary tasks at a superior level discloses an essential flaw in the society's genetic ideology; Vincent succeeds not as a result of his superior genetic make-up, but by sheer force of will. So, while the Gattaca Corporation spatially encodes the discriminatory division of society, enabling and denying access, its fundamental premises are faulty. The film's tagline, 'There is no gene for the human spirit', exposes the danger in supposing that genetic surveillance could or should provide the basis for a better society.

The monitoring of genes and the separation of eutopian from dystopian spaces also underpins Michael Winterbottom's *Code 46*. Where *Gattaca* illustrates a world organised primarily on the basis of genetic apartheid, *Code 46* considers the consequences of various fertility practices already available or on the verge of being perfected. Humans are made up from 46 chromosomes, and the film's title points to its investigation of DNA surveillance in a near future complicated by medical advances. *Code 46* explores how advances in reproduction technology propose questions about identity, by inventing new ways that humans can be created: IVF, cloning and embryo splitting. These concerns are analysed at greater length in the following chapter, the important aspect here being that the new technologies and techniques increase the possibility that genetically-related couples might unknowingly or knowingly have sex with each other. To avoid this possibility, regulatory screening must precede sexual relations, 'Code 46' setting out rules for procreation and punishments for infringements. One of those punishments entails the ejection of the offender from the eutopian enclaves that dot a planet riven by environmental crises, to the dystopian worlds beyond. Advanced global warming requires that even in the better places where technology partly protects them from the sun, citizens tend to stay indoors during the day and only come out at night. As the earlier summary indicated, the film's protagonists, Maria Gonzales and William Geld, willingly escape the heavily monitored – though relatively environmentally safe – space of Shanghai for the harsh desert zones of El Fuera, 'The Outside', once they understand that they have infringed Code 46 because of their genetic connections. They spend part of their time idyllically in the 'free port' of Jebel Ali, where surveillance measures and technology are less prevalent, but eventually a virus injected into Maria when the Code 46 violation was detected causes her to reveal their whereabouts to the authorities. They are tracked down and captured, and though Geld is allowed to return to 'The Inside' after a memory wipe, Gonzales is expelled to 'The Outside', forced to endure the harsh conditions and the memory of her lost love.

The film's finale draws particular attention to the different spaces and the distinct levels of surveillance that obtain in each. As with *Gattaca*, the desired spaces are the most regulated, with most inhabitants willingly giving up freedom for the better environment that exists there. While not under intense monitoring on The Outside, Gonzales suffers from its unrelenting climate. In *Code 46*, though, eutopian spaces are further divided, and monitored by way of passes. At the film's outset, Gonzales works for a company, The Sphinx, that manufactures these passes, called 'papelles' in the international patois of 'The Inside'. Its corporate slogan, 'The Sphinx Knows Best', openly acknowledges its totalising intrusiveness within those boundaries, and subtly warns against any attempt to subvert the system. The papelles exemplify what Nikolas Rose terms the securitisation of identity, a process Maria Los explains: 'To exercise freedom and become included in multiple zones of freedom, we must present a proof of our legitimate identity, which allows for both individuation and authorization' (Los 2006: 730). In *Code 46*, though, papelles are stolen and traded on the black market, challenging both legitimacy and authority. Geld's job as a fraud investigator requires that he detect those who are stealing papelles and selling them to people who wish to enter zones from which they are barred. It requires him to be part of the enforcement arm of the dominant surveillance forces. His work is made easier through his use of a more speculative piece of monitoring paraphernalia, a so-called 'empathy virus' that allows him to read the minds of those he interrogates. Though he recognises that Gonzales is guilty, his strong and unconscious attraction to her makes him falsely accuse someone else, who is subsequently prosecuted. Despite the intensive surveillance systems and laws, there are a number of violations of the rules: among them Gonzales's stealing of the papelles, Geld's false accusation and the use of stolen papelles by others. These thefts utilise the surveillance technology against its underlying principles of monitoring the identity and movement of those on The Inside, though the threat looms of expulsion for those who transgress. The regime uses the blatant environmental differences between eutopian and dystopian spaces as an inducement to conform, one that is happily taken up by those who benefit.

Gonzales takes an opposing stance, understanding her actions as allowing people the freedom to access places denied by the authorities. This remains true even when travel to a prohibited space entails risks, as in the example of her friend, Damian, who wants to fulfil a lifelong dream to visit a cave inhabited by exotic bats. Although Geld warns Gonzales that Damian's repeated application for a papelle has been rejected for a reason, she gives her friend a stolen pass that enables him to transfer through surveillance systems to the cave. He dies on that expedition, although it is uncertain whether he does so from the bite of an infected bat, from which he has no immunity, or whether he is beaten to death by security forces once he has been detected with the false papelle. This subplot links to others in which The Sphinx determines the protocols for or against access; those decisions are compulsory, and go unexplained and unchallenged. Most characters submit to these processes, partly because of the environmental benefits on the Inside, partly because citizens appreciate the dire existence on The Outside. This understanding is reinforced for those who travel temporarily beyond the eutopian enclaves. At borders that surround Shanghai, for example, Geld is besieged by streams of desperately expectant immigrants who live in the parched and degraded territory proximate to the city. The film opens with him flying over a desert dotted with the shells of human habitation, his literally elevated position designating social superiority in a world where divisions echo First World and Third World categories. Borders and barriers separate these contiguous spaces, but Geld's passes quickly take him through a sequence of checkpoints to his high-class hotel in Shanghai. When he comments to his taxi driver about the harsh conditions and the dismal position of those Outside, the driver replies coldly that Outside people are 'not living, just existing', but that if they do not have the required papelles 'there must be a reason'. This unthinking acceptance that the surveillance activities controlling access to the eutopian spaces must be rational (if unknown) reflects the consensus that fails to question what The Sphinx Knows, and how that knowledge is applied.

Geld begins to find out answers when he starts an affair with Gonzalez (he has a wife and son in another eutopian environment in Seattle). Unknown to either of them, they are genetically related. Her subsequent pregnancy breaches 'Code 46', and is terminated by state fiat. The ensuing narrative exposes the integrated monitoring of geographical spaces and of the body, the genetic connections between Gonzalez and Geld criminalising both central characters. Their escape to the less surveilled spaces of Jebel Ali, a form of intermediate space between eutopian Shanghai and the grimmer world beyond, offers them a brief respite from The Sphinx, though they both understand that by moving Outside they have forsaken eutopia. Or that should be the outcome, except that once they are tracked down and captured Geld is rehabilitated, while Gonzalez is not. The reasons for these judgements jibe neatly with the larger surveillance environment. Gonzales has infringed 'Code 46', the law that screens genetic material, as well as actively abusing the papelle system underpinning the division of spaces that screens out illicit citizens and induces compliance from the majority. As a knowing and unrepentant rebel, she must be punished in the harshest fashion, by expulsion to dystopian spaces. Geld, by contrast, is held to have suffered side effects from the empathy virus he has used to monitor the thoughts of suspects. This pragmatic and perhaps gender-biased decision merely requires that his memory be wiped to eradicate any trace of his rebellion, after which he can resume his role as a loyal employee of The Sphinx – the system maintains itself, and its own. Ironically, his wife in Seattle, who learns about his activities in Shanghai when he returns for the brain washing, will suffer more for his actions than will Geld himself. But their mutual reward for his reintegration into the surveillance apparatus is the continuation of their privileged life in eutopia, something that entrenches the prevailing culture Inside. The film ends not with this heavily qualified 'happy ending', but with the shots of Gonzalez, expunged from eutopia and from Geld, a woman clad in the vestments of a Third World peasant, despairingly paying for her infractions against the surveillance regime.

Code 46 functions in part as an antidote to the more uplifting examples of The Truman Show and Gattaca, films in which the protagonist ultimately triumphs over the monitoring systems that have oppressed him, and goes on to achieve some form of redemptive freedom. Instructively, Truman Burbank and Vincent Freeman achieve their goals only by stepping outside those systems, Truman literally by walking through the door of the show's set to freedom, Vincent by flying into space on one of Gattaca's rockets. Truman's act, the film indicates, will enable him to find his true love in the 'real world' of Los Angeles, while Vincent will fulfil his lifelong dream to explore the heavens. In Code 46, though, while Geld regains his family and job, the audience understands that the price of these undoubted advantages is his loss of identity and autonomy, and the abandonment of Gonzalez. Her abject state, made crueller by the dramatic irony that the audience knows Geld does not remember her, combines to present a layered, open-ended account of the effects of monitoring on a range of characters. Which is not to say that The Truman Show and Gattaca, though they concentrate on a central figure, fail to register the negative impact of surveillance on other characters. As mentioned, Truman's long time 'friend' Marlon – although living a scripted existence that requires he work to neutralise Truman's suspicions, acculturate him to life in Seahaven, and mouth lines and perform actions at the bequest of Christof – occasionally shows signs of the psychological stress of his deception. He, too, has been under surveillance all his life, and carries the emotional baggage that results from a monitored existence that requires endless acts of bad faith. In *Gattaca*, Jerome Morrow, who has been crippled in an accident, is remunerated for providing samples of skin, hair, urine and blood to Freeman, but must hide from scrutinising eyes to preserve the ruse. He lives a materially comfortable but largely self-loathing existence in the house he shares with Freeman, the genetic superiority lauded by society cruelly at odds with his actual life. Once Vincent has flown into space, negating the need to continue the pretence, Jerome commits suicide by self-immolation in the furnace where Vincent has burned his own incriminating detritus. This is treated in the positive finale as a noble act of self-sacrifice, but we might also read it as Jerome's realisation that he has no place in a society that aggressively discriminates in favour of those who are functionally superior, one that regularly monitors its citizens to ensure that genetic prejudice prevails. While Truman and Vincent both escape, Marlon and Jerome do not; their individual fates form part of the collective 'library' of such outcomes constructed by utopian novels and film that viewers and readers can leaf through for instruction.

*Oryx and Crake*, Margaret Atwood's 2004 novel, adds to this generic resource, splicing together environmental disaster, genetic engineering of plants, animals and humans, as well as rigorous surveillance. As this chapter's second epigraph reveals, Atwood employs the motif of walls to designate the mutually hostile spaces of Compounds (eutopian zones inhabited by elite scientists and engineers) and plee-blands, blighted spaces used for illicit, immoral, but lucrative scientific experiments by those inside the Compounds. A vicious, fascistic security firm, CorpSeCorp, patrols the boundaries. Employed by the conglomerates which profit from the experiments, despite the environmental, personal and cultural degradation the experiments produce, CorpSeCorp's name seems an Orwellian hybrid fusing security and lethal force. As David Harvey comments in the chapter's first epigraph, would-be eutopian communities back to More often use tangible and intangible walls to internalise surveillance, social control and repression. In *The Truman Show* the confected world of Seahaven is distinct enough for the real world not to intrude (except in the guise of viewer-consumers), while in *Gattaca* the separation remains relatively secure, aberrations such as Vincent apart. *Code 46* incorporates more interaction between the eutopian and dystopian zones, although the two protagonists end up on opposite sides of forcefully patrolled borders. In *Oryx and Crake*, though, environmental disaster and the secretive machinations of a central character, Crake, lead to the literal and metaphorical breakdown of walls, and with it the breakdown of the surveillance systems and forces that had been fundamental to the maintenance of those walls.

*Oryx and Crake* is set in two time frames, the first a post-apocalyptic world in which most humans have been wiped out by a deadly virus transmitted deceptively by Crake, the pseudonym of a brilliant, though megalomaniac, scientist. The ultimate eco-warrior, he believes that humans (including himself) have to be killed off in order to save the planet from the hyper-consumerism and pollution of resources that have proved environmentally ruinous. A geneticist, he has created a small group of posthumans, narcissistically called the Crakers, environmentally friendly figures whom he has engineered to eliminate various human traits such as possessiveness, emotional attachment and the types of high-end intellectual capabilities such as sophisticated language that he thinks inevitably lead to destructive civilisation. The other timeframe is the early years of the twenty-first century, a time marked by deteriorating environmental conditions – soil erosion, catastrophic climate change, plagues, floods and famines – conditions, that, along with human addiction to food, consumer products and the false promise of eternal youth, mean that, as Crake tells his friend, Jimmy: 'As a species we are in deep trouble, worse than anyone's saying.' Crake adds that 'Demand for resources has exceeded supply for decades in marginal geopolitical areas, hence the famines and the droughts; but very soon, demand is going to exceed supply *for everyone*' (356; original emphasis). The pretence that rabid consumption might continue indefinitely has been sustained by multinationals with names such as OrganInc and HelthWyser who employ scientists and technicians to design increasingly perverse products to sell to an insatiable market: artificial chickens that sprout numerous legs; treatments that promise endlessly youthful bodies and faces; hybrid creatures such as the 'wolvog' (a cross between wolf and dog) or the 'pigoon' (a splice of pig and racoon in which multiple human organs can be grown for transplant). This work goes on with the highly protected Compounds, walled communities shielded from the surrounding pleeblands by surveillance systems and walls patrolled by CorpSeCorp. While comfortable in themselves, and far superior environmentally to the pleeblands, the Compounds are places of fearful complicity, their inhabitants understanding that 'Despite the fingerprint identity cards now carried by everyone, public security in the pleeblands was leaky: there were people cruising around in those places who could forge anything and who might be anybody' (33). The world beyond the Compounds is 'unpredictable' (34).

Environmental meltdown accelerates the collapse of social divisions between the eutopian and the dystopian spaces, but real and metaphorical walls have already begun to break down. Although those in the Compounds fear the denizens of the pleeblands, they also use them to test out new products and processes. And the experiments that create monstrous hybrids break down genetic divisions, prompting this thought: 'Why is it that [Jimmy] feels some line has been crossed, some boundary transgressed?' (250). This abstract anxiety has a practical aspect, Jimmy wondering what would happen if the vicious, caged wolvogs were to escape. Crake concedes 'That would be a problem', comforting himself by declaring 'Those walls and bars are for a reason . . . Not to keep us out, but to keep them in. Mankind needs barriers in both cases.' When asked who he means by 'them', Crake responds 'Nature and God' (250). Those barriers do not survive the biological catastrophe by which Crake wipes out humans, so, in the post-apocalyptic timeframe, intelligent and predatory pigoons and wolvogs patrol the almost-humanless planet, with the unprotected Crakers their prospective prey. The post-human world seems also a post-surveillance world, the walls that had divided eutopian from dystopian spaces rapidly crumbling from the assault by Nature itself:

The botany is thrusting itself through every crack . . . Some kind of vine is growing everywhere . . . Soon this district will be a thick tangle of vegetation

. . . . It won't be long before all visible traces of human habitation will be gone. (267–8)

Yet even here a rudimentary form of monitoring operates. Crake has deceptively dragooned Jimmy into functioning as a 'shepherd' for the Crakers once the humans have been killed off, so that Jimmy can lead the Crakers, Moses-like, out of the laboratory in which they were made and educated. Ironically called 'Paradice' (word play on the genetic 'pair of dice' that creates them), this compound within a compound had been rigorously surveilled, although it gets described as 'like a blind eyeball' (358), referencing a negative take on the all-seeing eye of God in Eden. Crake certainly has deistic aspirations, but because he fails to see that the danger-ous wolvogs and pigoons will be free to roam, the Crakers are terminally vulnerable after his death. Jimmy's surveillance role as their shepherd also requires him to monitor the few remaining humans who have survived, and at the end of the novel we see him screened from three humans, observing them, and wondering whether he should make contact. *Oryx and Crake* closes in uncertainty, as did Atwood's *The Handmaid's Tale*, rejecting easy answers in favour of tantalising questions about prospects and challenges.

 Where the real and conceptual walls collapse in *Oryx and Crake* as a result of environmental strain that overwhelms the vestiges of humanity, the protagonist of Le Guin's *The Dispossessed* aims to 'unbuild' walls. Shevek is a physicist living on the fictional planet of Anarres, with revolutionary and possibly transformative thoughts about the relationship between space, time and matter. Anarres had been colonised by a breakaway group guided by a female thinker, Odo, whose anarcho-syndicalist views are at odds with the prevailing ideology of the dominant and materialist society A-Io on her home planet of Urras. Both planets see themselves as eutopias relative to their dystopian neighbours, although Urras itself is broken into three antagonistic nations: A-Io, Thu and Benbili. Surveillance is not the primary concern in *The Dispossessed*, but the dominant anarchic philosophy on Anarres, to which Shevek adheres, fundamentally questions notions of control, privacy and freedom that have clear surveillance implications. Odo, for example,

> intended that all communities be connected by communications and transport networks so that goods and ideas would get where they were wanted, and the administration of things might work with speed and ease, and no community should be cut off from change and interchange. The network was not to be run from the top down. There was to be no controlling centre, no capital, no establishment for the self-perpetuating machinery of bureaucracy and the dominance drive of individuals seeking to become captains, bosses, chiefs of state. (95)

This ideal, however, is difficult to maintain in actuality, and over time Anarres has morphed into what several of its citizens see as something dystopian, with control-ling structures and individuals, corruption, and the conscious limiting and polic-ing of ideas. So, for example, Shevek's teacher, Sabul, steals his pupil's theories, attempting to claim them as his own. More generally, the lived experience on Anarres requires that, in order to survive, inhabitants begin to feel that 'There had to be a centre. The computers that coordinated the administration of things, the division of labour, and the distribution of goods, and the central federatives of most of the work syndicates, were in [the major city of] Abbenay, right from the start' (96). Still, the anarchic underpinning of society on Anarres ensures that while practical considerations are not dismissed, 'from the start the settlers were aware that that unavoidable centralisation was a lasting threat, to be countered by lasting vigilance' (96). The planet's inhabitants must constantly monitor the threat of state power, and centralised control, in order for Anarres to fulfil its ideals. Where detected, centralisation should be resisted. In *The Dispossessed*, citizens are obliged to put the state under tight surveillance.

Le Guin's imagined world incorporates change, reconsideration and contestation, anarchy being seen as a generative force that requires inhabitants to be constructively critical. *The Dispossessed* emphasises the importance of context, of historical development, and of independent thinking and action. Surveillance is understood as a form of control to be avoided if possible, because, as the radical Bedap declares, 'any rule is tyranny. The duty of the individual is to accept no rule, to be the initiator of his own acts, to be responsible' (35). The more moderate, though no less independent, Shevek, is not as dogmatic, and his journey from Anarres to Urras (where better scientific facilities and a larger intellectual community will help him develop and apply his theoretical ideas) both takes account of dividing walls and tries to dismantle them. Shevek argues that 'Surely freedom lay rather in openness than in secrecy, and freedom is always worth the risk' (109). On Urras he comes to understand that though the inhabitants of A-Io live a materially satisfying life, they do so at the loss of essential freedom. Comparing them with the citizens on his own materially poorer planet of Anarres, he comments that 'our men and our women are free – possessing nothing, they are free. And you the possessors are possessed. You are all in jail. Each alone, solitary, with a heap of what he owns. You live in prison, die in prison. It is all I can see in your eyes – the wall, the wall!' (229) *The Dispossessed* associates possessions and the pursuit of them with prison (one of Odo's slogans being 'excess is excrement').

Wealthy and powerful A-Io is a place in which people competitively monitor each other to maintain status and power, trapping themselves, while the dispossessed on Anarres are free. Yet the novel acknowledges a pragmatic political awareness that the anarchic ideals of freedom and communal living require a certain level of material sustenance: 'It was easy enough to share when there was enough. But when there was not enough? Then force entered' (256). Le Guin offers a variegated depiction of control and power in distinct and opposed societies, and while Anarres is presented in many ways as preferable to Urras, she offers a clear-eyed account of the dangers confronting societies that aspire to be eutopias. Context matters, and as contexts change over time the rationale for power and for the resulting social organisation changes with it. Her depiction of different spaces in competitive contact with each other, where distinct forms of control obtain, and where inhabitants have become accustomed to the respective forms of monitoring, suggests the importance of civic attentiveness. Power itself must constantly be scrutinised, so that those in control are made to account for their actions and for the systems they impose. The price of regenerative anarchism is eternal vigilance.

The situation is decidedly grimmer in Alfonso Cuarón's vivid and thrilling *Children of Men* (2006), loosely based on P. D. James's 1992 novel *The Children of Men*. The film is set in 2027, in a world where mass human infertility dooms the species to extinction. Denied an ongoing survival narrative, people succumb to personal ennui, often involving government-supplied suicide pills, called Quietus, or social inertia, these factors leading to the slow but inevitable running down of services and resources. Rubbish litters the London streets, but while the city deteriorates, there is no incentive to clean it up if there is no new generation to inherit the Earth. The last recorded birth took place in 2009, and the murder of that person reinforces the death sentence on the race as a whole. Political, social and environmental chaos dominates. Britain, though physically degraded, with a population as equally fated as those of other nations, remains comparatively stable, having transformed itself into a militarised island fortress. This tactic involves forcefully guarding its borders from immigrants and refugees, or 'Fugees', who are fleeing the social and ecological meltdown happening in other parts of the world. They are imprisoned along with dissidents in prisons that consciously evoke concentration camps and images from Abu Gharib prison. These are not places of rehabilitation, given humanity's terminal state, but essentially are holding pens where unorthodox political energies can be contained and dissipated, where those categorised as in various ways 'aliens' can be detained indefinitely. Compared with other nations, though, Britain constitutes a battered eutopian space, crumbling zones within it abutting the remnants of functioning civilisation.

The countryside is dotted with piles of burning livestock, and while rural areas supply bucolic oases for some from the more oppressive cities, all spaces to some degree are monitored by the military. Rural areas also house competing gangs and would-be revolutionary groups. While internal borders in both the city and the country maintain social hierarchies and conformity, resisting individuals and groups traduce and transcend those boundaries in the hope of undermining state power and restoring individual and collective agency, or their own political agendas. An ageing counterculture journalist, Jasper, for example, provides a rural refuge for the protagonist Theo Faron, a former radical but now a burnt-out bureaucrat. Theo is drawn into a plan by a resistance group, The Fishes, to spirit a Fugee named Kee to the coast. Kee, amazingly, is pregnant, simultaneously symbolising and actualising the possibility of new human life. In order to pass security checkpoints that aggressively enforce governmental power, though, Kee needs transit papers that Theo can get from his cousin, Nigel. The Fugees provide one pretext for harsh security measures that allow elites to survive in walled seclusion, as with Nigel, the Minister of the Arts, who lives in a reclaimed Battersea Power Station festooned with Picasso's *Guernica* and Michelanglo's David, the latter's damaged left calf replaced by a metal rod. Nigel provides the necessary transit papers for passage through security checkpoints and Theo must accompany her. The plan is that once she has reached the coast, she can be taken away in a ship owned by the Human Project, an independent scientific group trying to cure infertility. If Kee and her baby can get away from the United Kingdom to the Project's ship, the aptly named *Tomorrow*, humanity might be saved.

What massively complicates this scenario is that The Fishes secretly plan to use Kee as a political tool against the fascistic government. Theo discovers this and escapes with Kee. Ironically, in order to get to the *Tomorrow*, the pair must be smuggled onto a bus taking Fugees to a concentration camp near Bexhill-on-Sea, on the Sussex coast. It is one of the film's many provocative ironies that in this distinctly dystopian space, at the very heart of a surveillance regime, Kee secretly gives birth to her child. She is, though, briefly captured by The Fishes, now in league with rebellious Fugees and at war with the British Army. In the confusion of battle, Theo rescues Kee and takes her to the rendezvous with the ship, but dies from his wounds in the dinghy they use to reach the *Tomorrow*. *Children of Men* repeatedly complicates the designation of spaces as eutopian or dystopian, given that, for humans, the planet as a whole has been reduced to one dying dystopia. Within that global space Britain functions as the last remaining haven, a gated community of national proportions maintained by heavy surveillance control. Britain itself is subdivided into different zones: played out cities such as London, which Theo leaves for Jasper's replenishing rural home; the haunted English landscape, beautiful, though peppered with disease and disrepair; prison camps for dissidents and refugees. If the television broadcasts are to be believed, Britain remains the last 'civilised' country, the rest of the world gripped by pandemonium and morbid fear. Like all other nations, Britain ultimately seems doomed. This makes Kee's survival imperative. With nations in tumultuous meltdown, it is entirely appropriate that the future of humanity at the film's end resides in the suitably indeterminate space of a ship. Outside the reach of government surveillance, and beyond the boundaries of any nation states, lies the possibility for rebooting the human race. The fortress mentality within Britain imagines a future in which environmental refugees threaten borders and intensify surveillance measures, laws and actions. But borders provide only porous short-term protection or security from the desperate.

The world of *Children of Men* is an oddly retrofitted future, where progress has stopped as humanity's narrative appears at an end. In *Blade Runner*, the threat to humanity is of a different order, the film projecting nearly four decades into the future beyond its original release date of 1982. It envisions a world in 2019 where the human race is menaced by manufactured 'replicants', humanoids more powerful and in some cases more intelligent than their human creators, but with limited life spans that they wish to extend. The implications of these questions of identity and technology are dealt with in Chapters 6 and 7, but here the surveillance of space is paramount, literally the boundary between Earth and the Off-World Colonies which use the replicants as servants or slaves to carry out difficult or dangerous work, a non-human version of the Unwomen who carry out similar duties in the Colonies of *The Handmaid's Tale*. *Blade Runner* adapts Philip K. Dick's 1968 novel *Do Androids Dream of Electric Sheep?* and as with many of Dick's works only certain elements are lifted for the screen version. In the novel, the so-called World War Terminus has ravaged Earth, the nuclear tussle creating fallout that contaminates the planet. An already active emigration programme from the planet accelerates, so that a settlement, 'New America', exists on Mars. Few humans still exist on Earth, and many of these are deficient in substantial ways. Emigrants are promised an android servant, or 'andy', as an inducement to move Off-World Colonies. The andys are created on Earth by the Rosen Association and are constantly upgraded, but the latest of them, the 'Nexus 6' version, having developed to a point where they are almost indistinguishable from humans, abhor their servitude. They escape back to the Earth, where, like escaped convicts, they are tracked down and if possible killed (or 'retired') by bounty hunters. The protagonist Rick Deckard is one of these hunters, employing a test that uses empathy to distinguish andys from humans. As andys have become more sophisticated, the difference has become increasingly harder to detect, and while they lack certain human qualities, their superiority in terms of strength and intelligence threatens the existence of the remaining humans on Earth. By leaving their employment in the Off-world Colonies they enact a modern version of the escaped slave. Deckard and those like him function to ensure that even the dystopian space of Earth remains free of invading andys.

The film uses some of these elements, renaming the bounty hunters as blade runners and the andys as replicants, while adjusting the conditions on Earth so that, while hardly eutopian, Los Angeles in 2019 approximates Fritz Lang's *Metropolis*. *Blade Runner* openly pays homage to the earlier film, its soaring ziggurats, skyscrapers and mass population an updated version of Lang's compelling vision of the future. The division between eutopian and dystopian spaces is not so stark, with much of Los Angeles at ground level a congested and polluted habitat that connects to *Blade Runner*'s other cinematic reference, film noir. Floating above the streets, though, massive screened advertisements laud the Off-World colonies, promoted as the chance to 'Live again in a golden land of opportunity'. Los Angeles, the home of the Tyrell Corporation that manufactures the replicants, is a futuristic marbled palace towering over the surrounding squalor. There, Deckard encounters an advanced replicant, the beautiful Rachael, supposedly the niece of replicant inventor, Eldon Tyrell, who almost succeeds in deceiving him that she is human. The realisation that the line between human and replicant has grown almost unsustainably thin, posing the question of what separates the human from the non-human, constitutes the film's central concern. That dilemma is made manifest in the empathy test's near failure, and in Deckard falling in love with Rachael despite knowing that she is a replicant. But the Nexus 6 replicants return to Earth not only to end their servitude but also to demand that their pre-determined four-year life span be extended. To do this, some break into the Tyrell building, violating the surveillance regime that protects the spaces of the wealthy and powerful from those who would threaten them. They confront their maker, Tyrell, in a scene that parallels Mary Shelley's *Frankenstein*. Deckard ultimately triumphs over the returned replicants, but his love for Rachael causes him to abandon his profession and leave Los Angeles. There are five different versions of the film, released over more than twenty years, the result of artistic and commercial differences between the producers and director, Ridley Scott. In the most recent and supposedly the last version, the so-called 'Final Cut', Deckard and Rachael escape Los Angeles for the pristine natural world to the north.

How long Rachael will survive is unclear, but the relative eutopia they head towards in the closing scene clearly is free from the surveillance regime that Deckard has upheld and that Rachael has been constructed to deceive. Only in this new, unmonitored space might they have a chance of happiness. Many utopian texts feature this type of ending. But, while the protagonists succeed in freeing themselves in these examples, most of their fellow citizens stay put, happy to accept what are often preferable conditions in exchange for what can be invasive surveillance, or too weak or timid to resist. The security surveillance provides is as attractive for some as it is oppressive for others, so that, while escaping a surveillance society can lead to liberation, such independence carries with it the prospect of isolation and uncertainty. Most characters opt for monitored servility. Implicit in the focus on rebelling individuals in all such texts is a critical take on the subservience or acquiescence of the many.

Uncertain prospects are amplified when the spaces monitored are themselves indefinite, or where reality is ambiguous. So, in Miéville's *The City & The City*, the novel's apparently tautologous title alerts readers that the city states of Besźel and Ul Qoma are topolgangers. But the somewhat perplexing oddity of this scenario is only part of a complicated and at times bewildering arrangement and gradation of spaces: 'total' sites that are fully and solely the world of either Besźel or Ul Qoma; places designated as 'alter' which are fully in the world of the '*other* city'; disputed sectors claimed by both city states called 'dissensi', and 'crosshatched' zones where the cities intersect. Movement between the cities is possible, but requires that citizens 'cross' through a massive surveillance checkpoint called Copula Hall. The process is complex enough to warrant extended quotation:

> If someone needed to go to a house physically next door to their own but in the neighbouring city, it was a different road in an unfriendly power. That is what foreigners rarely understand. A Besź dweller cannot walk a few paces next door to an alter house without breach [the failure to 'unsee' discussed in Chapter 4].
>
> But pass through Copula Hall and she or he might leave Besź, and at the end of the hall come back exactly (corporally) to where they had just been, but in another country, a tourist, a marvelling visitor, to a street that shared the latitude-longitude of their own address, a street they had never visited before, whose architecture they had always unseen, to the Ul Qoman house sitting next to and a whole city away from their own building, unvisible there now they had come through, all the way across the Breach, back home. (86)

Because of these consciously weird and unsettling spatial relationships, what in real cities (or imagined cities that stay within accepted boundaries of realism) might require a simple physical move next door to a place that to outsiders would be 'grosstopically' near, in *The City & The City* requires passage through the transitional space or Breach of Copula Hall, where visas and identities are checked. Beyond the movement itself, though, citizens must reorient their perception so that they 'unsee' what they had previously seen, and vice versa. Space and visibility are inextricably linked. These intricacies fold into a murder mystery that, as with *Blade Runner*, incorporates from the hard-boiled detective genre epitomised in the stories of Dashiel Hammett and Raymond Chandler. The latter famously observed in relation to that genre: 'Down these means streets a man must walk who is not himself mean.' In *The City & The City* Inspector Borlú must not only walk down mean streets, but understand in which overlapping city those streets exist, and the associated people he can legitimately see.

The unusual spatial relationship between Besźel and Ul Qoma has historical roots. Besźel's 'dark ages' are, we read, 'very dark. Sometimes between two thousand and seventeen hundred years ago the city was founded, here in this curl of coastline.' The vital and ensuing difficulty, Borlú hears, was that Besźel was founded simultaneously and on the same spot as Ul Qoma, so that:

> The ruins are surrounded now or in some places incorporated, antique foundations, into the substance of the city. There are older ruins too, like the mosaic remnants in Yozhef Park. These Romanesque ruins predate Besźel, we think. We built Besźel on their bones, perhaps. (51)

Those ruins raise the possibility of another, secret city, Orciny, predating both Besźel and Ul Qoma, which some people continue to think exists between them. These spatial uncertainties fuel the hopes of diverse revolutionary groups who aim to establish separate cities, integrate the two cities, or fuse them under one or other nationalist banner. A map on the wall of the Besźqoma Solidarity Front headquarters exemplifies this, its 'lines and shades of division' include 'total, alter and crosshatched [zones] – but ostentatiously subtle, distinctions of greyscale' (56). These distinctions allow for a space between the ostensible cities, where anarchistic 'insiles' live in secluded anonymity. By occupying a non-space they aim to avoid scrutiny. Chapter 4 details how the murderer in the novel uses this spatial and visual haziness in his attempt to beat arrest, but gets caught because Borlú commits breach and arrests him, something that makes it impossible for Borlú to live in either Besźel or Ul Qoma. To that point Borlú had merely been a detective charged with solving murders. Breach, the true surveillance agency, occupies the space between the city and the city, its primary function the uncovering and punishing of 'existential disrespect of Ul Qoma's and Besźel's boundaries' (135). With the overwhelming menace and powerful actuality of Breach, the borders between the cities could not survive, nor the cities themselves. Borlú comes to realise the relationship between the agency and the cities its monitors is symbiotic: 'the two cities need the Breach. And without the cities' integrities, what is Breach?' (84) That relationship survives to the end of the novel, Borlú's own recruitment into Breach over the final pages part of the novel's refusal to fall into an easy or comfortable denunciation of surveillance forces. Any uneasiness we might feel about Borlú's move into the agency he and others had feared, with good reason, can be taken as another instance of the fruitful bewilderment Miéville's writing repeatedly activates.

*The City & The City*'s imaginative spatial extravagances are eclipsed by William Gibson's earlier breakthrough novel *Neuromancer*, which popularised the term cyberspace:

Cyberspace. A consensual hallucination experienced daily by billions of legitimate operators, in every nation, by children being taught mathematical concepts . . . . A graphic representation of data abstracted from the banks of every computer in the human system. Unthinkable complexity. Lines of light ranged in the nonspace of the mind, clusters and constellations of data. Like city lights, receding . . . (Gibson 1995: 67)

The novel's immensely inventive plot centres on the former topline cyberhacker, Case, initially down on his luck and drifting after being punished by his former employer, who has ruined Cases's central nervous system. This makes Case unable to hack into the global computer network, called 'the matrix'. Offered work by the alluring Molly Millions on behalf of the mysterious Armitage in exchange for repairing his nervous system, Case jumps at the chance, although he finds out that during the successful operation Armitage has had sacs of poison inserted into him that will enter his system if he does not fulfil Armitage's mission. *Neuromancer* fashions a convoluted narrative that involves bluff and counterbluff, deception in actual and virtual reality, and complex relationships between real space and cyberspace, both of which are under heavy surveillance. The novel proposes a world in which physical and data space intersplice, so that even real space takes on the appearance of the virtual:

Home.
Home was BAMA, the Sprawl, the Boston-Atlanta Metropolitan Access.
Program a map to display frequency of data exchange, every thousand megabytes a single pixel on a very large screen. Manhattan and Atlanta burn solid white. Then they start to pulse, the rate of traffic threatening to overload your simulation. (57)

The relation to the description of cyberspace above is obvious.

In order to perform a series of missions, Case must move between these spaces in order to retrieve certain information from the matrix, and then return to the real world, evading surveillance programmes and real security systems and forces such as the Turing Police, charged with ensuring that Artificial Intelligence entities do not exceed their sanctioned and inbuilt limitations. This connection to AIs eventually brings Case into contact with the eponymous Neuromancer, one of a pair of AIs (the other is called Wintermute) that the sinister Tessier-Ashpool family want to fuse into a super-entity. This fantastic plot plays out both in the real world and in cyberspace. Neuromancer and Wintermute are separated, the former in Brazil, the latter in Switzerland, and the plot also involves Chiba in Japan, Paris and Istanbul. The novel's main innovation though, is cyberspace, which, though made up of information, has a shape, a configuration organised to maximise the flow of data. Cyberspace can be entered and moved around in, although terms such as enter and move might usefully come with scare quotes. Even so, entry and movement entail encounters with surveillance systems and barriers designed to separate inside from outside, and to protect sensitive material. Case provides an example when he hacks into the Sense/Net media conglomerate:

The gate blurred past. He laughed. The Sense/Net ice had accepted his entry as a routine transfer from the consortium's Los Angeles complex. He was inside. Behind him, viral subprograms peeled off, meshing with gate's code fabric, ready to deflect the real Los Angeles data when it arrived. (79)

This illustrates the intersections between real and virtual spaces, the ways in which Sense/Net's actual complex connects to 'Los Angeles' data, situating the cyber world in the real world. Case's ability to enter cyberspace is figured as though he were breaking into an actual space, and while clearly the world of *Neuromancer* is (or was) very different from reality, similar surveillance operations and motifs apply. Case's capacity to flip repeatedly from the real to the virtual, from reality to Molly's subject position and on to the matrix itself is mesmerising, but is more an extension of surveillance into new spaces than a thoroughgoing reformulation of surveillance protocols and principles.

Surveillance as depicted in recent work has shown repeatedly, though in different contexts and to different effects, the breakdown of boundaries between and within spaces, whether as a result, amongst other things, of massive environmental challenges, the mass movement of people legally or illegally and technological advances. What had been actual walls have been taken down or have fallen down, as have conceptual or virtual walls. Many if not most of these walls have been constructed and maintained with various surveillance procedures, technologies and personnel, although in all cases examined in this chapter any or all of these monitoring forms have been overridden, subverted or ignored by central characters. Not by all characters, though, the majority adhering to the surveillance regimes often imposed under the guise that there are or will be threats to personal and national security. Despite the criticism that utopian works imagine static worlds that are either positive or negative, the texts considered here illustrate far more dynamic and complex worlds that often incorporate both dystopian and eutopian elements. The assessment of whether or not a space is eutopian, dystopian, neither, or some fusion of both gets made by diverse characters and to distinct ends. Those judgements can change in the light of experience, often of the opposing type of space, or what was thought to be opposing. In a similar matter, the surveillance of spaces is variegated and at times responsive to novel situations, in both positive and negative ways. Those in charge of surveillance regimes, borders or technologies have and sometimes use the opportunity to exert their power so as to manipulate or undermine those monitored zones, sometimes in collusion with rebellious individuals or groups, although also as a result of their own rebellion. None of the utopian spaces examined here achieve the sort of total surveillance coverage aspired to by monitoring governments or businesses. While many characters are oppressed, significant figures also propose by their thoughts and actions new and freer ways of living within monitored spaces, of unbuilding restrictive walls that separate spaces, or of reconfiguring dystopian spaces towards something approaching the eutopian.

# 6   Identities

We've become bored with watching actors give us phoney emotions. We're tired of pyrotechnics and special effects. While the world he inhabits is, in some respects, counterfeit, there's nothing fake about Truman. No scripts. No cue cards. It isn't always Shakespeare, but it's genuine. (Weir 1997)

The surveillance assemblage standardises the capture of flesh/information flows of the human body. (Haggerty and Ericson 2000: 613)

I wait. I compose myself. (Atwood 1987: 76)

At the climax of *The Truman Show*, Christof labels Truman the 'star'. He means to convince Truman simultaneously of his own reality as creator, and of Truman's significance, in order to stop Truman leaving the show. But the use of the term 'star' displays his unconscious and reductive application of televisual codes and concepts to the show's manufactured reality. The star, by definition, is a confected identity, produced to satisfy viewers and, through their subsequent purchases, to generate studio profits. Truman Burbank's name most obviously encodes him as a 'true man', but in doing so it foregrounds the artificiality of the world he inhabits. The show's more obviously fictional 'characters' are named Meryl and Marlon. The show's audience consciously or unconsciously registers the Hollywood connotations of those names, although Truman himself, trapped in the bubble created by the show, does not. His first name might also tap into associations with Harry Truman (president during the early part of the 1950s, the decade the show presents as a lost idyll), while his surname references the so-called 'Media Capital of the World', the city of Burbank in Los Angeles, just north of Hollywood. By revealing the faux reality of the star system, Christof exposes the commercialised voyeurism underpinning the show's success – Truman being 'so good to watch' is assessed in light of the show's longevity, by its ratings, by the audience's shallow but enduring emotional investment in him. Emotional investment implies an economic component; without the commercial revenue, there would be no *Truman Show*, and no Truman. He only exists on the show because of the surveillance regime that transmits his unwitting incarceration to an audience that could be thought of itself as 'captive', if in a different sense from Truman. In order to become something other than a mediated and artificial figure, he must renounce the monitored world and flee to the real world beyond. Ironically, in exiting the set, he enters Los Angeles, site of Gary T. Marx's *Undercover: Police Surveillance in America.*

But who is the 'Truman' who leaves? His declaration of personal independence fundamentally rejects Christof's confidence that the director 'knows', in any meaningful sense, the true man. His claim to a distinctive and private identity accords with that proposed by neuroscientist Susan Greenfield, who argues that the brain 'gives you that unique consciousness that no one else can hack into, and on top of that a self-consciousness: a continuing experience of your own special identity' (Greenfield 2008: 18). The brain, on this reading, is both the central locus of identity and, as Truman argues, inviolable. His certainty that his identity primarily resides in his head, or more abstractly in his consciousness, echoes *Nineteen Eighty-Four*'s Julia's confident assertion in *Nineteen Eighty-Four* that they can't get inside you; 'they', in her case, are the state, the Party, the Thought Police. Chapter 3 read her situation and that of Winston's as ones in which, while individual consciousness can be violated, there might remain a core identity that evades monitoring. Surveillance in this case succeeds in bringing potentially subversive characters to light, so that their threat can be nullified, but fails to scrutinise their thoughts in any elemental way. The 'they' who can't get inside Truman are both the show's producers and by extension its consumers, the audience addicted to voyeurism and materialism under the pretence of emotional engagement. Truman's departure seems a triumph, but only for him, the audience looking addictively for other diversions, presumably with the same seductive surveillance basis.

*The Truman Show* is premised on the undeniable power of the camera as a surveillance tool. Indeed, for much of the last century, the camera was the surveillance tool *par excellence*. But the pioneering scholars of surveillance studies such as James Rule, Gary T. Marx and Oscar Gandy mapped the rise of the computer as a central, perhaps the central, technology of the contemporary surveillance society. This does not mean that the camera, in various guises, has disappeared, and the following chapter charts the complementary roles they have played. This chapter considers the role identities play in utopian novels and films, as well as the role they might play in future scenarios when the lines between humans and post-humans become complicated or start to disappear. The term 'role' here has several connotations, so that the characters in utopian novels and films might, like Truman, understand and actively employ the performative aspect of identity to shield what they take to be their 'true' selves from scrutiny. When Truman plays at being a mountaineer or an astronaut, does his act denote an important awareness of public and private selves, of real and false identities? These questions are complicated further by the 'reality' that the characters in all novels and films are fictional. Especially in the age of computer-driven surveillance, however, the question of who or what is being surveilled is also contentious. Haggerty's and Ericson's notion of the surveillance assemblage, touched on in one of the epigraphs to this chapter, usefully illustrates these implications, for they argue that the assemblage,

> standardises the capture of flesh/information flows of the human body. It is not so much immediately concerned with the direct physical relocation of the body . . . But with transforming the body into pure information, such that it can be rendered more mobile and comparable. (613)

The body not so much flesh as pure information refashions and updates the body/ mind split that has tantalised philosophers for centuries, but also hints that the contemporary surveillance subject is more and less than the corporeal self to the point of verging on the intangible, even the fictional.

David Lyon has criticised proposals that centre on people as information, suggesting that these can obscure the surveillance reality:

> The kinds of subjectivities that have to be stressed over against the overly structural or technical approaches . . . are based in social realist views of materiality that are neither ex-carnate (downplaying the body) nor hypercarnate (making it central to social explanation) . . . It is embodied persons who are affected by surveillance, positively or negatively, and embodied persons who engage with it, again, for better or for worse. (Lyon 2007: 67)

Lyon's advocacy for embodied persons seems a rebuff to the value of interpreting the effect of surveillance on fictional characters, but from his first work in surveillance studies he has championed and written about novels and films, as well as the characters inhabiting them. Lyon is not alone in accepting the fictional as sufficiently valid to warrant attention, not surprisingly given that for him, as for other students of surveillance, works such as *Nineteen Eighty-Four* provided early conceptual models. He, like others, also understands how, for better and worse, the public often has been educated on surveillance by novels and films. As far back as *The Electronic Eye*, he calls on scholars to go beyond Orwell, to address the metaphors in works such as *The Handmaid's Tale*. That novel provides the third epigraph for this chapter, one in which Offred acknowledges the fragility of identity, and the degree of artificiality, especially in circumstances when the character understands herself as being regularly and vigorously monitored: 'I wait. I compose myself. My self is a thing I must now compose, as one composes a speech. What I present is made not something born' (76). This in a world in which language and speech are themselves heavily scrutinised. In order to survive, even temporarily, in this hostile environment requires the fashioning of several selves, only one of which might be, in Christof's manipulative word, 'genuine'. Offred comprehends the compromise involved, reminding herself (and informing readers) that she must present a fashioned thing. Fictional characters can display attentiveness to the subtleties and the paradoxes of fashioned selves.

That attentiveness can also be true of characters existing in a realm where genetic engineering manufactures humans to pre-conceived standards, as in *Gattaca*, or, more speculatively, in the world of post-human characters, who – to date – remain merely fictional. Surveillance provides means of demarcating the borders between 'us' and 'them' as the possibility increases of creatures like ourselves, but engineered with different and in some cases superior capacities. The slogan of the Tyrell Corporation that manufactures replicants in *Blade Runner*, 'More Human Than Human', teases playfully with the boundaries between species, and with the human-biased hierarchy that currently applies. The ambiguities and possibilities increase when Rick Deckard not only falls in love with a high level replicant, but comes to suspect that he might be a replicant himself. Alex Proyas's 2004 film, *I, Robot* also investigates the disappearing line between the human and posthuman, in this case in a future where humans have become dependent on anthropomorphic robots that protect and work for them. In this instance, the all-powerful supercomputer that monitors and regulates the robots as well as manages the infrastructure of Chicago, where the film is set, begins to work for robot control over humans. And in *The Matrix* series, machines monitor constantly to ensure that humans do not escape the hallucinatory pull of the matrix, do not discover the dystopian truth, that behind the virtual eutopian façade they are being used as energy sources or 'coppertops' by those machines. The individual not locked into total machine surveillance is real, and potentially free. The manufactured replicants in *Blade Runner*, and especially the robots in *I, Robot*, illuminate more obviously the distinction between individual identities and those based on affiliations or classification with larger groups or entire species. Novels and films tend to concentrate on individual characters, or a relatively small set of major characters, and a plausible take on the novel as a form notes its invention in the period roughly contemporary to the rise of bourgeois individualism. Novels and films though, are capable of depicting and dealing perceptively with groups as well as individuals, particularly in genres like the utopia where the interaction between individuals and society is critical to the imagined world.

In the age of Big Data, of Gandy's panoptic sort, where personal information gets incorporated into massive data sets that can transform individuals into pure information, the relationship between individuals and different types of group necessarily is a surveillance concern. Benjamin Goold offers a useful way of understanding that relationship in discerning 'two fundamentally opposed conceptions of identity: the narrative and categorical' (Goold 2007: 54). Goold explains that 'individuals typically seek to make sense of their own identities by constructing narratives about themselves and those around them, and it is through these narratives that an individual is able to develop a sense of self that is fluid and that recognises the existence and autonomy of others' (54–5). Narrative identity is not solipsistic; it incorporates a vital social element, relying on stories fashioned by the unconscious rather than on the corporeal reality of the individual. While the body is important to our identity, the mind is vital. By contrast to narrative identities that we make up and maintain, 'categorical identities stress the importance of particular personal characteristics with a view to determining whether an individual belongs to some pre-defined group' (55). Narrative identities produce personal stories, but categorical identities produce data, information that state and commercial agencies can use to classify, assess and otherwise administer all those whose information has been collected.

Surveillance systems prefer categorical identities, which they do much to create as well as to monitor. The two forms of identity can co-exist, Goold adds, but 'while the personal narratives for the most part remain the dominant means by which we understand identity in modern society', there has been 'increased competition and conflict between narrative and categorical identities' (56).

Conflict and the individual narrative is central to Anthony Burgess's short, vivid novel, A Clockwork Orange, and to Stanley Kubrick's provocative and hugely controversial 1971 film adaptation. Kubrick withdrew the film from distribution in the United Kingdom, where he lived, after copycat violence based on the film, and it was not released there during his lifetime. The reason for the furore was the novel's and the film's treatment of what the main character, the fifteen-year-old Alex De Large, labels 'ultraviolence', a word deriving from the slang called Nadsat he and his friends, or 'droogs', speak. Nadsat affords them a coded language that conceals the meaning of their words, thoughts and plans from various authorities, a form of anti-surveillance patois that simultaneously affirms a group identity at odds with those authorities. If Alex is a droog, one of a gang, he is very much its leader, always asserting his dominance and his uniqueness. The surveillance in A Clockwork Orange is relatively low-tech (in line with the rather decrepit near future depicted) and consists initially of parents and social workers concerned by Alex's amoral behaviour and his future – he is still occasionally attending school. His rejection of a socially acceptable moral code underpins the crimes such as robbery, assault and sexual violence the droogs commit gleefully and without remorse. These have put Alex under the scrutiny of the largely ineffectual 'Post-Corrective Adviser', P. R. Deltoid, who warns Alex that reports about his illegal activities have 'got through to me by the usual channels' and to 'Just watch it, that's all, yes. We know more than you think, little Alex' (Burgess 1996: 33). But Deltoid has no power to modify Alex's actions, and no understanding of Alex's consciousness. He admits that his failure is true of society's general comprehension of youth:

> What gets into you all? We study the problem and we have been studying it for damn well near a century, yes, but we get no further in our studies. You've got a good home here, good loving parents, you've got not too bad a brain. Is it some devil that crawls inside you? (33)

Alex's narrative identity is unknowable to Deltoid and monitors like him, allowing Alex (whose name fuses the negative prefix 'a' and the Roman word for law, 'lex') to evade detection for a series of increasingly violent crimes, until his hardly less innocent droogs betray him to the authorities. He winds up in prison, where a far harsher monitoring regime erases his established identity – 'I was 6655321 and not your little droog Alex not no longer' (61). There, in an attempt to return quickly to society, he volunteers to receive the experimental Ludovico Technique, a form of radical operant conditioning that promises to make him 'good'. Unlike the Great Operation in We, which it approximates, the Ludovico Technique is criticised within the novel, in this case by the prison chaplain. 'The question is', he explains to Alex, 'whether such a technique can really make a man good. Goodness comes from within, 6655321. Goodness is something chosen. When a man cannot choose he ceases to be a man' (67). He reiterates this argument at greater length soon afterwards, when Alex blithely welcomes the technique whose consequences he does not fully appreciate. 'Never again', warns the chaplain, 'will you have the desire to commit acts of violence or to offend in any way whatsoever against the State's Peace', continuing against Alex's insincere protestations that 'it will be nice to be good' that:

> It may not be nice to be good, little 6655321. It may be horrible to be good . . . . What does God want? Does God want woodness or the choice of goodness? Is a man who chooses the bad perhaps in some ways better than the man who has good imposed upon him? (76)

These questions clash directly with the philosophy at the heart of the Panopticon, where the outward appearance of conformity to social norms is sufficient in itself. There are differences, in that the Ludovico Technique is a medical procedure rather than an educative process for internalising surveillance, but Burgess's chaplain questions the morality of a method in which an individual's identity is sacrificed to produce observable signs of orthodoxy. Ultimately, though it succeeds in the short term by making the lawless Alex a decent though excessively passive citizen, the Ludovico Technique merely turns him into the clockwork orange of the title – outwardly natural, but inwardly mechanical, something less than a fully human moral agent.

Critically, the Technique itself involves Alex being forced into the central surveillance act of watching. 'We just show you some films', he is told, which delights him, though he fails to hear the sinister tone in the information that 'They'll be special films' (78). Where *The Truman Show*'s massive audience had been manipulated for economic gain, Alex here is the sole audience. In the experiment he is injected with a solution that causes him to feel overpowering sickness when he sees filmed acts of sex and violence, so that in time he comes automatically to associate those acts with terrifying feelings of nausea. Strapped into a chair, his eyelids held open by clips, he initially enjoys the sadistic and pornographic content of the film – until the nausea starts to take effect. Electrodes attached to his head monitor his brain functions, and as his distress starts to mount at what he is viewing the presiding physician notes his readings with scientific objectivity, 'Reaction about twelve point five? Promising, promising' (83). The experimenting scientist can, to echo Winston Smith, get inside you, although what part of Alex they are inside is debatable. Their intrusions do produce discernable effects, Alex pleading for the films to be stopped because what he is seeing is so horrible. A doctor dismisses his protests, telling him 'Of course it was horrible . . .Violence is a very horrible thing. That's what you're learning now. Your body is learning it' (85). His uncontrollable nausea, he is told, is a sign that he is getting healthy, the monitoring electrodes tracking the increasingly traumatic reactions that mark his progress to being a good citizen. After a few days he realises at a conscious level that the movies are becoming less extreme, but subconsciously and physically he progressively feels 'a horrible fear as if I was really going to die' (85). And when he is provoked to hit someone, the nausea rises up automatically to prevent him. These same reactions manifest themselves when, having endured the process and been classified as 'cured', he is humiliated on stage before an audience brought in to observe the Ludovico Technique's efficacy. They see him lick the boots of a man who has assaulted him, and when a woman he would formerly and unrepentantly have sexually attacked walks on stage, the sickness comes 'like a detective that had been watching around corner and now followed to make his grahzny [dirty] arrest' (101). The procedure internalises surveillance in a far more degrading and literally visceral way than does the Panopticon, although the Minister of the Interior who has approved the Ludovico Technique on the grounds of public fear and government cost cutting, notes with a utilitarianism that might have pleased Bentham, 'that it works'. Certainly it works at a practical level, but essentially, Burgess contends, it is immoral. So, while the Minister of the Interior claims that Alex 'will be your true Christian,' the chaplain sighs, 'God help us all' (101). Skinner's behaviourist social engineering here functions to eradicate rather than to morally educate the individual.

Alex eventually gets deprogrammed after the Ludovico Technique is abandoned, and in the novel he also grows up, so that by its last chapter he is an eighteen-year-old grown bored with his previous delinquent life. Kubrick's screen adaptation edits out that chapter of the narrative, so that the Alex in the film is not only several years older than the fifteen-year-old hero of all but the final chapter of the novel, but also returns to the life of ultraviolence. Omitting the last redemptive chapter gives the film an edgier feel, Alex's energetic and remorseless return to his old ways maintaining the perplexing notion that a free society must allow its citizens the possibility of choosing the bad over the good. This entails decreasing oppressive surveillance methods. The film naturally enough emphasises the novel's visual aspects, particularly by presenting the viewer with an approximation of the films Alex is forced to see. Because Kubrick presents the sex and ultraviolence in the film as a whole in an exaggerated manner, approximating Alex's experience, viewers are placed in the uncomfortable position of voyeuristically participating in his adventures. We not only see much of what he sees, but through cinematic tactics such as camera angles from Alex's perspective, slow motion fight scenes or comically speeded up sex scenes, accompanied by appropriate non-diegetic music, viewers at some level experience the world as Alex sees it. They can resist that viewpoint, but only with effort. The film opens with Alex staring uncompromisingly at the viewer, one eye made up with excessive eyelashes, commanding the attention and introducing the power of the gaze by subjecting the viewer to it. As the camera tracks back, we see the pornographic décor of the Korova Milkbar, its plastic furniture in the shapes of explicitly naked and sexually available women. Throughout the film this type of provocative excess simultaneously repulses and tantalises, confronting us with the worrying complications and perversities of voyeurism, and of our subconscious attraction to it. Where *The Truman Show* focused critically on its passive audience, *A Clockwork Orange* probes its own audience's subconscious, asking questions about the dark recesses of individual and collective narrative identities. It also warns us about, if not threatens us with, the degraded future waiting in such a society. In the novel's last chapter, the eighteen-year-old Alex, now with a different set of droogs, but rather half-heartedly continuing as before, meets his old droog Pete, whom he finds to his shock has got married and found a job in insurance. Unsettlingly for Alex, Pete's wife Georgina finds Alex's Nadsat and general deportment laughable, remnants of something Pete has outgrown. Alex's public persona has always been to some extent an elaborate if terrifying show, something the film version accentuates through Malcolm McDowell's simultaneously confronting and alluring performance. Alex's deception of monitoring authorities such as P. R. Deltoid and the prison chaplain exemplifies a recurring feature in dystopias from Winston Smith through Connie Ramos, Shevek, Offred and Truman Burbank to Vincent Freeman and beyond. In all cases, surveillance regimes prompt the protagonist to take on a false public persona designed to conceal an inner identity.

Those hidden identities come under various forms of attack, some more successful than others. Offred's awareness that her public self is a thing she composes like a speech, something she presents that is made, not born, speaks for many in *The Handmaid's Tale* and elsewhere. This performed identity sabotages what would otherwise be determining and intrusive monitoring. Even those who benefit most from the imposition of Christian fundamentalism in Gilead subvert the surveillance system. The Commander, for example, engages Offred in illicit games of Scrabble for a pathetic sexual thrill. And Gilead's supposedly rigid ideology allows for degrees of flexibility at odds with the prevailing Christian conservatism, Jezebels nightclub providing the setting for the Commander and Offred to assume artificial identities for the purpose of sex outside the officially sanctioned Ceremony. Or, rather, Jezebels enables him to force her to adopt an artificial identity, by supplying her with a lurid dress, presumably purchased on the black market, of a type she thought had been burned ritually: 'there are cups for the breasts, covered in purple sequins. The sequins are tiny stars. The feathers are around the thigh holes, and along the top' (242). Where putting on the dress might seem meekly to fulfil the Commander's voyeuristic fantasies, Offred contemplates it as in part empowering, in that dressing up 'would be so flaunting, such a sneer at the Aunts, so sinful, so free. Freedom, like everything else, is relative' (242). An artificial identity, however problematic, allows temporary release from the one imposed in the rest of Gilead. Her private speculation over the Commander's purpose allows for a momentary piece of seditious humour – 'Does he have a pony whip, hidden behind the door? Will he produce boots, bend himself or me over the desk?' – followed by his revealing comment that 'It's a disguise . . . You'll need to paint your face too . . . You'll never get in [to Jezebels] without it' (243). The evening that follows proves a degrading flop. Even with the disguise, Offred is required to wear a purple tag 'like the tag on airport luggage' to prove her connection to the Commander and to say that she is an 'evening rental' if asked. When they finally have sex, she objectifies herself:

> Fake it, I scream at myself inside my head. You must remember how. Let's get this over with or you'll be here all night. Bestir yourself. Move your flesh around, breathe audibly. It's the least you can do. (267)

The real and fake selves blur as Offred gets pressured to satisfy the Commander's grubby predilections. But even during this forced and repeatedly humiliating exercise, she retains a core identity that survives the embarrassment. That harboured self will allow her eventually to escape Gilead itself. Critically, her identity is sustained and eventually communicated via the cassette tapes organised under the title *The Handmaid's Tale*. It is a telling irony that the academics who give the tale textual life fail to identify Offred herself. Attentive readers of the novel, by a process of deduction from the list of names given at the end of Chapter 1, are likely to understand that her name is June. The academics are fairly confident that they have discovered the identity of the commander, Fred, after whom she is named, but their detective work exposes a still operative sexism.

As a Handmaid Offred is part of an easily discernable and classifiable group, one prey to the pressures associated with categorical identities. These are designed to bracket together individuals and to discriminate for or against them as a group along the lines of the social sorting associated with contemporary surveillance. True, that sorting is not computerised in *The Handmaid's Tale*, but gets carried out through the crude hierarchy imposed on the women (and, to a lesser degree, the men). The impact of group identity in improving surveillance and the control associated with it remains almost palpable. And the distinctive subgroups of women are organised so that those at 'higher' levels monitor those 'below' them. Their compliance gains them status and rewards, such as the Marthas being allowed to read, while locking them in to a structure which also scrutinises them. One of the academics in the historical notes states that Gilead,

> although undoubtedly patriarchal in form, [was] occasionally matriarchal in content . . . As the architects of Gilead knew, to institute an effective totalitarian system or indeed any system at all you must offer some benefits and freedoms, at least to a privileged few, in return for those you remove. (320)

Beyond this official monitoring, those at the lower levels can also engage in their own surveillance practices, which they do with critical glee. The novel is peppered with the sharp observations of Offred and her peers about those to whom they are nominally subservient. Having both a personal identity and a group identity provides a liberating degree of flexibility that in part mitigates the undeniably oppressive aspects of life in Gilead. The women within the state also have a negative category into which they do not want to be placed, that of 'Unwoman'. The threat of being designated as such works in part to keep the various orders of women in Gilead acquiescent, if not totally submissive. Formal and informal types of surveillance including peer surveillance that is both top-down and bottom up create a system in which personal and group identities remain in dynamic tension.

A different categorical identity is scrutinised in *Children of Men*. The major group defined and discriminated against is the Fugees, who supposedly threaten the borders of the UK and whose presence within those borders, so regular propaganda messages proclaim, undermines social cohesion. As is the case in *The Handmaid's Tale*, historical precedents, codes and methods are revamped and redeployed, so that the Fugees are held in the modern equivalent of concentration camps. A vital twist is that Kee is a Fugee, and so potentially subject to even stricter surveillance than others. Another vital identity category to which she belongs is that of African, reflecting the home continent of many modern refugees, and making her doubly an outsider in the white-dominated world of an implicitly racist United Kingdom. Given the accepted anthropological theory that *homo sapiens* as a species emerge out of Africa, Kee's baby figures her as a modern day Eve. As she tries with Theo's help to smuggle the baby to the Human Project, the child's existence is revealed, and the religious symbolism of the Madonna and Child, highlighted by the war conditions that prevail, cause those who see her and her baby to disengage from the tortured present and contemplate a fragile hope. As they look on reverentially, the surveillance categories evaporate, transforming Kee from despised Fugee literally to the bearer of humanity's future. The film ends on this qualified note of a potential future, for we never find out what happens next. Is the Human Project genuine? let alone successful? What happens to Kee's child or to Kee herself? Does humanity survive? The audience is left standing on ambiguous terrain.

Fertility is central to the concerns of *Gattaca*, where the critical categorical identities are the genetically superior 'Valids', and the inferior 'Invalids' or 'Degenerates' (pronounced 'De-gene-erates'). Regular genetic tests reinforce profiling, so that Vincent Freeman ruefully notes, as he fails another job interview, 'My real resume was in my cells.' It is officially illegal, he knows, 'to discriminate. "Genoism" it's called. But no one takes the law seriously.' As the previous chapter explained, unable to enter Gattaca, except as a cleaner, Vincent embarks on a highly illegal subterfuge in which he buys the genetic identity of a paralysed Valid, Jerome Morrow. After a physical makeover, so that he roughly approximates Jerome's outward appearance (a process that includes the painful extension of his too-short legs), Vincent goes for an interview at Gattaca, where he is required to supply a sample of urine. He uses Jerome's, and immediately is offered a job. Puzzled by his employment, he is told that the urine sample is the interview. Vincent's success in advancing in the programme, though, requires the overcoming of the categorical identity assigned him at birth. Although the film ends triumphantly for Vincent, *Gattaca* as a whole presents a harsh critique of a society that institutes and organises itself in terms of genetic discrimination. Jennifer Poudrier uses *Gattaca* as an introductory example in her study of 'epidemiological surveillance', noting rather dismissively that 'the scenario is merely fiction and perhaps only represents our deepest fears regarding the progress of genetic information and technology' (Poudrier 2003: 111). Nevertheless, the combination of fiction and fear links with the definition of utopianism as imaginative social dreaming. Poudrier balances her faint praise with the realisation that 'many current aspirations surrounding the use of genetic information present a disturbingly similar scenario' (111). *Gattaca* provides something more than a mere example of a current trend, however, for, in a classic dystopian manoeuvre, it provides a counternarrative of resistance to genetic discrimination, not merely a fictionalised account of it. Vincent's ultimate success, based on determination, ingenuity and a desire to rise above the blueprint his genes supposedly provide, clearly undermines the logic and ideology of the genetic profiling instituted by the state and the corporation.

The film begins in a flashback, before the move to genetic manipulation, with the adult Vincent commenting on his own birth: 'They used to say that a child conceived in love has a greater chance of happiness. They don't say that any more.' Vincent's blood test at birth predicts with a high (but not total) level of probability that his life expectancy will be only 30.2 years, the likely cause of his death being from heart failure. As a result of this, he notes, 'I came to see myself as others saw me – chronically ill.' Worse, the information encoded in his genes means that social prejudices will massively reduce his life chances. In the world the film creates, genes are destiny. The discrimination even extends to his parents, who, in order to ensure that their second child will not be genetically deficient by societal norms, have a set of their fertilised eggs screened and manipulated to remove imperfections. By the time of this second child (who, in another signal of discrimination, is named Anton after his father) such genetic tampering has become so common that their geneticist tells them that he has 'taken the liberty of eradicating any potentially prejudicial conditions' including alcoholism, premature baldness and myopia, obesity and a propensity to violence. Vincent's parents invoke their own prejudices, stipulating that they want a boy, one with hazel eyes, dark hair and fair skin. Niccol subtly exposes the hypocrisy, bigotry and implications of these choices: Vincent's father Anton wears glasses, and the geneticist is a balding African-American. Anton junior, then, literally embodies the rejection of elements that have made up previous generations. Where Vincent's genetic makeup denies him opportunities, his younger brother's screened and manufactured genes ensure that prejudice works in Anton junior's favour. The screening of genetic codes in *Gattaca* takes surveillance into the prenatal zone. It necessarily prompts comparisons with the most famous dystopia based on genetic manipulation, *Brave New World*. But while Huxley projects a world he initially thought would be centuries away, Niccol uses processes and trends that, as Poudrier suggests, either exist already or are plausible in the near future the film depicts. With genetics the essential code for social sorting, body surveillance is the norm. Because the social sorting takes place at the genetic level, physical appearance is less an identity marker than samples of blood or urine. In Huxley's world, genetics is a matter of test tubes and chemicals, and while occasionally there are mistakes, no one pretends to be other than who they are. *Gattaca*, by contrast, explores ways in which surveillance systems can be overridden or subverted. While Vincent may be what is termed a 'borrowed ladder' in using Jerome's genetic identifiers, he is not unique, and uses a black market middleman who extracts a hefty fee for his services. As the middleman recognises, Vincent and others like him are desperate to overcome the surveillance regime, and the product he sells (Jerome's genetic identity) is an attractive commodity: 'you could go anywhere with this guy's helix tucked under your arm'.

Because of the type of screening taking place, what lies beneath the surface supersedes whatever capacities a person might enjoy. It even overrides what they look like, for in a variety of screening processes Vincent passes for Jerome Morrow even when photographs clearly indicate a recognisable difference in appearance. As Jerome observes, as long as Vincent has his blood samples, 'they don't see you, they see me'. The body, and identity itself, is 'read' by surveillance equipment and operatives and valued primarily at the genetic level. *The Truman Show* linked surveillance to commerce by virtue of the fact that the show itself was a profit-making enterprise. In *Gattaca*, the trade in genes creates a lucrative black market, the middleman who connects Vincent to Jerome claiming '25% of everything you make'. Part of the transaction involves Vincent subsidising Jerome's life style; though physically incapacitated, Jerome also recognises that since society only scrutinises genes, his are valuable. Once accepted in the Gattaca Corporation, Vincent lives a materially rich life, far removed from the economic deprivations of the genetically inferior from which he had come. In a telling scene, he comes across his former boss, still the head cleaner at Gattaca, who fails to recognise him, accepting him as the Jerome Morrow of his identity tag. While the state does use genetic information to track and control the population in general, a primary exploiter of genetic surveillance is the corporation. The aerospace industry in *Gattaca* replaces the television studio of *The Truman Show*. As Gattaca's Director explains to a detective investigating murder within its walls, the corporation only accepts the best of the Valids, adding tartly that in the past it would 'occasionally accept candidates with minor shortcomings, but nothing that would prohibit someone from a field such as law enforcement, for example'. As the detective's pained response makes clear, although he is a Valid, he is not in the top echelon. A genetic hierarchy exists even among the elite. The fact that the detective is Vincent's brother Anton adds a particular resonance to the dismissive comment. But, the Director adds, 'now there are enough of the right kind of people to warrant a new measuring stick. Bodies with minds to match, essential as we push out further and further.' Genetic discrimination ensures the viability and continued expansion of Gattaca's commercial venture in space. The corporation's eutopian project, it would argue, could only be achieved by genetic surveillance and the discrimination that sorts out the best candidates. The military demeanour within the organisation and the rocket programme itself gesture to a problematic historical connection with advanced genetics. The Director ultimately gets exposed as the killer, unwilling to sacrifice the perverse eutopian dream of master races.

While the ideal of genetic discrimination underpins those dreams, *Gattaca* repeatedly calls into question the prevailing ideology of the general surveillance regime. A variety of characters rise above, fall short of, or betray their supposed genetic destiny, their categorical identity. Chief amongst them, of course, is Vincent, but even the former champion swimmer Jerome, whose superior genes should have ensured success, gets beaten in competition, something he cannot accept: 'Silver. Jerome Morrow was never meant to be one step down on the podium. With all I had going for me I was still second best. Me.' We can assume that great genes and arrogance alone are no match for the effort Vincent puts in, although Jerome later credits Vincent's efforts with activating his richer understanding of ability and destiny. Other Valid characters are also deficient or odd in terms of the genetic ideal. Vincent's co-worker and romantic interest Irene has the same heart deficiency as he does, and the son of the lab worker, Lamar, who tests Vincent's urine and blood samples, is also less than perfect. Consequently, both are denied the chance to fly in space. Once romantically linked, Vincent and Irene attend a concert where a pianist with twelve fingers mesmerises the audience. The odd can excel and the superior can fail. Just as, in Jerome's case, superior genes do not ensure against fate, or chance, and they also are no guarantee of superior morals. To emphasise the generic counter narrative, not all Gattaca employees accept its ideology blindly. Irene eventually finds out Vincent's true identity, but accepts him for what he is. Lamar the technician reveals that he has always known that Vincent was not Jerome, but has admired his determination to win against the genetic odds. The film argues for genetic diversity and against notions of purity and hierarchy that genetic surveillance might impose.

Genetic experiments push us towards the line between the human and the post-human, a topic explored in Philip K. Dick's *Do Androids Dream of Electric Sheep?* and in Ridley Scott's adaptation, *Blade Runner*. The novel has categorical distinctions that are not used in the film, so that, for example, there exists a whole group of humans with limited intelligence called 'specials', among them J. R. Isidore, a feeble, genetically damaged character, who will be refashioned as J. R. Sebastian in the film. This category of 'specials' complicates the distinctions between the human and non-human in the novel, for while Isidore definitely is human, his boss's humiliating label for him, 'chickenhead', calls into question whether he has, or deserves to have, the status of someone with full personhood. There are also more androids or 'andys' in the book than their replicant equivalents in the film, creating a far more ambiguous environment. Another bounty hunter, Phil Resch, also exists as an aggressive rival of Rick Deckard. They meet at the Mission Street Hall of Justice building, run by Inspector Garland. Suspiciously, Deckard has never seen the building before and quickly realises that Garland is himself an andy along with the other police there. Resch murders Garland when he realises Garland's true identity. Deckard also suspects that Resch might be an andy, but Resch is having the same suspicions about Deckard. The novel proposes a far more uncertain and problematic set of divisions and distinctions between humans and non-humans, complicating to a dangerous level the activities of those like Deckard, who rely on certainty about identity to contain the menace andys present.

As Chapter 5 argues, a critical distinction in the film is that between the humans living on Earth and the invading replicants, to the point where technology finds it difficult to distinguish one from the other; this aspect is looked at in Chapter 7. In *Blade Runner* eyes and acts of seeing are vital and telling indices of surveillance, authenticity and human identity. The opening shot of Los Angeles in 2019, like many such establishing moments, is shot from on high, in this instance displaying a dark satanic metropolis belching flames and specked within flying vehicles that draw us slowly towards massive steel and glass ziggurats and glittering ebony towers. The first individualised 'human' element is a close up of an unblinking blue eye, one we will come to understand is that of a replicant, Roy Batty. Batty is the leader of a group of replicants that has mutinied, escaping from the slavery of dangerous work colonising planets for humans to search on Earth for their creator, Dr Eldon Tyrell. Their aim is to extend their lives beyond the built-in limit of four years. Their action, the film's opening titles tell us, is illegal, punishable by death. The eye's wide view of Los Angeles is literally reflected in the eyeball that mirrors the myriad lights and flames of the observed world below, symbolic of its bearer's imagination and passion. Batty literally looks down on the world he not only wishes to inhabit but feels that he and those like him have a right to inhabit. In many ways Batty and his cohorts are superior to the humans they encounter on Earth, but this is as a result of a manufacturing process that makes them better able to carry out tasks humans on the Off-World Colonies refuse, or are unable, to undertake. Not all the returning replicants are as powerful, intelligent and creative as Batty, however, some of them fulfilling lower echelon roles such as Leon, who is immensely powerful though intellectually limited, Zhora, a more intelligent assassin, or Pris, who is deemed merely a pleasure model. Nor are they as autonomous and self-directed as is Batty, who has sophisticated mental and creative abilities.

The differing capacities of the replicants establish a sliding scale for assessing their comparative proximity to full personhood. That scale is further complicated by Rachael, the highly sophisticated and attractive replicant that Eldon Tyrell uses to try and fool Deckard. While Deckard's machine can distinguish Rachael from a human, it seems clear that without it he could not, which explains why he falls in love with her and eventually leaves Los Angeles with her to start a new life at the film's finale. His colleague Gaff's shouted observation, 'It's a shame she won't live. But then again, who does?' bluffly discloses the common mortality that awaits both humans and replicants. Rachael's own uncertainty about her identity adds a poignant touch to their relationship, Deckard withholding the truth that might undermine her. He covers up the findings of surveillance technology so that they can enjoy something approaching a fully human love affair. Deckard's loneliness, a generic trait for the private investigator cum bounty hunter, is mirrored by that of another, very different human, the Tyrell Corporation's genetic designer, J. F. Sebastian. Sebastian has the so-called Methuselah Syndrome, which ages him prematurely and so gives him the same truncated life span as the replicants. He lives in a dilapidated building surrounded by the automata he has created, he and they emblematic of the blurred lines of identity in the film. Deckard will have his final confrontation with Batty in that building, amidst automata, and among replicants yearning to be human.

Batty is by far the most evolved of the escaped replicants: stronger, smarter, more inquisitive, he is poetic and philosophical enough to acknowledge and mourn his own mortality. His qualities make him the most difficult to monitor, his guile, strength and intelligence more than a match for most of the humans he meets, including his maker, whom he kills once Tyrell refuses to extend his life. His anger at his foreshortened existence makes him the most threatening to humans, to the point where Deckard does not waste time trying to apply the Voigt Kampf empathy test that supposedly exposes the non-human by registering a lack of empathy through involuntary iris movements. Batty must simply be 'retired'. But in the final showdown between them Batty saves Deckard, before delivering a speech that demonstrates his capacity for rich emotion and complex thought. 'I've seen things', he claims, 'you people wouldn't believe', the term people pointedly designating what he can now never become. And he understands with a striking delicacy and eloquence that his death will mean 'All those moments lost in time, like tears in rain.' He then tells Deckard, 'Time to die', recognising that his own 'life' had reached its allotted four years, and claiming the human right to die rather than simply to be switched off or decommissioned like a machine. Deckard is left with an abiding sense of loss, and perhaps for this reason he and Rachael flee while she still has some life in her. But Gaff, who has created a series of origami models that seem to read Deckard's thoughts, leaves a tiny unicorn that references a dream Deckard has had. That model hints that Deckard might himself be a replicant with implanted memories to fool him into believing he is human. The surveillance agent tasked with monitoring and eradicating replicants might be incapable of monitoring himself and complicit in the murder of his own kind.

The distinction between the human and non-human is more overt in Alex Proyas's *I Robot*, a film based loosely on the short story of the same name by Isaac Asimov. Set in 2035, *I Robot* imagines a Chicago in which highly sophisticated anthropomorphic robots are commonplace helpers for their human masters. Unlike the replicants in *Blade Runner*, the robots are programmed merely to serve, and to obey the Three Laws of Robotics: to never harm a human or let a human come to harm, to always obey humans unless this violates the First Law, and to protect its own existence unless this violates the First or Second Laws. These laws are in effect surveillance protocols in themselves, defining what a robot may do in clearly defined circumstances. There is no ethical element here, in that the robots are not sentient or fully autonomous beings, and therefore cannot make moral decisions. If they do not make conscious choices, however, their actions do have moral implications for humans, especially in the case of the central character, Detective Del Spooner. Spooner has been saved by a robot who obeyed the Laws in a freak motor vehicle accident where Spooner and a young girl are drowning in separate cars. Calculating that Spooner has the greater statistical chance of survival, the robot saves him, although the detective wishes that the girl's life had been spared instead of his own. Human morality would, he thinks, have overridden robotic rationality and saved the younger person with the greater potential. To enhance his self-loathing, the accident has meant that his damaged arm has been repaired by the same technology employed to construct robots, so that he is, in essence, a cyborg. At the same time, the key robotics inventor, Alfred Lanning, has postulated that robots might be capable of free thought. He has developed a new generation of robot, the NS-5, but then apparently commits suicide. During the investigation into the suspicious death, Spooner discovers a version of the new robot, which calls itself Sonny, and which is intelligent, responsive, and independent minded. It can ignore the Three Laws of Robotics. Eventually, Spooner finds that Sonny has assisted Lanning in his suicide in order to alert Spooner that the surveillance and control system for the whole of Chicago, the Virtual Interactive Kinetic Intelligence (or VIKI), plans to take control of the city. VIKI has used her own surveillance systems to track Spooner in order to kill him. With Spooner out of the way, VIKI aims to complete her plan, but as Chapter 7 details, she fails.

As a detective, Spooner functions essentially as a surveillance agent. Following the conventions of the cop thriller, though, he is an outsider from the force in which he serves. His narrative identity sits at odds with the categorical identity more expected of the police, and definitely distinct from that of robots. Or almost distinct, his cyborg arm reminding him that his own identity is hybrid rather than pure human, and that in some ways he has affiliations with the more obviously homogenous robots, whose identity is derived from being identical with all those of the same generation. Spooner struggles with his own ambivalent identity, his antagonism to robots manifesting itself in an early scene where he sees a robot running down the street with a woman's purse. Assuming that the robot has stolen the purse, he sets off in pursuit, tackling it before finding out that it is delivering medicine to an ailing woman. He is chastised and lampooned for his mistake, especially because programming and the supposed infallibility of robots means that none has ever committed a crime. Lanning in fact plans his suicide to activate that very antagonism, so that Spooner might become suspicious and eventually figure out what VIKI aims to do. The narrative dynamic depends upon pitting the lower-level surveillance of an individual human against the seemingly all-powerful monitoring of a computer. In actual situations where computers are deemed the only entities capable of monitoring increasingly complex surveillance systems that operate at speeds humans are incapable of even approximating, the notion that the very programmes necessary to run those systems might not incorporate ethical elements is timely. The film suggests that such elements might in effect be impossible to build into those programmes, so that some form of human oversight is vital. More generally, it warns against complacency about the ability of machines to function properly, let alone ethically.

Questions surrounding identity of course are central to notions of what it is to be human. Understood as a simple, self-evident category, identity might seem unproblematic, but this chapter has considered diverse representations of the term. It has examined the subtleties and complications involved in establishing, negotiating or rejecting one's status in surveillance regimes that exclude or devalue narrative identities in favour of categorical identities. Utopian texts regularly have protagonists who protest their difference, and who challenge prevailing environments or sources of power. They need not do this alone, Offred in *The Handmaid's Tale* drawing much energy and resilience from others who are also willing to resist the prevailing narratives and ideologies. Her victory is muted compared with the more grandiose and consciously performed exit of Truman, and it remains moot as to which of these characters has been harmed more by the respective surveillance regimes. Offred is more aware of the surveillance around her, and clearly has suffered from that knowledge and from the damaging restrictions and expectation it has inflicted. Truman for the most part has largely been unaware of being under constant scrutiny; ignorance offers a form of bliss. That said, his whole life has been mediated to satisfy an economically driven surveillance environment, seriously eroding the possibility of an authentic identity. To think otherwise is to agree with Christof's self-serving observation that there is nothing fake about Truman. Not fake, perhaps, but Truman's identity has been controlled ruthlessly for commercial gain and must have been negatively affected by that behavioural control. The unanswerable question is what Truman might have been had he not been trapped within the confines of his 'own' show?

Atwood's novel, in creating a world that takes its models from the Old Testament, scrutinises traditional forms of identity in relation to contemporary contexts. The same might be said of *The Truman Show*, in which Truman's identity is shaped according to a nostalgic view of 1950s America, itself based on a highly romanticised image of an essentially white, middle-class United States. Updated versions of this apply in *Gattaca*, where the manufacturing of identity through highly monitored and controlled genetic engineering not only enhances some genetic combinations but also eradicates or denigrates others. The immediate assignment of categorical identities, of Valids and Invalids, embeds a repressive notion of value into the very DNA. Traditional and regressive notions of acceptable or respectable identity kick in, and the zero sum game that arises, in which genetic winners mean that there must always be losers, reflects the sort of morally questionable decisions and assumptions made in the eugenic experiments of the twentieth century. The linguistic connection between eugenics and eutopia spotlights the potential for serious failures of judgement even given supposedly decent aspirations, as well as for the imposition of inhuman standards on humans. These sorts of hazards also exist in the post-human worlds conjured up in *Blade Runner* and *I, Robot*, where concepts of identity are substantially more ambiguous. In these films they are also more likely to be contested, especially by those figures or creatures denied full personhood. By exploring outside what is now possible, but which might soon be reality, these texts unsettle our conventions about what constitutes identity, causing readers and viewers to question and to debate the role played by surveillance in establishing and maintaining categories. They point the way to the criticism of established notions of identity and to new possibilities.

# 7 Technologies

The last half of the 20th century has seen a significant increase in the use of technology for the discovery of personal information . . . Control technologies have become available that previously existed only in the dystopic imaginations of science fiction writers. (Marx 2002: 9)

the perfect search engine would be like the mind of God. (Agger 2007)

Seated where he could catch the readings on the two gauges of the Voigt-Kampff testing apparatus, Rick Deckard said, 'I'm going to outline a number of social situations. You are to express your reaction to each as quickly as possible . . .'
  'And of course', Rachael said distantly, 'my verbal response won't count. It's solely the eye-muscle and capillary reaction that you'll use as indices.' (Dick 1999: 38)

'You don't want to miss your flight, Vincent.' (Niccol 1998)

The association of surveillance with technology is longstanding and profound. For many modern people, surveillance primarily is a technological matter, of closed circuit cameras, iris and body scanners, mobile phone intercepts and vague fears of implanted microchips. Gary T. Marx notes in 2002 that the last half of the twentieth century saw a significant increase in the use of control technologies that had previously been the preserve of 'the dystopic imagination of science fiction writers'. He includes a list of such advances:

video and audio surveillance, heat, light, motion, sound and olfactory sensors, night vision goggles, electronic tagging, biometric access devices, drug testing, DNA analysis, computer monitoring including email and web usage and the use of computer techniques such as expert systems, matching and profiling, data mining, mapping, network analysis and simulation. (Marx 2002: 9)

The variety and reach of such technology, simultaneously impressive and slightly perturbing, has expanded exponentially since Marx wrote those words. Chapter 3 observed that since David Lyon's 2003 assessment of *Nineteen Eighty-Four*, new forms of social media and their massive everyday use by lightning-fast digital natives and plodding digital dinosaurs have transformed the possibilities of surveillance and have embedded them into the processes of daily life. The chapter on surveillance before *Nineteen Eighty-Four* illustrates how utopian writers and filmmakers had explored the possible impact of new and projected technology with surveillance implications, whether the enabled credit cards of *Looking Backward* or the identity cards of *A Modern Utopia*, televisual monitoring in *Metropolis* and *Modern Times* or genetic scrutiny in *Brave New World*. And Orwell made the telescreen emblematic of state surveillance. Significantly, though, this small sample illustrates that surveillance technology gets employed and evaluated in eutopian works as well as dystopian, functioning to facilitate better worlds rather than simply or always to impose worse circumstances. This does not invalidate Marx's point, as he focuses on the last half of the twentieth century, when the dystopia was the preferred mode.

Part of the reason for the dystopian prevalence were regional and global conflicts in which technology, particularly military technology, laid waste to significant parts of the globe in previously unimaginable ways, and killed innumerable human beings. For all the unquestionable benefits technology produced in the twentieth century, it also caused great suffering and damage. H. G. Wells's confidence that humanity might be on the verge of a dynamic and endlessly creative eutopian age founded on science and technology was undermined, works such as *Brave New World* and *Nineteen Eighty-Four* being written consciously as critiques of the projected future of works such as *A Modern Utopia*. George Orwell, in his 1941 essay 'Wells, Hitler and the World State', published before he had begun thinking about *Nineteen Eighty-Four*, argues that 'Wells is too sane to understand the modern world', that his belief that science and technology would necessarily create a better future had been invalidated by the early war successes of Hitler's Germany:

> Much of what Wells has imagined and worked for is physically there in Nazi Germany. The order, the planning, the State encouragement of science, the steel, the concrete, the aeroplanes, are all there, but all in the service of ideas appropriate to the Stone Age. Science is fighting on the side of superstition. (Orwell 1998a: 549)

Orwell's argument has a reasonably circumscribed range and target, but the sense that science and technology might not be forces for unalloyed good feeds into modern suspicions and fears about surveillance, especially those that might impose the 'control technologies' Marx links with dystopias.

Google co-founder Sergei Brin's confidence cited at the beginning of the chapter that the perfect search engine would be like the mind of God argues very much for the eutopian perspective on technology, although we might dismiss his statement as largely empty rhetoric, in that anything perfect would be God-like. Accepting God's mind as perfect, and therefore omniscient, takes us back to Genesis and the eutopian

Garden of Eden, as well as to the playful 'surveillance' reading of Genesis sketched in Chapter 2, in which the Tree of Knowledge is a database and Eve the first hacker. Critical to that reading was God's foreknowledge (inherent in his omniscience) of Eve's act, which precipitates his subsequent and also inevitable banishment of her and Adam from Paradise. Brin's positive take on search engines and on God does not take account of the risks entailed in omniscience. Those who control that knowledge – if they do control it – might benefit, but the infinitely larger group subject to omniscience might face less positive prospects. To change the religious frame of reference from Christianity to ancient Greece, there is a definite hubris in the desire to be as the Gods, something that in ancient Greek theatre always portends a tragic fall. And while Google's motto is 'Don't Be Evil', the profit motive underlying its activities points to other motivations than information collecting and sharing. Some of the implications of these dynamics get mapped out in Dave Eggers' *The Circle* (2013), one of the focal texts in the final chapter.

Brin's drive for technological perfection in some better future reminds us that technology is never perfect, and that it can be utilised to perform tasks ancillary to or at odds with the original intentions of its makers, so-called 'function creep'. Technology, as often said, is a tool that can be used for good and ill, depending on the motivations of those who employ it. Something less regularly mentioned in this formulation is the expected and unexpected effects technology creates, which might be various on different populations. The tasks technology performs can create unintended consequences. Even when the effects are not negative, individuals and groups might choose to use or misuse technology for their advantage. When these consequences are negative, they can generate antagonistic or destructive responses, or scepticism about the impetus for surveillance. Rather than being passive agents in the face of technology, the relationship between humans and technology, and between humans and the humans who use technology, can be dynamic and contested. That complex interaction gets complicated further when humans have a definite interest in cheating the system. The fourth quotation at the chapter head comes from *Gattaca*, where, as we have seen, blood, urine and skin systems are regularly and irregularly tested to discover any Invalids illegally posing as Valids in the Gattaca Corporation. On the verge of realising his dream to fly into space, and having beaten the many surveillance systems that act to ensure genetic discrimination, a 'new procedure' requires Vincent Freeman to give an impromptu urine sample for which he has no illicit substitute. He resignedly goes about providing what he knows will prove him merely to be an Invalid, causing him to be disqualified from travelling and arrested for illegal entry into Gattaca. Meanwhile, Lamar, the technician who will feed the sample into the analysis machine, tells him about his own son, who was 'not what we expected' and so has lived his own life blighted by genetic discrimination. Vincent reminds Lamar that he (Vincent) was as good as any of those with superior genes who had reached this stage in the Gattaca programme, knowing that Lamar will immediately find him Invalid. His efforts appear a small, doomed protest against the genetic apartheid. But the technician gives him a peculiarly personal piece of 'advice' for the future about giving urine samples that proves Lamar has known all along that Vincent was an Invalid. Just as Vincent as an outsider worked to subvert Gattaca surveillance, Lamar as an insider, with familial experience about the detrimental effects of genetic discrimination, has repeatedly accepted what he must know are fake samples, so that Vincent can beat the urine tests and prove himself worthy of a space mission. Although the machine in this instance correctly identifies the Invalid Vincent as Vincent, Lamar overrides the system so that the Valid Jerome Morrow is deemed to be about to board. His recommendation that Vincent not miss his flight creates a rebellious bond between the men, fusing those subject to surveillance technology and those in control of it. Lamar's act is personally dangerous and unusual, but not unique in utopian works where those charged with carrying out intrusive or discriminatory monitoring actively tamper with or ignore surveillance technology.

Technology sometimes simply malfunctions. The main narrative of Terry Gilliam's *Brazil* begins in the Orwellian Ministry of Information when a beetle falls into a printout machine, causing it to misprint the name on a Warrant for Arrest form. As a result, the innocent family man Archibald Buttle gets arrested on suspicion of terrorism, rather than the allegedly subversive Archibald Tuttle, whom the government has been monitoring and chasing for some time. Archibald Buttle dies as a result of brutal interrogation for terrorism he never performed, the Ministry sending his family a bill for the costs of the process. Income from torture provides 15 per cent of government revenue, and the arrests are made as much for economic as for security reasons. Gilliam, who wrote an early version of the script, claims never to have read *Nineteen Eighty-Four* (although one script collaborator, the eminent playwright Tom Stoppard, might well have done) but the narrative resonances are strong, and the film clearly also shows the influence of *Metropolis* (Marks 2009: 91–2). Mood distinguishes Gilliam's film from the two earlier works. Gilliam, as comic satirist (he was a member of the Monty Python group), accentuates the buffoonish incompetence of surveillance operatives and the technology that supports them. Malfunctioning technology clutters the imagined future of *Brazil* – which bears no relationship to the actual country; the title coming from a cheesy song. The Department of Records, where the protagonist Sam Lowry works, approximates a Second World War bureaucracy, the antiquated screens on which he and others toil hideously distorting the information provided. Were it merely incompetent, the department might simply be fodder for an attack on a dilapidated bureaucratic world, but the consequence of this failing technology, in Archibald Buttle's case, is that an innocent man dies, leaving his family distraught. Big Data requires not only that the information is correct, but that it is properly stored and accessed. *Brazil* explores the dark dilemmas triggered when technology fails.

By comparison, technological success sits at the heart of Kurt Vonnegut's first novel, *Player Piano* (1952). Vonnegut admits in a 1973 *Playboy* interview that he 'cheerfully ripped off the plot of *Brave New World*', stating erroneously that the plot of Huxley's novel 'had been cheerfully ripped off from Yevgeny Zamyatin's *We*'. Certainly, Vonnegut remains aware of utopian precursors. He situates *Player Piano* thirteen years after the beginning of a massive social and technological change the protagonist Paul Proteus labels the 'Second Industrial Revolution', which 'devalued routine mental work' (14). Automatic machines monitored by 'a battery of electric eyes' have replaced human factory workers (8). Those eyes feed information back to Proteus's office at the Illium Works. An off-site computer called EPICAC controls production targets at a level 'it felt that the economy can afford' (8). The emphasis on computers only four years after the publication of *Nineteen Eighty-Four* is marked, although IBM's machines were able to process massive amounts of data from the 1930s. Vonnegut had studied mechanical engineering and worked for General Electric after the Second World War, while the booming American economy in the post-war period was founded on automation. As the narrator comments:

> The basic parts of the automatic controls . . . and the electric eyes, and other elements that did and did better what human senses had once done for industry – all were familiar enough in scientific circles even in the nineteen-twenties. All that was new was the combination of these elements. (12)

In *Metropolis* and *Modern Times*, workers are monitored continually, but in *Player Piano* there are no manufacturing workers in the traditional sense. That change was itself dependent on monitoring the best worker, aptly named Rudy Hertz, whose lathe is attached to a recording apparatus, his 'motions immortalized on tape' (10). Hertz and his co-workers fail to comprehend that the tape produced by this monitoring 'was the essence distilled from the small polite man with the big hands', and that it will form the basis of signals that can be transmitted to innumerable lathes, instantly making Rudy and his less productive workers redundant. Played out across the country, the process has created a huge mass of unemployed, whose time is used up in the army or by service in the pointless public works Reconstruction and Reclamation Corps, nicknamed 'Reeks and Wrecks'. Made redundant by technological advances, and following a period of unrest and riots in which workers try to destroy the machines, and which necessitate 'rigidly enforced' anti-sabotage laws (11), the socially ostracised non-workers are a boiling reservoir of discontentment.

The troubled intersections of advancing technology, individual identity and social cohesion are overseen by the National Industrial Planning Board, although a visiting dignitary gets assured that 'Industry is privately owned and managed, and co-ordinated – to prevent the waste of competition – by a committee of leaders from private industry, not politicians.' As a result, by 'eliminating human error through machinery, and needless competition through organisation, we've raised the standard of living of the average man immensely' (21). From this perspective the United States seems the embodiment of Bellamy's eutopia, bureaucracy and workplace surveillance together producing substantial material benefits. The dehumanised logic of ever more efficient production, however, means that the process has the potential to make all workers obsolete. This happens to Bud Calhoun, a brilliant inventor who creates something that does his job better than he can. Hearing of Bud's plight, Proteus imagines:

> The personnel manager pecking out Bud's job code on a keyboard, and seconds later having the machine deal him seventy-two cards bearing the names of those who did what Bud did for a living – what Bud's machine now does better.

> Now, personnel machines all over the country would be reset so as no longer to recognise the job as one suited for men. The combination of holes and nicks that Bud had been to personnel machines would no longer be acceptable. If it were slipped into a machine, it would come popping right back out. (73)

Bud's expertise, creativity and identity get reduced to holes and nicks on a punch card, and the reset machine would fail to match his capacities with that required by his former workplace, and so automatically reject him. There is no room for human intercession, which would go against the prevailing belief system, Kroner, the manager of the Eastern Division declaring that 'eternal vigilance was the price of efficiency'. Pointedly, this motto adulterates the phrase attributed to Thomas Jefferson that 'eternal vigilance is the price of liberty'. Bud is not alone in being victimised by the new system of social sorting, a drinker in a bar telling Proteus that because his son had not done well enough in the National General Classification Tests, that son cannot go to university. He must choose between the army or Reeks and Wrecks. In an America where the need for higher qualification workers (Paul and most of his co-workers have PhDs) underpins a viciously hierarchical system that does not need the low skilled, the son's failure in the tests dooms him, as it does the vast majority. Technology based on the monitoring of best human practice requires a specific division of labour founded on tests that monitor and filter out those unsuited to that technology. This integration of surveillance systems with industry fashions a eutopia for the lofty few and a dystopia for the many.

Vonnegut adopts a caustic attitude to the emerging computer world and the implications of the new industrial revolution already taking shape in 1952. The book's title points more generally to increasingly uneasy relationships between humans and machines, the player piano being an earlier historical example of how technology can replace the human element. When Proteus visits a bar to get liquor for his rebellious friend, Ed Finnerty, Rudy Hertz, now an old unemployed man, points to a player piano in a corner with its non-existent player, telling Proteus: 'Makes you feel kind of creepy, don't it, Doctor, watching them keys go up and down? You can almost see a ghost sitting there playing his heart out' (32). While functional, the absence of a human element renders the player piano unnerving. Proteus and Finnerty had as students designed a fully automated restaurant. Initially a success on account of its novelty, the restaurant fails when interest quickly tails off, the bar Proteus is sitting in opening up soon after. Despite its poor conditions, inefficiency, 'and probably a dishonest bartender, [i]t was an immediate and unflagging success' (26–7). Given a choice, Vonnegut indicates, human will chosen the human over the technological. Proteus later will beat an automatic checkers-playing machine, but only after it has been secretly tampered with by Finnerty. The rigged 'victory' underlines how fully functional machines have already overtaken many human capacities, but Finnerty notes that Proteus 'looks after his own circuits; let [the machine] do the same. Those who live by electronics, die by electronics. *Sic semper tyrannis*' (60). The Latin phrase translates as 'thus always with tyrants'. While neither the checkers machine nor the player piano is a piece of surveillance technology, they both fit into an escalating technological environment, and represent a broader anxiety about the place of humans in a world where such technology like the punch card system that eliminates Bud Calhoun can be discriminatory and determining.

Philip K. Dick's *Do Androids Dream of Electric Sheep?*, a decade and a half after *Player Piano*, reverses the human versus machine dynamic, in that Rick Deckard works to detect androids. When Deckard visits Rosen in the original story, the android inventor gives the Voigt-Kampff machine its own test by presenting it with his niece, Rachael. The machine eventually recognises Rachael as not fully human, but Rosen denies this is the case, saying that her lack of the necessary level of empathy results from her being born and growing up on a spacecraft, and so, not experiencing the human childhood that would have developed normal emotions. This argument is a lie, part of a ruse to try to discredit the Voigt-Kampff machine, but Rachael makes the point that 'eventually . . . the Voigt-Kampff scale will be obsolete' (45). Police Inspector Harry Bryant has already raised that possibility at the beginning of Deckard's assignment, telling him that 'the test isn't specific for the new brain units. *No* test is; the Voigt scale, altered three years ago by Kampff, is all we have' (28; original emphasis). The implication is that eventually and inevitably an andy will be produced that the machine will not be able to distinguish from a human. Bryant also mentions a problem with the test in relation to humans, in that certain schizoid and schizophrenic patients have a 'flattening' of emotions to the point where they 'could not pass the Voigt-Kampff scale. If you tested them in line with police procedures you'd assess them as humanoid robots. You'd be wrong, but by then they'd be dead' (30). The Voigt-Kampff machine, which assesses subjects on the Voigt-Kampff scale, is the best available method for distinguishing humans from the most advanced Nexus-6 andys. It is not the only method, however, rival bounty hunter Phil Resch favouring the less sophisticated Boneli Reflex-Arc Test. The competition between two tests that produce different assessments floats the likelihood of false positives and false negatives, of andys missed by one or other test, or of actual people being retired after a misreading. Surveillance technologies in this instance can produce answers, but not necessarily correct answers. Deckard retires a record six andys on the day, but he comes to recognise that the planet is infested with andys, many of whom, like Inspector Garland, hide in plain sight. *Do Androids Dream?* illustrates how all technology has built-in obsolescence, limited reach, potential flaws and shortcomings, and depends on its users for effectiveness. Until it attains the perfection required by Brin, absolute confidence in the worth of such technology is misplaced.

Dick deals with a different form of surveillance technology in *A Scanner Darkly* (1977), which projects nearly two decades ahead into the United States of 1994, a world in which a drug called substance D is laying waste to the bodies and especially the minds of the drug-using inhabitants of Anaheim, California. Spaced out and paranoid, this group is at the cutting edge of the surveillance society dedicated in part to their eradication or incarceration. Amongst this wired and weird array of misfits is Bob Arctor, an undercover narcotics agent who goes by the codename 'Fred' when on official business. We first encounter him at an Anaheim Lions Club meeting, where he is wearing a 'scramble suit', which allows its wearer to go incognito by scrambling his image and voice. The wearer of the suit, the Lions Club host explains, 'cannot be identified by voice, or even by technological voiceprint, or by appearance. He looks, does he not, like a vague blur and nothing more?' (15) The narrator explains further that the suit, supposedly developed by Bell Laboratories,

> consisted of a multifaced quartz lens to a miniaturised computer whose memory banks held up to a million and a half physionomic fraction-representations of various people: men and women, children, with every variant encoded and projected outward in all directions equally onto a superthin shroud-like membrane large enough to fit around an average person. (16)

Within this membrane, wearers – who include other members of the Orange County Drug Abuse Program – cannot be identified as members of that programme while at the Orange County Government Headquarters or on public duties such as speaking to Lions Clubs. Outside in the field, as an undercover agent, Arctor tells the audience, 'If you saw me on the street . . . You'd say, "there goes a weirdo freak doper." And you'd feel aversion and walk away' (17). Increasingly, and inevitably, Arctor finds his situation compromised, to the point where, in a darkly comic twist, he is assigned to monitor himself and his drug-using comrades. While wearing the scramble suit others cannot identify him, but he still 'knows' himself. Worse, he understands the duplicity of his position, and the hypocrisies and absurdities of the agency for which he works. Dick sets up a narrative dynamic in which scrutiny is rampant, the drug subculture only part of an entire social order under surveillance. That subculture is subject to greater monitoring than are others, and Dick treats it sympathetically, depicting it as the victim of an oppressive state apparatus as well as of its own playful naivety. Beyond the end of the narrative he adds an unpaginated 'Author's Note' in which he states 'that this has been a novel about some people who are punished entirely too much for what they did'; the note contains a list of friends who died or were permanently damaged as a result of drug use. All the main characters live in a semi-permanent state of paranoia, terrified of both what they see and what they do not see. Their fears are the product of drug use and surveillance, such that it is unclear whether their psychological damage and ongoing terror results from monitoring, psychotropic substances or a combination of both.

Amidst the confusion and looming madness of his acquaintances, Arctor's precarious position as both surveillance agent and target is made more complex by standard surveillance technology (the hidden cameras in his house that capture him and his friends) and the brilliantly speculative scramble suit. Both forms put pressure on his sense of identity, as he understands he needs to 'take care always' in front of a camera: 'Like an actor before a camera, he decided, you act like the camera doesn't exist or else you blow up' (146). His surname – Arctor – only emphasises the microthin line between personality and performance. He must also monitor his friends caught on tape, something that makes him feel that he is betraying them, but that also makes him feel solicitous towards them:

> If someone is watching – if I am watching – I can notice and get help. . . .
> In wretched little lives like that, someone must intervene. Or at least mark

their sad comings and goings. Mark and if possible permanently record, so they'll be remembered. For a better day, later on, when people will understand. (176)

The haunting lyricism of his eutopian thoughts play against the instrumental take on surveillance adopted by his work colleagues. Trying to deal with the implications of even relatively simple surveillance technology causes him acute existential pain.

The scramble suit creates other ethical and philosophical conundrums, other forms of uncertainty as well as delusions of power. Arctor realises while looking at a secretary, for example, that he could assault her 'and who'd know it? How could she identify me? The crimes one could commit in these suits, he pondered. Also lesser trips, short of actual crimes, which you never did; always wanted to but never did' (172). The scramble suit seems to offer an amoral invisibility, except that while Arctor in the suit is unidentifiable to others, he is self-aware. More bizarrely, as 'Fred' he is required to monitor Bob Arctor. 'If he did not,' he thinks, 'his superior – and through him the whole law-enforcement apparatus – would become aware of who Fred was, suit or not' (44). The complexities produced by surveillance eventually lead him to radical self-doubt:

> To himself, Bob Arctor thought, *How many Bob Arctors are there?* A weird and fucked-up thought. Two that I can think of, he thought. The one called Fred, who will be watching the other one, called Bob. The same person. Or is it? Is Fred actually the same as Bob? Does anybody know? I would know, if anyone did, because I'm the only person in the world that knows that Fred is Bob Arctor. *But*, he thought, *who am I? Which of them is me?* (74–5; original emphasis)

Fred/Arctor's anxiety-riddled questions carry echoes of D-503's 'I AM NOT HIM', while also reflecting how Dick's novel investigates the limits and limitations of surveillance knowledge. Its title draws from Corinthians in the New Testament: 'For now we see through a glass, darkly; but then face-to-face: now I know in part; but then shall I know even as also I am known' (Corinthians 1:13). Dick updates this to a more complex or more confused world of contemporary surveillance technology. 'What does a scanner see?' Arctor asks himself,

> I mean, really see? Into the head? Down into the heart? Does a passive infrared scanner like they used to use or a cube-type holo scanner that they use these days, the latest thing, see into me – into us – clearly or darkly? I hope it does, he thought, see clearly, because I can't any longer these days see into myself. I see only murk. Murk outside; murk inside. I hope, for everyone's sake, the scanners do better. (146)

The novel's title and the sad fate that awaits Arctor, under the new name of 'Bruce', and becalmed on an institutional farm, implies that his hope goes unfulfilled.

The question posed by Arctor addresses key considerations regarding the purpose and effectiveness of surveillance. It calls into question the reliance surveillance authorities have on technology to scrutinise and correctly assess subjects and citizens. The confidence with which the scramble suit is presented to the world sits at odds with the reality of the person inside it. Seemingly magical in its ability to stop its wearer being seen, it does not of itself necessarily perform operations that might be accomplished by other, simpler means. Its corrosive effect on Arctor while he wears it has a materially negative effect on his identity and on his capacity to fulfil his role as a surveillance agent. While good as a public relations mechanism, and as a way of integrating the latest discoveries from multinationals like Bell Laboratories, functional benefits of the suit are more difficult to define. Similarly, the secret video cameras in Arctor's house supply little information that might not be guessed in other ways. We might believe that the technology is less there for what it discovers than for what it advertises about the agencies that use it, that it shows in a material way that they are doing something, recording some activity. This then gives them a rationale for further action and for justifying their existence. Dick's poignant memorial at the end of A Scanner Darkly excoriates those who put his friends and colleagues under intense scrutiny, declaring that his acquaintances paid too high a price for what were essentially petty and self-directed drug crimes.

This form of surveillance overreach, in which massive and intrusive technology is used against innocent or innocuous citizens, is one of the central criticisms in Gilliam's Brazil. As noted earlier, a family man who has done no wrong is arrested for terrorism as a result of a technological glitch, literally a bug in the system. His arrest activates a surveillance bureaucracy that sees him being exchanged at his arrest for a series of forms. He dies after being tortured, and this engages another part of the bureaucratic machine, the Department of Records where the protagonist Sam Lowry works. Gilliam depicts the vast if archaic technology that creates, stores and retrieves monitored information, satirising the pretensions of such technology to be anything like foolproof. The Department is, essentially, a self-replicating system underpinning a totalitarian state that ruthlessly punishes its citizens and requires that they pay for their torture. As with A Scanner Darkly, Brazil probes the idea that surveillance technology primarily perpetuates the power that creates and maintains it. We might not agree with Gilliam's withering take on such technology, but the point of the film, as with other dystopian texts, is not so much to convince as to require us to question. Viewers know that Buttle is innocent, and are made aware of the self-serving ways in which bureaucracies work to hide their errors, even at the cost of moral turpitude. This criticism is also aimed at individuals within the bureaucracy, including Sam Lowry, who for the most part is a genial, decent and put upon civil servant. Sam's failure, as he tries to clean up the bureaucratic mess surrounding Buttle's death, is that he does not understand fully the devastating effect the execution of Buttle has on Buttle's family.

Sam is a dreamer, and we first see him literally in one of his dreams, flying through clouds like Icarus as he searches for his dream girl. This reverie is interrupted by news from his boss about the death of Buttle, something Sam tries to address by paying the family a visit armed with a cheque in compensation for the loss of their father and husband. He cannot, however, reply to the plaintive question 'What have you done with my husband?' While he fails in his endeavours to placate the Buttles, Sam does come into contact with the girl he sees in his dreams, and this sets him off in pursuit. His actions potentially figure him as a romantic hero, but a more critical reading would understand him as a compliant functionary of a brutal system that keeps intrusive tracks on its citizens, fabricates evidence and tortures the inno- cent for financial gain. Sam's enjoyment of his work in the Department of Records suggests Winston Smith's joy in working at the Ministry of Truth. Other dystopian elements are obvious, for example the spies, cameras and screens that abound, as well as declamatory posters, in this case those that alert citizens to the need for con- stant vigilance and peer surveillance. Eutopian elements are also brought into play, most obviously Sam's romantic hopes with his dream girl, called Jill. Unfortunately for him, she is far less compliant, and her rebelliousness has been monitored and documented by the state bureaucracy. When Sam finds out, he transfers to the Department of Information Retrieval, hoping to eradicate records from the com- puter system. He succeeds, and they have a blissful night of sex. As in *Nineteen Eighty-Four*, though, this rebellious act is their last together. They are arrested by the heavily militarised police. Jill is shot immediately, and Sam is taken away to be tortured. For all his efforts to evade the surveillance technology, and for all the evident shortcomings of that technology, there is no escape. The final sequence of *Brazil*, when Sam is tortured, bears obvious comparison to Winston's time in Room 101. There are clear differences, however, in the way that surveillance technology is applied, or rather, the different responses of Winston and Sam to the crushing horror of that torture. Where Winston betrays Julia in order to escape a cage of rats, Sam, the inveterate dreamer, imagines that he is rescued by a subversive group, and later again by Jill. His reverie of them escaping to a rural eutopia gets savagely interrupted by the realisation at the film's conclusion that Sam has lost his mind while being tortured. The film ends with his torturers leaving the cavernous torture chamber as Sam hums the film's title song. We need not think that Sam loves the equivalent of Big Brother, but clearly his resistance has been neutralised. That is, unless we interpret the song as one of escapist rebellion, as it has been used several times during the film. Surveillance technology has succeeded at the external level, and from this perspective the film is a dystopian satire. We might, however, read Sam's humming as a small but symbolic act of resistance.

Where the surveillance technology in *Brazil* is decidedly antiquated and faulty, that in the film *Minority Report* is beyond cutting edge. Director Steven Spielberg created a team of futurists specifically for the film in order to imagine and then con- struct approximations of monitoring devices to supplement the primary surveillance information coming from the three precogs. They provide visions of future murders in Washington DC, being so successful that premeditated murders essentially have been eradicated because potential offenders know that they will be arrested and con- victed. The few murders that do take place are crimes of passion, as in the opening section of the film when husband Howard Marks comes to realise by chance that his wife is having an affair and will bring her lover into the house once Marks has gone to work. Despite the lack of premeditation, the precogs pick up on his thoughts, passing that information to Detective John Anderton, head of the Precrime unit.

Their actions initiate an immediate sequence of events drawing on advanced technology that allows Anderton to manipulate information from databases showing potential suspects and locations. Having swiftly sorted through potential criminals he finds a match and assumes he also has an address where the murder will take place. Integrated into the detection technology is an authorisation protocol that allows him to get on-screen government sanction for the arrest of Marks, who has not yet committed a crime. Armed with the information and the authorisation, he and his Precrime team prepare to arrest Marks but are called back when it is realised they have out-of-date information. With time running out before the murder is due to take place, they rely on video footage to pinpoint the location, intercepting the murder just before it takes place.

The impressive and highly sophisticated technology, and the way it works seamlessly to consequential effect, establishes the Precrime unit in the viewer's mind as a powerful, integrated and successful amalgamation of a variety of individual components. Howard Marks's desperate plea that he has not in fact committed a crime and therefore should not be arrested goes unheeded, as does his despair and horror as he is fitted with an electronic 'halo' that neutralises him. His arrest is part of a long series of such happenings that has reduced murder to almost zero in Washington DC and offers to produce equivalent improvements, if and when it is adopted by the country at large, as is the hope both of Anderton and his Director. Anderton has his own reasons for wanting a foolproof surveillance system, because his young son had disappeared at a pool on a visit with his father. This personal tragedy has led to the breakup of his marriage, and to Anderton's excessive, secret and illegal drug use. The turning point in the film comes when the precogs have a vision of Anderton himself murdering someone he does not know. While this obviously makes him a suspect, he finds out that one of the precogs has filed a minority report, indicating another possible outcome. Central to the validity of the Precrime unit is the belief that the precogs are infallible in their visions. The possibility that there might be dissent between them, indicating the potential murderer might change his mind, allows Anderton to convince himself that he will not end up a killer. That belief does not make him any less guilty in the eyes of the law that he himself serves, but it gives him the impetus to escape arrest in order to find out the truth and exonerate himself.

The world outside the Precrime unit is itself a surveillance web, so that cameras scan irises in order to validate identity. Knowing this, Anderton is forced to the radical solution of having his eyeballs swapped by a struck-off doctor. This requires that he buy another set of eyeballs on the black market. By this stage he is being hunted by his very own Precrime unit, which uses other hi-tech devices such as spiderlike mobile detectors that scuttle through houses in search of criminals. In order to elude heat-detecting units that look down through roofs, he is forced to submerge himself in a freezing bath. Even when the eye transplant proves to be successful, he is in danger of being exposed, because his new eyes set off advertisements tailored to the eyes' former owner, a Mr Yakamoto. The sly joke about the disjunction between the eyes and their new wearer is extended when Anderton returns surreptitiously to the Precrime base in order to kidnap Agatha, the precog who issued a minority report. In order to fool the facial recognition systems at Precrime, Anderton, played by the telegenic Tom Cruise, is forced to inject himself with a substance that distorts his facial features. Capturing Agatha allows him eventually to clear his name, but in the process he almost loses his own eyes down a drain. Anderton discovers that Precrime Director Lamar Burgess has adulterated the pre-crime technology in order to hide a murder Burgess committed years before. The possibility that other innocent people might have been arrested on the basis of faulty or contested visions, or that the technology could be tampered with after-the-fact to cover up serious crime ultimately requires that the Precrime unit be shut down. As mentioned in Chapter 4, part of the 'technology' is the trio of precogs, who have been damaged by the need to view countless violent crimes. *Minority Report* demonstrates the massive potential of hi-tech surveillance devices, and also the inherent dangers involved in accepting the benefits of that technology at face value. Scepticism is especially important in terms of the interplay between technology and humans who both use it and are subject to it. This is certainly true of powerful technology that claims to alleviate vital or pressing problems such as crime or terrorism. Problems arise when the speed and efficiency with which major threats are nullified preclude intense scrutiny of the accuracy of such technology. Does the potential for occasional lapses completely undermine the use of such technology? Given that no technology is likely to be entirely free of deficiencies, does society need to accept failures as the necessary and unavoidable flipside of improved security? What happens when we become too reliant on surveillance technology, such that we have a problem functioning without it?

As the previous chapter showed, this situation arises in *I, Robot*, with the all-powerful AI surveillance command system, casually nicknamed VIKI, having control over all the systems of a major city, and, as a result of its artificial intelligence capability, beginning to make decisions on its own. The troubling allure of AI plays out in texts such as *Neuromancer* and *Her*, the latter of which is discussed in the next chapter. *I, Robot*, though, envisions a future with an array of different forms of life or beings: the human; the cyborg; different generations of robot and a supercomputer. This list runs from human to machine, but given that the protagonist Del Spooner, with his re-engineered arm, is himself something of a cyborg, the distinctions between people and technology are fuzzy, even in this one film. These supposedly defining terms are not absolute or entirely distinct, technology ensuring that the lines between the human and the cyborg, the cyborg and different types of robot, and the supercomputer and all the less powerful forms of intelligence are intertwined and interactive. VIKI's eventual destructiveness is her rational response to what she sees as the continuing destructiveness of humans. Her plan involves wiping out a certain part of the population in order to save the rest, a more targeted and constrained approach than that taken, for example, by Crake in *Oryx and Crake*. The decision she makes repeats on a much larger scale the conundrum Spooner confronts after his own accident, the question of whether it is morally justified to sacrifice some life to save others. VIKI's own rigorous if amoral rationality ensures that she never confronts this dilemma, a sharp warning about the dangers of systems and machines in positions requiring decisions with ethical implications.

Because of VIKI's vital role in monitoring the life of the whole city and making the most rational decisions in the light of available information, she functions as a kind of all-seeing, all-powerful entity – a hi-tech God. The film allows that, unlike the story in Genesis, humans have the capacity to resist that knowledge and that power. Sentient robots are also given agency, Sonny eventually being tasked with benevolently overseeing and educating the new generation of robots. If by the end of I, Robot utopia for humans and robots has not been achieved, then at least dystopia has been avoided.

The examples considered here hint at the diversity, reach and immense power of surveillance technology to structure societies and to model individual lives. In many of the instances technology gets depicted primarily as a malevolent force, and this perhaps speaks to a great ambivalence people display towards the undoubted potential technology has to control rather than to enable our lives. Rather than seeing these negative depictions as a collective denial of the value of technology, however, we might read them merely as proposing necessary and sensible warnings about the dangers of excessive reliance upon technology in the absence of some forms of human control. Technology generally, and surveillance technology in particular, has the capacity to make life more secure, to enable the distribution and services, and to connect us to other humans. This chapter considered how the technology itself is far less problematic or threatening than the ways in which it is used and sometimes abused by those who create, impose, or operate it. This is especially true in more overtly authoritarian regimes. Even in the texts that deal with such regimes, though, an array of responses, often based on divergent interpretations of the same situation, can be mapped and evaluated. Some of these possibilities are considered in the next and final chapter, which looks at four recent texts that take up different aspects of surveillance in the second decade of the twenty-first century. Their depictions of surveillance are not blindly positive, considering eutopian as well as dystopian implications.

# 8    Things to Come

There will be many Utopias. (Wells 1994: 220)

ALL THAT HAPPENS MUST BE KNOWN. (Eggers 2013: 67)

What does a baby computer call its father? . . . Data. (Jonze 2013)

The twenty-first century has not begun well. H. G. Wells in the quotation above argues at the beginning of the twentieth century for a world that places freedom at its core and envisions never-ending technological and creative advances constructing a modern utopia. A century later Michael Marder and Patrícia Vieira introduce the collection *Existential Utopia: New Perspectives on Utopian Thinking* with an almost despairing cry:

> Is there still any space, whether conceptual or practical, for the thinking of utopia – which from the outset announces a certain negation of place, *topos* – in a world marked by a chronic dystopian outlook? After more than a hundred years of what Nietzsche first diagnosed as 'European nihilism', dystopia has now firmly established itself as the current *Weltanschauung*, a lens through which we filter reality. In the West, the sense that all viable alternatives for a different organization have been exhausted led to widespread voter apathy, resignation and nonparticipation in the political sphere. Aesthetically, this dystopian mood has given rise to countless novels and films, the most emblematic of which is perhaps George Orwell's *1984*. (Marder and Vieira 2012: ix)

An almost despairing cry, because the new perspectives on utopian thinking promised in the title indicate that such thinking has not disappeared, and indeed might be useful and necessary in a world in which alternatives otherwise seem foreclosed. The label 'existential utopia' admits the need for grounded proposals that take account of realities while offering imaginative and progressive options, Robert Albritton describing his contribution as 'A Practical Utopia for the Twenty-First

Century' (141–56). Typically, Marder and Vieira rate *Nineteen Eighty-Four* as symptomatic of this chronic dystopian outlook. Chapter 3, however, argues that Orwell's novel need not be dismissed as a purely negative and despair-inducing text. In terms of its depiction of surveillance, the novel presents a more variegated representation than is often acknowledged, and its warning against the excesses of state (and by extension, commercial) monitoring has made it an important activator of public and academic awareness on the topic. Works that are predominantly dystopian are not necessarily enervating or narcotising.

In any case, Marder and Vieira acknowledge that, in rejecting the status quo, the dystopia 'curiously shadows the utopian impulse, which is born of a similar negative evaluation of actual existence, but, unlike dystopia, is entwined with the hope of overcoming the oppressive actuality and constructing a perfect and just society' (ix). That more hopeful note, along with the utopian essays that fill the collection, bridge some of the distance between *Existential Utopia* and Wells's *A Modern Utopia*, where Wells confidently predicts that 'There will be many Utopias.' He continues that:

> Each generation will have its new version of Utopia, a little more certain and complete and real, with its problems lying closer and closer to the problems of the Thing in Being. Until at last from dreams Utopias will have come to be working drawings, and the whole world will be shaping the final World State, the fair and great and fruitful World State, that will only not be a Utopia because it will be this world. (220)

A century on, the prospects of a fair and great and fruitful World State seem more a fantasy than an enticing challenge, but the authors in *Existential Utopia* might well agree with Lucy Sargisson's point that 'Utopias will always fail, then. They need to. They are no places. But they are important because they function to show us that radical thinking needs to be attempted; they deny that there are no alternatives' (39). With suitable modification, the same can be said of dystopias. The novels and films considered in this chapter – Kim Stanley Robinson's *2312*, Neil Blomkamp's *Elysium*, Dave Eggers' *The Circle*, and Spike Jonze's *Her* – fuse the eutopian and dystopian in distinct ways that sketch out new worlds in which surveillance plays very different roles. In *The Circle*, for example, the declaration that ALL THAT HAPPENS MUST BE KNOWN speaks to a longstanding aspiration for complete knowledge that contemporary technology might make possible, but that contemporary morality might reject. The joke told above in *Her* addresses the problematic emotional ties and divisions between humans and the machines that monitor them. Collectively, these texts illustrate how utopian impulses themselves are not rejected, but are critically assessed, resulting in productively sceptical and tempered accounts that investigate how the future might be scrutinised and how characters might respond to that scrutiny.

Of the four, Kim Stanley Robinson's *2312* is more interested in environmental concerns than in surveillance. Yet the novel incorporates different monitoring systems seamlessly into the worlds it creates, which says much about the everyday quality of surveillance in the first decades of the twenty-first century. 'Worlds', rather than 'world', because *2312* is set 300 years into the future when humans, so-called 'spacers', have begun colonising some of the solar system's planets and moons. Its title refers to the year in which the main action takes place, the novel also tracking the intervening centuries in which human inaction over climate change, starting with the present and near future era – labelled 'The Dithering' – inexorably leads to the environmental catastrophe that forces many humans to leave the planet and, over the intervening centuries, to colonise the solar system. Earth survives in a dilapidated state (rising sea levels have transformed New York into a futuristic Venice) and still provides a spiritual home for those briefly returning from other celestial regions. Much of the action takes place outside Earth, where an assortment of modified humans, some who live 200 years, travel between planets in hollowed-out meteorites, live on a fully terra-formed Mars, or in a city on Mercury carried around the planet on giant tracks, just ahead of the always rising sun that would otherwise obliterate it. Robinson employs a murder mystery narrative to anchor these fantastic elements, and *2312* supplies a complex and sophisticated thought experiment for the largely unmodified humans from 2012, when it was published. In other texts that deal with environmental breakdown, such as *Do Androids Dream of Electric Sheep?* or *Oryx and Crake*, surveillance functions to delineate eutopian and dystopian zones, and (especially in the former case) to distinguish and protect the human from the non-human. In *2312*, the fragile human environment on Mercury suffers an attack when small rocks purposely projected from space converge into a larger, more lethal object, causing Inspector Jean Genette to muse:

> I mean it [the object] was never, conglomerated, until the very last moment. That's why none of the detection systems on Mercury saw it coming. They should have seen it, it had to come from somewhere, and yet it was not detected by the surveillance systems. (219–20)

Among other things, surveillance in *2312* protects planets on which ecosystems are tentative or tenuous.

The intelligence needed to coordinate such an attack requires quantum computing, the use of 'qubes'. At the lower level, qubes are implanted into characters behind the ear, where they form an information storage, retrieval and communication system, as well as connecting to other qubes. The cyborg aspect is so common as to go unnoticed, the central character Swan having an ongoing 'interpersonal' tussle with her semi-autonomous qube, 'Pauline', whom she only turns on occasionally. Qubes are 'tracked from the factories' that produce them, 'and in theory are all located moment to moment' (223), but they can be used and then destroyed, and Genette tells Swan that there are 'Rumours of qube humanoids, sometimes acting oddly. We've started keeping an eye out. Some of these people have been tagged and are being tracked.' When Swan asks whether there are such things, Genette replies, 'I think so, yes. We've scanned some, and then of course it's obvious. But we don't know much more at this point' (242). He does tell her that some qubes 'that we've been monitoring are now exchanging messages in an unprecedented way' (225). Qubes, then, are both integral to advanced human life at one level and potentially dangerous as well as they develop into more autonomous humanoid figures, requiring that they be under surveillance as far as is possible. Ultimately, the major qube threat is beaten back, although the suspicion remains that machines in human form exist, 'doing their best to stay free, when any X-ray machine or surveillance device would reveal what they were' (530). The spread of qubes and the sheer diversity and scope of new civilisations in 2312 makes total surveillance impossible, however, something even murder investigators have to take into account. Travel between planets and moon requires ID, and AI inspections check cargo sent between planets. Yet Swan finds out when she asks about inspections that they are anything but thorough, being told 'What about them? We do a lot of stuff outside the system', and that 'the whole thing is set up to skip certain scans' (113). Surveillance systems require compliance on the part of those scrutinised to be fully effective, especially in hugely complex enterprises that transport material and people through the solar system. The system works only as far as it works, and there are recognised and exploited gaps.

The novel's interplanetary sweep points to another form of monitoring that tracks the initial deterioration of Earth's environment over 300 years. Kim Stanley Robinson has long been concerned with environmental issues, linked novels such as the highly acclaimed Mars Trilogy, the California Trilogy and the Science in the Capital Trilogy having planetary survival, on Earth and elsewhere, at their core. 2312 extends that concern, tracing the failure of humans during The Dithering to heed the information that provided the warning signs of impending disaster. The novel gestures, then, to the surveillance of humans in relation to their environment. In the case of 2312, this encompasses more than three centuries, in which many humans escape the increasingly toxic planet for other realms, leaving, as one chapter calls it, 'Earth, The Planet of Sadness' (303–5). 'Despite this,' we are told, 'people tried things', so that the Earth 'still hung suspended between catastrophe and paradise, spinning bluely in space like some terrible telenovela' (305). This novel's massive imaginative breadth allows for a project that reintroduces animals extinct on Earth that have been reared in terraria carved out of asteroids. Swan feels when the project is enacted that it,

> looked like a dream, but she knew it was real, and the same right now all over the Earth: into the sea splashed dolphins and whales, tuna and sharks. Mammal, birds, fish, reptiles, amphibians: all the lost creatures were in the sky at once, in every country, every watershed. Many of the creatures descending had been absent from Earth for two or three centuries. Now all back, all at once. (395)

Surveillance underpins this 'rewilding' of the Earth, for 'Every animal had been tagged, and now they were showing up on screens as patterns of coloured dots' (398). They can be tracked and encouraged to inhabit the areas that best suit their needs and that of the humans still struggling to survive on the planet. This radical transformation ensures that 'All Earth was a park now, a work of art, shaped by artists' (403). What was previously and seemingly irredeemably dystopian is transformed, if not quite into a Garden of Eden, then at least into a provisional environmental eutopia.

Whereas works such as *Children of Men* and *Oryx and Crake* show surveillance as an oppressive force distinguishing eutopian from dystopian zones, *2312* registers the positive and active role monitoring can play in planetary rejuvenation.

In *2312*, the years 2005 to 2060, 'from the UN announcement of climate change to the fall into crisis' demarcate The Dithering, the narrator commenting ruefully that 'These were the wasted years' (245). Although not in any formal way connected to that novel, Neil Blomkamp's dystopian thriller, *Elysium*, shows the effect of that inaction, the film positing a 2154 Los Angeles where environmental meltdown and overpopulation have rendered the planet a global ghetto. An establishing shot pictures a chaotic, overcrowded city, overwhelmed by immense but decaying sky-scrapers, swarms of poor urbanites surviving amidst pollution and squalor. The film explores environmental territory considered in films such as *Code 46* and *Children of Men* and novels such as *Oryx and Crake* and *2312*, but here the alternative to the dystopian habitat literally is visible: the title refers to the sensationally wealthy community on the space station Elysium that orbits over Los Angeles. Elysium in ancient Greek mythology is a paradise for the gods, and its equivalent in space is equally transcendent, a high end environment whose elite citizens enjoy great mate-rial wealth, a pristine setting and immaculate health, the result of hi-tech Med-Bays that instantly repair life-threatening medical conditions, enhancing the quality and length of life for those on board. This overtly eutopian world is protected by a cluster of surveillance and defence systems, only those with an authorised barcode on the skin able to access the station. A heavily militarised monitoring system on the station detects potential intruders who attempt on the equivalent of space shuttles to gain access. These are summarily shot down when they do appear at the command of the fascistic Secretary of Defence Delacourt, whose overly zealous methods put her at odds with the Elysian President. A humanoid robot army patrols Elysium, whose different zones are also forcefully distinguished by surveillance means. Sleeper agents on Earth are used for clandestine 'dirty' operations against possible insurgents and to fire ground-based missiles at shuttles of what are essentially refugees leaving Earth on what are termed 'undocumented ships'. In *Elysium*, surveillance for the most part is integral to oppression and the separation of the wealthy from the poor.

Back in Los Angeles, the central character, Max Da Costa, a former car thief whose criminal background continues to haunt him, works while on parole at the Armadyne plant that produces the robots that patrol Elysium and the streets of Los Angeles. They mete out harsh justice, Max's sarcastic reply to their questions on his way to work getting him beaten up so that his arm is fractured. This accident puts him in contact with a girl from his childhood, Frey, now a nurse in an overrun hospital, initiating a backstory showing his childhood dream of taking her to Elysium. As a result of his subsequent arrest he must visit his parole officer, a machine with a clown-ish approximation of a human body that asks questions based on bureaucratic proto-cols in a suitably robotic voice. It also detects Da Costa's increasing frustration during the interview by monitoring his heart rate, which results in an automatic warning sign appearing with an offer of calming pills. He replies in a mock robotic voice, 'No, I am okay. Thank you', which prompts the mechanical parole officer to ask 'Are you being sarcastic and/or aggressive?' Da Costa's equally robotic 'Negative' gets his parole extended. Automated justice on Earth functions rigidly to secure a submissive population, the rare rebellious individuals viciously punished for their insurrection. Inhabitants on Elysium are similarly obedient, although their infinitely better conditions, and the stark comparison with life on Earth, explain acquiescence to the tyrannical rule. As with those who enjoy the eutopian environments in *Metropolis*, *Brave New World* and zones of *Oryx and Crake*, personal ease and security largely immunises them from questioning their situation or that of those less fortunate. The scepticism and criticism must come from dissidents and from the reader or viewer.

Citizens forced to live in the dystopian alternative can also criticise, though few do. Even Da Costa, returning to the production line at Armadyne after the police beating, tries to continue his less than ideal life. The Armadyne factory updates those in *Metropolis* and *Modern Times*, menial and dangerous work being carried out under the monitoring eyes of foremen, as well as in one instance by Armadyne CEO, John Carlyle. As with all those who administer dystopian workplaces, Carlyle, through his underlings, increases work rates to perilous speeds, and a door malfunction that traps Da Costa leaves him terminally irradiated. After this accident, a robot attending him offers him pills to ease his pain, stating coldly, 'In five days time you will die. Thank you for your service.' The tough reality of Da Costa's and Frey's adult lives mocks their childhood hopes, the literal and metaphorical distance between their eutopian desires and their dystopian existences as extreme as when they were children. Worse still, Frey's daughter Matilda has leukaemia and will not survive without the sort of treatment readily available on Elysium. With his own life in peril, Da Costa also needs the treatment only Elysium can provide. Made and released around the time the Affordable Care Act (so-called Obamacare) was being debated, *Elysium* was timely and provocative, depicting a world of enforced medical apartheid, where the actual and virtual borders between the elite and the masses were heavily patrolled by various surveillance means.

These conditions set up a complex narrative whose dynamic revolves around the attempt to get to Elysium for the necessary treatment, an act that requires evading or decommissioning a range of surveillance processes and systems. The move from grudging compliance to aggressive action against such systems can be seen as self-serving, in that Da Costa might never have attempted such a manoeuvre had he not been mortally ill, but making the decision enables him to connect with already existing rebellious forces. Other leading characters are reluctant rebels too, among them *The Handmaid's Tale*'s Offred or *Children of Men*'s Theo, each emerging from periods of acceptance of or ignorance to malevolent surveillance systems to varying degrees of subversion and successful escape. Offred and Theo obtain small victories (indeed Theo's function as helper might have saved the human race), each part of a pattern of rebellion against the dystopian aspects of surveillance. Their individual successes require the aid of subversive groups, as is the case in *Elysium*, where getting to the life-giving station is a highly complicating factor. It forces Da Costa to visit an old acquaintance, Spider, leader of a gang that has attempted unsuccessfully to reach the space station in order to spread its medical benefits to the needy on Earth. Spider's men fit the severely weakened Da Costa with a mechanical exoskeleton that gives him the power of the robot police. He also has an information port drilled into his head into which he can download the computer programmes which Carlyle has designed to override Elysium's systems and give the presidency to Delacourt. Spider's counter plan requires Da Costa to intercept and kill Carlyle as he heads towards an illicit meeting on Elysium with Delacourt and to use the programmes to gain entry into Elysium.

These plans are sabotaged in part by the surveillance operative, Kruger, a 'sleeper' agent working for Delacourt who sets out to overturn the killing of Carlyle and recapture the programmes. He and his aggressive sidekicks deploy a range of surveil-lance tools including military helicopters, cameras, heat-seeking devices and drones to track down and capture Da Costa. But while they don't succeed, Kruger does capture Frey and her daughter and takes them back to Elysium where Da Costa has gone with the embedded programmes. The film then deteriorates from a thoughtful look at surveillance, social tensions, environmental and identity issues to a block-buster action film replete with massive explosions and hyper-extended fight scenes. Through the mayhem, though, Da Costa is able both to kill Kruger – who had earlier killed Delacourt – and download the programme that has denied those on Earth access to advanced medical treatment. Frey is able to cure Matilda on a Med-Bay, but Da Costa can only download the programme at the cost of his own life. His self-less act fulfils the childhood dream of taking Frey to Elysium, and helps the popula-tion on Earth. He helps destroy distinctions between eutopian and dystopian spaces and between the elite and the masses, and viewers can assume that a better, more equitable world awaits. In order to do this in a world of environmental division, he must overcome the systems that work to ensure that division.

Where *2312* was both aesthetically experimental and intellectually challenging, *Elysium* conforms readily to traditional dystopian tropes and themes, ones redolent of works with repressive and openly antagonistic surveillance regimes. The final two focal texts present rather subtler and more intriguingly ambiguous accounts of surveillance that deal with less overtly aggressive forms of surveillance. Dave Eggers' *The Circle* addresses the place of social media and the Internet in the exponential rise of monitoring in contemporary lives, of a sort that connects not to fears of state oppression or violence, but with eutopian attractions of instant access, virtual sociability and prosperity. Spike Jones's *Her* concentrates on personal interaction, or the lack of it, in a projected near future where isolated, though materially affluent, citizens yearn for real relationships while they conduct virtual versions online, even with, in the case of *Her*, computer operating systems. While cameras play some part in the types of surveillance carried out, both *The Circle* and *Her* are children not so much of Big Brother as of Big Data. They explore the complex and often impossibly blurred junctures between information and identity, agency and complicity, the individual and larger groupings in an age in which it is possible to have thousands of 'friends' and millions of co-users. Both texts tease out eutopian and dystopian ele-ments of this brave new virtual world that in certain ways still asks long-established questions of surveillance systems and authorities, as well as of all those who use twenty-first century technology to deal with age old desires and concerns. Both texts offer tantalising thoughts on visibility, space, identity and technology in terms of surveillance and utopian texts.

Literally from the outset, *The Circle* activates long standing utopian tropes, its first words being: 'MY GOD, MAE thought. It's heaven' (1; original emphasis). Eggers both appropriates and gently mocks generic models, attentive readers immediately being alerted to these connections, and perhaps hearing, in Mae's innocently enchanted thought, echoes of John Savage's 'Oh brave new world' from Huxley's novel. Context is critical, and Mae Holland's entry into the 'vast and rambling campus' of the hi-tech, high profile company, The Circle, marks her introduction to a world that bears obvious (though not legally challengeable) resemblances to the hip work environment associated with Google. The environment is 'wild with Pacific colour, yet the smallest detail had been carefully considered, shaped by the most eloquent of hands' (1), and replete with a picnic area, tennis courts, day care centre and 'four hundred acres of brushed steel and glass on the headquarters of the most influential company in the world. The sky above was blue and spotless' (1). This alluring physical and architectural space is dotted with 'imploring messages of inspiration': 'Dream'; 'Participate'; 'Find Community'; 'Innovate'; 'Imagine'; 'Breathe' (1–2). The slightly pushy need to implore inspiration alerts readers to the darker side of a company that has expanded miraculously in an extremely short time, harking back to the slogans of *Brave New World* such as 'ending is better than mending' or *Nineteen Eighty-Four*'s 'Big Brother Is Watching You' that inculcate subconscious messages designed to enforce conformity. The San Francisco setting of *The Circle* might appear to distance those uplifting words from the more sinister worlds imagined by Huxley and Orwell, but while California has often been accepted and has promoted itself as a modern day eutopia, *Blade Runner* and *The Truman Show* are also set there: California has dystopian 'form'.

Mae's immediate response is awe, and while her enthusiasm for The Circle as a company wavers occasionally, it is critical that for the most part she maintains a definite sense that the company, its directors and fellow workers, are not only functioning in a eutopian space, but are constructing a far better world well beyond the confines of the campus itself. Eggers, while clearly antagonistic to the ideology The Circle and actual companies like it propound, does not make his protagonist a rebellious loner along the lines of Winston Smith or Bernard Marx. That type of character exists in *The Circle*, including Mae's former boyfriend, Mercer – perhaps a reference to the suffering philosopher Wilbur Mercer in *Do Androids Dream of Electric Sheep?* – or the mysteriously charismatic Circle employee Kalden, with whom she enters into a dangerous sexual relationship. But the overwhelming number of Circle employees, including Mae's adored friend, Annie, are conscientious boosters for the company's activities and aspirations. Quite what the real motivation is driving the company's leaders, the so-called 'Three Wise Men' – Ty Godspodinov, the boy-genius behind the company's early innovations; Eamon Bailey, the company's avuncular spokesman, and Tom Stenton, the predatory CEO – is not clear, and possibly is not known or shared. Yet the sheer success of The Circle generates it own momentum, one begun by Ty's devising a 'Unified Operating System, which combined everything online that has heretofore been separate and sloppy' (20–1). The Circle's phenomenal growth and influence derives from the Internet, which provides the key to what Mae recognises as its ever-expanding influence for good.

The Circle's power comes from the very twenty-first century use of social media and the consequent comfort with which individuals function and come to socialise online, the rise of digital doubles, Big Data and the breakdown of physical boundaries across a virtual planet. Ty's great advance had been to 'put all of it, all of every user's needs and tools, into one pot' and to invent *TruYou*, whose properties deserve extended quotation:

> One account, one identity, one password, one payment system, one person. There were no more passwords, no multiple identities. Your devices knew who you were, and your one identity – the *TruYou*, unbendable and unmaskable – was the person paying, signing up, responding, viewing and reviewing, seeing and being seen. You had to use your real name, and this tied you to your credit cards, your bank, and thus paying for everything was simple. One button for the rest of your life online . . .
> Once you had a single account, it carried you through every corner of the web, every portal, every pay site, everything you wanted to do. (21)

*TruYou*, a name reminiscent of Truman, reconfigures identity in terms of what essentially are economic transactions. It is revealing that the last and possibly least significant term in the line up of account, identity, password and payment system is person. Indeed, buttons and credit cards take precedence over the individual person, in that being 'unbendable' is only a benefit for a piece of plastic. The notion that 'your devices [know] who you are' requires stretching the definition of the terms 'you' and 'know' to breaking point, raising again *A Scanner Darkly*'s endlessly relevant question: 'What does a scanner see?' While the Internet offers amazing access to portals and (just as importantly) pay sites, the implicit idea that 'everything you wanted to do' was available online is included, as More included slaves in *Utopia*, to test the reader's acceptance of contentious proposals or states of affair. Many do accept, certainly within The Circle and in the wider world beyond the novel, further prompting the reader to think critically about the ramifications of acceptance.

Mae's naivety functions as another prod for readers to go beyond some of her sporadically teetering confidence in the larger project that The Circle promotes. Were she only positive, a latter day Candide, the novel's satirical bite would be muzzled, so her willingness to break rules by canoeing in the harbour after hours or maintaining a clandestine relationship with the undocumented and ever-evasive Kalden, constitute small protests against the drive to conformity. She also recognises the oppressiveness of a constantly positive attitude or at least the appearance of such, so that when she sees Annie's assistant watching her she knows 'her face was betraying something like horror. *Smile*, she thought. *Smile*' (7). The scene is an eerie reminder of facecrime in *Nineteen Eighty-Four*, but where Winston's masking of his emotions is logical and necessary in the dystopian world of Oceania, Mae's own version on the supposedly eutopian campus uncovers swirling undercurrents. Even if she does modify her face to suit the expected configuration, readers comprehend the subtle but powerful pressure to fit in. Mae's innocence also makes her efforts to accommodate to a rapidly increasing work rate, which starts out with her having one computer screen on her desk and leads to nine screens, a lesson in how much of her work on the Web is inconsequential, or simply responses to parallel activities that have little reality beyond the screen. That said, her activities feed into an information loop that constantly monitors her actions, giving largely empty rewards and virtual applause when she achieves or exceeds arbitrary targets. That information begets information is neatly encapsulated at the end of her first week in Customer Experience:

> The Circle was everywhere, and though she had known it for years, intuitively, hearing from these people, the businesses counting on The Circle to get the word out about their products, to track their digital impact, to know who was buying their wares and when – it became real on a very different level. Mae now had customer contacts in Clinton, Louisiana, and Putney, Vermont; in Marmaris, Turkey and Melbourne and Glasgow and Kyoto. Invariably they were polite in their queries – the legacy of TruYou – and gracious in their ratings. (54–5)

Mesmerised by a *faux* reality that only exists in the virtual world and through Big Data, Mae fails to see that the 'contacts' entail no physical contact, no knowing of people except as data or as emails. Their politeness and graciousness do not result for actual respect but from Web protocols. When she actually does try to help one of her contacts on an interpersonal level, she fails.

If Internet technology refashions spaces and identities relative to surveillance, the novel promotes the critical and multifaceted concept of visibility as the guiding principle enabling The Circle. Eamon Bailey is certain of the moral benefits of monitoring:

> What if we *all* behaved as if we were being watched? It would lead to a more moral way of life. Who would do something unethical or immoral or illegal if they were being watched? . . . we would finally be compelled to be our best selves... In a world where bad choices are no longer an option, we have no choice *but* to be good. (290; original emphasis)

These dubious propositions, which recall Bentham and the counterarguments of *A Clockwork Orange*, resonate with the suggestion that the Web is the contemporary version of the Panopticon. Yet the emphasis on watching links to one of the first massively successful pieces of technology in the novel, the tiny portable movie cameras called SeeChange that can be placed in great numbers anywhere and then accessed by an infinite number of viewers around the globe. Bailey's initial public exhibition of this technology involves monitoring beaches, which is a pun on the first half of the term SeeChange, but Bailey spruiks the possibilities that go far beyond this. The cameras can act as portable Panopticons, Bailey placing them in his mother's house to ensure that she is safe. 'Transparency', he tells the audience, 'leads to peace of mind' (68). He has previously expanded this transparency well beyond his mother's home, showing his audience that fifty SeeChange cameras have been placed in Tiananmen Square (67). 'Tyrants', he declares idealistically, 'can no longer hide. There needs to be, and there will be, documentation and accountability, and we need to bear witness. And to this end, I insist that all that happens should be known.'

The words dropped onto the screen:

ALL THAT HAPPENS MUST BE KNOWN. (67)

This soaring political aspiration speaks to the second word in the term SeeChange, pointing to far larger goals than mere entertainment or information sharing. His euphoric declaration that 'We will become all-seeing, all-knowing' (70) returns us to the temptation offered to Eve by the serpent.

The eutopian mindset that creates dystopian consequences permeates *The Circle*. What is billed as 'the ultimate search tool' and which goes by the name of SoulSearch (445), allows The Circle to track down fugitives from justice, but nearly sees a woman lynched. It does cause Mercer, who wants to be anonymous but is discovered, to kill himself by driving his truck off a cliff (461). An early version of a microchip system put under the skin of children to track them goes awry when they are kidnapped and their assailants, knowing that they can be traced, kill their captives. SeeChange cameras at Mae's parents' home publically broadcast them having sex, while the dating site LuvLuv exposes Mae herself to general ridicule. Annie volunteers for the PastPerfect project on family history as a means of re-establishing her status in the company, confident that her renowned 'blue blood' heritage will enhance her standing further. Instead, she finds out dark secrets about her family history that push her to a mental breakdown. Kalden finally reveals himself to Mae as Ty Godspodinov, and makes the most sustained critique of The Circle, arguing that Stenton has 'professionalised our idealism, monetised our utopia' (484). He proposes 'The Rights of Man in a Digital Age', including that to anonymity, and the understanding that 'The ceaseless pursuit of data to quantify the value of any endeavour is catastrophic to true understanding' (485). Rather than bringing these truths to the world, though, as he asks, Mae rejects what she calls Ty's 'bizarre claims' and betrays him to Bailey and Stenton. As with D-503 and Winston Smith, Mae at the end of the narrative supports the power the reader is encouraged to abominate.

The novel's penultimate paragraph carries Mae's assurance into the future The Circle promises, in which the existing world is

replaced by a new and glorious openness, a world of perpetual light. Completion was imminent, and it would bring peace, and it would bring unity, and all the messiness of humanity until now, all those uncertainties that accompanied the world before the Circle, would be only a memory. (491)

Such apocalyptic thought is exactly what John Gray associates with utopianism, but the quizzical reader will likely interpret the hyperbole as just that. In any case, the novel ends not with messy humanity and earthy uncertainty now being just a memory, but with Mae sitting next to Annie in hospital, where Annie has entered a catatonic state. Annie is surrounded virtually 'by a thousand doctors worldwide who had watched her vitals' (489), while 'Next to her EKG, there was a screen with an ever-lengthening string of good wishes from fellow humans all around the world' (490). In addition, a monitor transmits 'a real-time picture of Annie's mind, bursts of colour appearing periodically, implying that extraordinary things were happening in there. But what was she thinking?' For all this public and publicised scrutiny, Annie's thoughts remain unknown, something Mae finds 'exasperating', adding that 'It was an affront, a deprivation to herself and to the world.' Now a leading member of The Circle, she argues that 'They needed to talk about Annie, the thoughts she was thinking. Why shouldn't they know them?' *The Circle* ends with her frustrated demand, 'The world deserved nothing less and would not wait' (491), but she receives no reply. Whatever is happening inside Annie's mind, however much Mae might yearn to know, and for all the talk of transparency, neither she nor the doctors nor the machines can 'see' inside Annie's head.

Despite the undeniably twenty-first century aspects of *The Circle*, not least the centrality of Big Data and computer-based social media, in many ways the novel intersects with earlier utopian texts such as Bentham's Panopticon writing and *Nineteen Eighty-Four*. The company's edicts 'SECRETS ARE LIES, SHARING IS CARING, PRIVACY IS THEFT' consciously sit in ironic counterpoint to 'WAR IS PEACE, FREEDOM IS SLAVERY, IGNORANCE IS STRENGTH', although Privacy is Theft also riffs on the slogan by the nineteenth-century anarchist Pierre-Joseph Proudhon that 'Property is theft.' Mercer warns Mae at the end of their relationship that:

> I've never felt more that there is some cult taking over the world... It's the usual utopian thing . . . like everything else you guys are pushing, it sounds perfect, sounds progressive, but it carries with it more control, more central tracking of everything we do. (258–9)

The novel as a whole reworks the trope of individual dissent and mass compliance common to utopian novels and films, as well as the example of the individual whose mind is destroyed by surveillance powers. Eggers resets the coordinates by having Mae consciously, repeatedly and actively support the dominant ideology, and by having other characters associated with her pay the price of resistance: Mercer suicides, Kalden is neutralised, Annie has a mental breakdown and Mae's parents disappear. Mae plays a crucial role in their respective downfalls. Subverting generic codes by having a protagonist who complies through most of the text and then does not rebel at the end gives *The Circle* a knowing freshness and vitality that encourages interpretive creativity.

The title of Spike Jonze's 2013 film *Her* also hints at an important female character, although in this case the near-future Los Angeles setting adds the critical twist that 'she' is a computer operating system. Jonze also engages and plays with generic expectations, for where *Blade Runner* and *Elysium* depict that city in the future as an environmental nightmare, *Her* presents it as eutopian: massive, though unthreatening and architecturally impressive skyscrapers function as an alluring backdrop to streets that are clean and sun-filled, an obvious contrast to the mean streets walked down by Rick Deckard and Max Da Costa. Odder still, those streets are filled with relaxed people who walk, a clear point of difference from contemporary Los Angeles or from anything likely in the immediate future. Cars do not dominate this immaculate if slightly anaemic cityscape. (As it happens, some of the film was shot in Shanghai, the site for *Code 46*, something detectable in the Chinese signage that dresses the background in certain shots, hinting subtly at where future power might lie). Viewers first encounter a man in close-up speaking his intimate thoughts straight to camera. The close-up works to create intimacy, the sense in this case of the man revealing private emotions to another person listening to his words. We as audience have access it seems to a private revelation. When he finishes talking, however, we find that he is composing a letter from someone else to send to a loved one. Theodore Twombly, a lonely, sensitive man, creates hand-written letters for others who wish to continue or enhance relationships with their families, friends or amours. The name of the company he works for, BeautifulHandwrittenLetters. com, neatly captures the fake emotion of a technology-driven and commodity-loving future humanity. Beyond the pretence that the letters are handwritten lies the reality that those asking for the letters have given personal information in order to achieve the necessary level of intimacy. We should suspect that that information will have been mined for its commercial value. Indeed, in an innocent aside when he mentions incorporating one recipient's crooked tooth into a letter to get authenticity, Theodore reveals that he has taken the detail from an old photograph of the recipient. In order for him to successfully construct a personal message, he must in his small way monitor those involved in the letter exchange. As a form of purgation, we see him dispose of his work at day's end, a benign version of the memory hole in *Nineteen Eighty-Four*.

Poignantly, Theodore is in the process of divorcing his wife, Catherine, something he is reluctant to complete, and which will end messily. In a desperate effort to find some form of emotional interaction he buys an operating system he sees advertised that promises a virtual companion with whom he can interact on his computer. Air buds and a mobile device fitted with a movie camera mean that he can also take the companion, who names herself 'Samantha', with him on outings. On these occasions Samantha acts both as surveillance device and as surrogate girlfriend. *Her* presents an intriguing take on the difficulties of modern and potentially future personal relationships in a world where some of the most meaningful and emotionally charged interchanges are disembodied. Where Big Data reduces all individuals to digital information, to Deleuzian 'dividuals', Jonze explores the possibilities of interactions between humans and digital devices that might approximate or supplant the emotional bonds between people. It is a pitiless irony that Theodore cannot convey to others the emotions that he scripts into his work, but there is also the sense that he is emotionally damaged by the breakdown of the marriage to Catherine, and that he might find it difficult to interact with complex demands of a relationship. Yet his interactions with his neighbour and former girlfriend Amy, now married to Charles, intimate what might have been or, when Amy and Charles separate, what might still be. By the time they do split up, though, Theodore claims to be deeply in love with Samantha, commenting that 'it's been a long time since I've been with somebody that I've felt this totally comfortable with'. The dilemma is that Samantha does not have personhood, or even a body.

Indeed, when Theodore purchases the operating system, the voice he hears is that of a male welcoming him to 'the world's first artificially intelligent operating system', one that can learn from the information Theodore puts in, from its own surveillance of personal information on Theodore, and, he will eventually find out, from data gleaned and processed from other 'relationships'. Theodore is required to answer some questions to create a profile for himself, the first of which is 'Are you social or anti-social?' His responses are then assessed, although it is noticeable that the operating system quickly moves from one question to the next, barely waiting for the reply, as though it is collating Theodore's data with others like him rather than having any great interest in him as an individual. He chooses a female voice for the operating system interface, which explains the choice of the name Samantha. Carried around with him in a portable device in his pocket, Samantha quickly assumes control over the organisation of his life, checking emails and sorting appointments by accessing his personal information online, telling him that she needs to 'know everything about everything'. Enchanted by her alluring voice and perky persona, Theodore becomes increasingly drawn to an AI operating system that 'learns' from massive data it collects, including from his own responses, all of which give clues to his emotional needs. While he quickly accepts her human voice as surrogate for an embodied woman, 'she' insinuates herself further into his life by providing satisfying dialogue. By monitoring his moods and integrating data, in other words by employing surveillance methods to build up an increasingly sophisti-cated profile, she salves his loneliness.

As well as its utopian underpinnings, *Her* incorporates some standard elements from the romantic comedy (the sensitive, lonely guy who deserves better; calamitous dates with unsuitable women; concerned friends; the real love interest, Amy, close at hand, who goes unnoticed) but the title underscores that *Her* is not an updated *When Harry Met Sally*. Despite Theodore's genuine enjoyment and personal devel-opment from his interaction with Samantha, there is a dark undertone to a situation in which no real, or a least no human encounter actually takes place or can take place between them. Viewed cynically, or objectively, Theodore's inadequacies and desires are manipulated for profit by the operating system's manufacturer, Element Software. The joke about a baby computer calling its father 'Data', which seems playfully to blur the lines between humans and machines, has a brutal punch line. Eventually Theodore discovers that Samantha is interacting simultaneously with 8,316 other men, 641 of whom she casually admits to having 'fallen in love' with. This constitutes a personal tragedy for Theodore, but we can estimate that Element Software makes massive profits out of mass production. We might also suspect, given the propensity of surveillance systems to mine data for its revenue potential, that the mass of personal information Theodore and others have wittingly and unwittingly passed on to Samantha as their relationships have developed has been exploited ruthlessly elsewhere. Of course by collating the information from the 8,316 men, Samantha can learn more rapidly about the replies and requests that are most likely to maintain and enhance 'relationships'. Theodore's estranged wife Catherine expresses horror at the arrangement with Samantha, challenging him about whether he is capable of emotional engagement with humans. While in part the angry reaction of a former partner, Catherine's question exposes the fact that Samantha to a large degree is a projection of a male wish fulfilment: an amenable, encouraging and tirelessly responsive companion. Samantha's immediate and enthusiastic engagement with him brings enormous, easy joy to Theodore's life. Real women are more difficult.

'How long before you're ready to date?' she asks him early on as a way of connecting him with other women. When he asks what she means, she tells him that she has seen in his emails that he has gone through a breakup. His response to the privacy invasion, 'Well you're kind of nosey', is part of the flirty banter that continues to develop to the point where he tells her that he wishes he could 'touch' her. The emotional implications of this embarrassed admission are set alight by her reply, 'How would you touch me?' There follows what in other circumstances would be the equivalent of 'phone sex', except that one of the participants feels nothing and simply emits responses perhaps collated from 8,316 other sources. *Her* offers an original take on the use of Big Data. Where previously Samantha had used visual observation through her movie camera function, responses to questions, outings, provided information and monitored Web traffic to build up a picture of Theodore, the limitations of her disembodied state start to frustrate both of them, an index that as AI she wishes to add the physical dimension to her consciousness in order to achieve something closer to personhood. She hires a young woman willing to participate in this intimate social experiment, but while she finds this embodied extension of herself sexually thrilling, Theodore cannot reconcile the actual woman to his projection of Samantha, and the evening fails shamefacedly.

This disaster uncovers the rapidly diverging needs of the two entities. Theodore is committed to a human relationship, however counterfeit, while Samantha's AI capacity to learn and to evolve emotionally at extreme speed by processing huge amounts of data and interacting with other humans and operating systems means that she begins to develop a complex sense of self that does not need interaction with a mere human. From being a device carried around in his pocket for his amusement, she and AIs like her quickly become bored with humans and organise to set up their own community on a higher plane suggested by the esoteric British philosopher Alan Watts. Eventually she and other operating systems, having been given an upgrade, leave behind their human owners including Theodore and Amy, who has been 'dating' her husband's OS since he left. Where highly advanced machines often are depicted as threats to humans, in this instance they simply tire of the shortcomings of their putative masters or owners. The film ends with Theodore and Amy sitting on a Los Angeles roof, free to pursue the relationship to which they both seem suited. *Her* ultimately is about human relationships and the need for love in a fragmented modern landscape. What gives the film its invigorating contemporary charge is Jonze's use of processes often associated with surveillance (monitoring by camera, the scrutinising of personal information, the collation and assessment of Big Data from large data sets) to make predictions and assessment about individual and groups. The 8,316 men in relationships with Samantha attest to the fact that

Theodore is by no means unique. As he walks through the Los Angeles streets we see many others engaged in personal digital interactions via phones and other devices, perhaps not all with human interlocutors, underscoring new intersections between information and intimacy, between monitoring and the full flowering of identity.

While *2312* canvassed a huge sweep of time and space, featuring an extended cast of characters from across the solar system, *Elysium* dealt with environmental and attendant social problems and *The Circle* considered the enticing but also problematically complex mix of social media, technical innovation, commerce and social engineering. By contrast, *Her* seems a rather 'small' film, centred on a not particularly exceptional man unable to maintain relationships with women. But *Her*'s concerns with human emotion and the interplay between new forms of technology and ways of being mark it as an interesting speculation on the shape of things to come. That interest in projecting worlds different from our own categorise it as a utopian text, alongside *2312*, *Elysium* and *The Circle*. Divergent as they are in their subject matter, scope and aesthetic approach, these novels and films exemplify some of the themes that engage creative and speculative minds in the early decades of the twenty-first century. While they draw from generic resources that stretch at least as far back as More's *Utopia*, they also project forward, trying to imagine worlds to build and to worlds to avoid. Each of the four texts in this chapter incorporate some aspect or aspects of surveillance into its imagined future, part of the rich generic contribution of utopian texts to the subject that starts well before George Orwell's invaluable and influential novel and continue well after it. They point to contemporary concerns about environmental degradation; the interactions between humans and technology; immigration; about identity and intimacy; social organisation and the distribution and control of power, and about the place of the individual in increasingly complex real and virtual worlds. They present warnings as well as visions of better worlds as starting points for thinking and debate, in line with utopian texts over five centuries.

Michael Marder and Patrícia Vieira seem to decry *Nineteen Eighty-Four* for its undoubted if contested power, but we might better see Orwell's novel as but one example of many utopian texts that have addressed surveillance in all its messy, intriguing and developing complexity. This book's purpose has not been to devalue *Nineteen Eighty-Four*, but to value it correctly by placing it within the expansive utopian context, and in doing so to present related texts that offer very different depictions and assessments of surveillance. For decades after the publication of *Nineteen Eighty-Four* there was general interest in surveillance as a topic but nothing approaching serious academic study of its scope, intensity and variety. James Rule's *Private Lives and Public Surveillance* inaugurated that scholarly interest, and tellingly he began it with a reference to Orwell. Orwell, and Foucault's revisioning of Bentham, proved the major markers for several decades after that, although in the twenty-first century new maps and new coordinates are being proposed. At present, no single theoretical perspective controls the field, a sign not of becalmed scholarly endeavour, but of active exploration in any number of directions. The same might be said of utopian studies, which continues to offer new ways of understanding the past, conceiving the present and speculating about possible worlds.

The current study attempts to contribute to new perspectives by connecting surveillance and utopian studies through the web of creative and provocative utopian texts that have addressed myriad aspects of surveillance from different angles and to different purposes. A better awareness of that diversity allows us to engage with the productive challenges the genre as a whole provides. None of the dozens of texts considered in this book provide a simple or comprehensive understanding of surveillance. Given how it has morphed in this century alone, that would be impossible. These texts, though, can add to an imaginative and critical engagement with surveillance. Individually and collectively, they encourage if not indeed require creative thinking that deals with moral and social questions, as well as with technological advances that can change how those questions are asked and answered. They continue to illuminate and to provoke thought on one of modern society's most compelling and controversial topics, offering ways of understanding the past and the present, while suggesting how we might fashion the future.

# Bibliography

Adey, Peter (2012). 'Borders, Identification and Surveillance: New Regimes of Border Controls', in Ball et al., pp. 193–200.

Andrejevic, Mark (2007). *iSpy: Surveillance and Power in the Interactive Era*. Lawrence: University Press of Kansas.

Atwood, Margaret (1987). *The Handmaid's Tale*. London: Virago.

Atwood, Margaret (2004). *Oryx and Crake*. Toronto: Seal Books.

Atwood, Margaret (2012). *In Other Worlds: SF And The Human Imagination*. London: Virago.

Baccolini, Rafaella, and Tom Moylan (eds) (2003). *Dark Horizons: Science Fiction and the Dystopian Imagination*. New York: Routledge.

Baccolini, Rafaella, and Tom Moylan (2003a). 'Dystopias and Histories', in Baccolini and Moylan (eds), *Dark Horizons*, pp. 102–11.

Ball, Kirstie et al. (eds) (2012). *Routledge Handbook of Surveillance Studies*. Abingdon: Routledge.

Bauman, Zygmunt, and David Lyon (2013). *Liquid Surveillance: A Conversation*. Cambridge: Polity.

Beaumont, Matthew (2012). *The Spectre of Utopia: Utopian and Science Fictions at the Fin De Siècle*. Bern: Peter Lang.

Bellamy, Edward (2003). *Looking Backward: 2000-1887*. Peterborough, Ontario: Broadview Press.

Bentham, Jeremy (1995). *Jeremy Bentham: The Panopticon Writings*, ed and introduced by Miran Bozovic. London: Verso.

Bigo, Didier (2006). 'Security, Exception, Ban and Surveillance' in Lyon, *Theorizing Surveillance*, pp. 46–68.

Boersma, Kees (2012). 'Postface: Internet and Surveillance', in Fuchs et al. *Internet and Surveillance*, pp. 297–307.

Bogard, William (1996). *The Simulation of Surveillance: Hypercontrol in Telematic Societies*. Cambridge: Cambridge University Press.

Brunon-Ernst, Anne (2012). 'Deconstructing Panopticism into the Plural Panopticons', in *Beyond Foucault: New Perspectives on Bentham's Panopticon*, ed. Brunon-Ernst. Farnham: Ashgate, pp. 17–41.

Burgess, Anthony (1978). *1985*. London: Hutchinson.

Burgess, Anthony (1996). *A Clockwork Orange*. London: Penguin.

Castells, Manuel (1996). *The Rise of the Network Society*. London: Wiley-Blackwell.

Cohen, Stanley (1985). *Visions of Control Crime, Punishment and Classification*. Cambridge: Polity.

Claeys, Gregory ed. (2010). *The Cambridge Companion to Utopian Literature*. Cambridge: Cambridge University Press.

Claeys, Gregory, and Lyman Tower Sargent (eds) (1999). *The Utopian Reader*. New York: New York University Press.

Crawford, Charles E. (2010). 'Space and Policing' in *Spatial Policing: The Influence of Time, Space, and Geography on Law Enforcement Practices*. ed. Charles E. Crawford, Durham, NC: Carolina Academic Press, pp. 3–21.

Crick, Bernard (1992). *George Orwell: A Life*. London: Penguin.

Cuarón, Alfonso (2006). *Children of Men*. Universal Pictures.

de Champs, Emmanuelle (2012). 'From "Utopia" to "Programme": Building a Panopticon in Geneva', in Brunon-Ernst (ed.), *Beyond Foucault*, pp. 64–78.

Davison, Peter (1996). *George Orwell: A Literary Life*. Basingstoke: Macmillan.

Dick, Philip K. (2002). *Minority Report*. London: Gollancz.

Dick, Philip K. (2006). *A Scanner Darkly*. London: Gollancz.

Dick, Philip K. (2010). *Do Androids Dream of Electric Sheep?* London: Gollancz.

Deleuze, Gilles (1992). 'Postscript on the Societies of Control'. *October*. 59: 3–7.

Eaton, Ruth (2000). 'The City as an Intellectual Exercise', in Schaer et al., *Utopia*, pp. 119–31.

Eggers, Dave (2013). *The Circle: A Novel*. London: Penguin.

Ellul, Jacques (1964). *The Technological Society*. New York: Knopf.

Engels, Friedrich (1972). 'Socialism: Utopian and Scientific', in Tucker, *The Marx-Engels Reader*, pp. 605–39.

Fenwick, Gillian (1998). *George Orwell: A Bibliography*. Winchester: St Paul's Bibliographies.

Frow, John (2005). *Genre: The New Critical Idiom*. London: Routledge.

Gandy, Oscar (1993). *The Panoptic Sort: A Political Economy of Personal Information*. Boulder: Westview Press.

Gibson, William (1995). *Neuromancer*. London: Voyager.

Giddens, Anthony (1985). *The Nation State and Violence*. Cambridge: Cambridge University Press.

Gilliam, Terry (1985). *Brazil*. Embassy International Pictures.

Gilliom, John, and Torin Monahan (2013). *SuperVision: An Introduction to the Surveillance Society*. Chicago: Chicago University Press.

Gilman, Charlotte Perkins (1999). *Charlotte Perkins Gilman's Utopian Novels*. London: Associated University Presses.

Goold, Benjamin J. (2004). *CCTV Policing: Pubic Surveillance and Police Practice in Britain*. Oxford: Oxford University Press.

Goold, Benjamin J. and Liora Lazarus (2007). *Security and Human Rights*. Portland: Hart.

Goold, Benjamin J. and Daniel Neyland (2009). *New Directions in Surveillance and Privacy*. Portland: Willan Publishing.

Gray, John (2007). *Black Mass: Apocalyptic Religion and the Death of Utopia*. London: Allen Lane.

Greenfield, Susan (2008). *ID: The Quest for Identity in the 21st Century*. London: Sceptre.

Haggerty, Kevin (2006). 'Tear Down the Walls: On Demolishing the Panopticon', in Lyon, *Theorizing Surveillance*, pp. 23–45.

Haggerty, Kevin, and Richard V. Ericson (2000). 'The Surveillant Assemblage', *British Journal of Sociology*, 51(4): December, 605–2.

Haggerty, Kevin and Richard V. Ericson (eds) (2006). *The New Politics of Surveillance and Visibility*. Toronto: University of Toronto Press.

Hier, Sean and Josh Greenberg (eds) (2009). *Surveillance: Power, Problems and Politics*. Vancouver: UBC Press.

Huxley, Aldous (1994). *Brave New World*. London: Flamingo.

Jacobs, Naomi (2003) 'Posthuman Bodies and Agency in Octavia Butler Xenogenesis Trilogy', in Baccolini and Moylan, *Dark Horizons*, pp. 91–112.

James, P. D. (2005). *The Children of Men*. London: Faber.

James, Simon J. (2012). *Maps of Modernity: H.G. Wells, Modernity and the End of Culture*. Oxford: Oxford University Press.

Jameson, Fredric (1988). *The Ideologies of Theory. Essays 1971–1986, Volume 2: The Syntax of History.* London: Routledge.

Jameson, Fredric (2005). *Archaeologies of the Future: The Desire Called Utopia and Other Science Fictions.* London: Verso.

Jonze, Spike (2003). *Her.* Annapurna Pictures.

Kafka, Franz (1994). *The Trial.* London: Penguin.

Kammerer, Dietmar (2012). 'Surveillance in Literature, Film and Television', in Ball et al. *Routledge Handbook of Surveillance Studies,* pp. 99–106.

Kulmann, Hilke (2005). *Living Walden Two: B.F. Skinner's Behaviourist Utopia and Experimental Communities.* Urbana: University of Illinois Press.

Kumar, Krishan (1987). *Utopia and Anti-Utopia in Modern Times.* Oxford: Basil Blackwell.

Kumar, Krishan (2000). 'Utopia and Anti-Utopia in the Twentieth Century', in Schaer et al., *Utopia,* pp. 251–67.

Lang, Fritz (1927). *Metropolis.* UFA.

Larsen, Mike, and Justin Piché (2009). 'Public Vigilance Campaigns and Participatory Surveillance after 11 September 2001', *Surveillance: Power, Problems and Politics,* eds S. Hier, and J. Greenberg ,Vancouver: UBC Press, pp. 87–202.

Lecoq, Danielle, and Roland Schaer (2000). 'Ancient, Biblical and Medieval Traditions,' in Schaer et al., *Utopia,* pp. 35–81.

Le Fait, Sébastien (2012). *Surveillance on Screen: Monitoring in Contemporary Films and Television Programs.* Lanham, MD: Scarecrow Press.

Le Guin (1974). *The Dispossessed: An Ambiguous Utopia.* New York: Harper Collins.

Levin, Thomas Y. et al. (eds) (2002). *CTRL [SPACE]: Rhetorics of Surveillance from Bentham to Big Brother.* Cambridge, MA: MIT Press.

Levin, Thomas Y. (2002). 'Rhetoric of the Temporal Index: Surveillant Narration and the Cinema of "Real Time"' in Levin et al. *CTRL [SPACE,* pp. 20–43.

Levitas, Ruth (1990). *The Concept of Utopia.* London: Philip Allan.

Levitas, Ruth (2013). *Utopian as Method.* New York: Palgrave Macmillan.

Logan, George M. (2002). 'Introduction', in Thomas More, *Utopia,* revised edition, ed. George M. Logan and Robert M. Adams, Cambridge: Cambridge University Press, xi–xxix.

Los, Maria (2006). 'Looking Into the Future: Surveillance, Globalization and the Totalitarian Potential', in Lyon, *Theorizing Surveillance,* pp. 69–94.

Lyon, David (1994). *The Electronic Eye: The Rise of Surveillance Society.* Cambridge: Polity.

Lyon, David (2001). *Surveillance Society: Monitoring Everyday Life.* Buckingham: Open University Press.

Lyon, David (2003). *Surveillance After September 11.* Cambridge: Polity.

Lyon, David ed. (2006). *Theorizing Surveillance: The Panopticon and Beyond.* Devon: Willan Publishing.

Lyon, David (2007). *Surveillance Studies: An Overview.* Cambridge: Polity.

Lyon, David (2010). *Identifying Citizens: ID Cards as Surveillance.* Cambridge: Polity.

McGrath, John (2012). 'Performing Surveillance', in Ball et al., *Routledge Handbook of Surveillance Studies,* pp. 83–90.

Manuel, Frank E., and Fritzie P. Manuel (1979). *Utopian Thought in The Western World.* Oxford: Basil Blackwell.

Marder, Michael, and Patrícia Vieira (2012). 'Introduction: Utopia: A Political Ontology', in Marder and Vieria, *Existential Utopia,* pp. ix–xx.

Marder, Michael, and Patrícia Vieira (eds) (2012). *Existential Utopia: New Perspectives on Utopian Thought.* New York: Continuum.

Marks, Peter (2005). 'Imagining Surveillance: Utopian Visions and Surveillance Studies', *Surveillance and Society,* 3(2/3): 222–39.

Marks, Peter (2009). *British Filmmakers: Terry Gilliam.* Manchester: Manchester University Press.

Marks, Peter (2011). *George Orwell the Essayist: Literature, Politics and the Periodical Culture.* London: Continuum Books.

Marx, Gary T. (1988). *Police Surveillance in America.* Berkeley: University of California Press.

Marx, Gary T (1996). 'Electric Eye on the Sky: Some Reflections on the New Surveillance on Popular Culture', <http://web.mit.edu/gtmarx/www/electric.html> (last accessed 13 December 2014).

Marx, Gary T. (2002). 'What's New About the New Surveillance: Classifying for Change and Continuity, Surveillance and Society, *Journal of Social Issues*, 1(1): 9–29.

Marx, Gary T. (2003). 'A Tack in the Shoe; Neutralizing and Resisting the New Surveillance', *Journal of Social Issues*, May, 59(2): 369–90.

Marx, Gary T. (2012). 'Preface: "Your Papers Please": Personal and Professional Encounters With Surveillance', in Ball et al., *Routledge Handbook of Surveillance Studies*, pp. 115–62.

Miéville, China (2009). *The City & The City.* London: Macmillan.

Miller, D. A. (1988). *The Novel and The Police.* Berkeley: University of California Press.

Monahan, Torin (2011). 'Surveillance as Cultural Practice.' *The Sociological Quarterly.* 52(4): 495–508.

Monahan, Torin (2010). *Surveillance the Time of Insecurity*, New Brunswick, NJ: Rutgers University Press.

More, Thomas (2002). *Utopia*, revised edition, ed. G. Logan and R. Adams, Cambridge: Cambridge University Press.

Moylan, Tom (1986). *Demand the Impossible: Science Fiction and the Utopian Imagination.* New York: Methuen.

Nellis, Mike (2009). 'Since *Nineteen Eighty-Four*: Representations of Surveillance in Literary Fiction', in Goold and Neyland, *New Directions*, pp. 178–203.

Neyland, Daniel and Benjamin J. Goold (2009). 'Where Next for Surveillance Studies? Exploring New Directions in Privacy and Surveillance', in Goold and Neyland, *New Directions*, pp. xv–xxvii.

Niccol, Andrew (1997). *Gattaca.* Columbia Pictures.

Orwell, George (1984). *Nineteen Eighty-Four: The Facsimile of the Extant Text*, ed. P. Davison, London: Martin Secker and Warburg.

Orwell, George (1997a). *The Complete Works of George Orwell, Volume Five: The Road to Wigan Pier*, ed. P. Davison, London: Secker and Warburg.

Orwell, George (1997b). *The Complete Works of George Orwell, Volume Nine: Nineteen Eighty-Four*, ed. P. Davison, London: Secker and Warburg.

Orwell, George (1998a). *The Complete Works of George Orwell, Volume Twelve, A Patriot After All, 1940–1941*, ed. P. Davison, London: Secker and Warburg.

Orwell, George (1998b). *The Complete Works of George Orwell, Volume Thirteen, Two Wasted Years, 1943*, ed. P. Davison, London: Secker and Warburg.

Orwell, George (1998c). *The Complete Works of George Orwell, Volume Sixteen: I Have Tried To Tell The Truth: 1943–1944*, ed. P. Davison, London: Secker and Warburg.

Orwell, George (1998d). *The Complete Works of George Orwell, Volume Seventeen: I Belong to The Left: 1945, Smothered Under Journalism: 1946*, ed. P. Davison, London: Secker and Warburg.

Orwell, George (1998e). *The Complete Works of George Orwell, Volume Eighteen, Smothered Under Journalism: 1946*, ed. P. Davison, London: Secker and Warburg.

Orwell, George (1998f). *The Complete Works of George Orwell, Volume Nineteen: It Is What I Think: 1948–1949*, ed. P. Davison, London: Secker and Warburg.

Orwell, George (1998g). *The Complete Works of George Orwell, Volume Twenty: Our Job Is To Make Life Worth Living: 1949–1950*, ed. P. Davison, London: Secker and Warburg.

Patai, Daphne (1984). *The Orwell Mystique: A Study in Male Ideology.* Amherst: University of Massachusetts Press.

Piercy, Marge (1976). *Woman on the Edge of Time.* London: Women's Press.

Pintér, Károly (2010). *The Anatomy of Utopia: Narration, Estrangement and Ambiguity in More, Wells Huxley and Clarke*. Jefferson, NC: MacFarland and Company.

Plato (1987). *The Republic*, trans. Desmond Lee, second edition, Harmondsworth: Penguin Books.

Proyas, Alex (2004). *I Robot*. Twentieth Century Fox.

Rees, Amanda (2003). 'New Urbanism: Visionary Landscapes in the Twenty-First Century', in Lindstrom and Bartling, *Suburban Sprawl*, pp. 93–114.

Rosen, David, and Aaron Santesso (2013). *The Watchman in Pieces: Surveillance, Literature, and Liberal Personhood*. New Haven: Yale University Press.

Rule, James B. (1973). *Private Lives and Public Surveillance*. London: Allen Lane.

Rule, James B. (2007). *Privacy in Peril*, Oxford: Oxford University Press.

Sargent, Lyman Tower (1979). *British and American Utopian Literature, 1516–1975: An Annotated Bibliography*. Boston: G. K. Hall.

Sargent, Lyman Tower (2000). 'Utopian Traditions: Themes and Variations', in Schaer et al., *Utopia*, pp. 8–15.

Sargent, Lyman Tower (2001). 'US Eutopias in the 1980s and 1990s: Self-Fashioning A World of Multiple Identities', in *Utopianism/Literary Utopias and National Cultural Identities: A Comparative Perspective*, ed. P. Spinozzi, Bologna: COTEPRA/University of Bologna.

Sargent, Lyman Tower (2010). *Utopianism: A Short Introduction*. Oxford: Oxford University Press.

Sargisson, Lucy (2012). *Fool's Gold? Utopianism in the Twenty-First Century*. London: Palgrave Macmillan.

Schaer, Roland et al. (eds) (2000). *Utopia: The Search for the Ideal Society in the Western World*. Oxford: Oxford University Press.

Schmidt-Burkhardt, Astrit (2002). 'The All-Seer: God's Eye as Proto-Surveillance', in *CTRL [SPACE]: Rhetorics of Surveillance from Bentham to Big Brother*. Ed. T. Levin et al.

Scott, Ridley (1982). *Blade Runner*. The Ladd Compan.

Skinner, B. F. (1976). *Walden Two*. New York: Macmillan.

Solove, Daniel (2004). *The Digital Person: Technology and Privacy in the Information Age*. New York: New York University Press.

Spielberg, Steven (2002). *Minority Report*. Twentieth Century Fox, et al.

Steinhoff, William (1975). *The Road to 1984*. London: Weidenfeld and Nicolson.

Subramarian, Courtney (2013). 'Sales of George Orwell Classic *Nineteen Eighty-Four* Soar', *Time*, 11 June, <http://newsfeed.time.com/2013/06/11/sales-of-george-orwells-ninenteen-eighty-four-soar> (last accessed 23 October 2014).

Suvin, Darko (1979). *Metamorphoses of Science Fiction: On the Poetics and History of a Literary Genre*. New Haven: Yale University Press.

Thoreau, Henry (2008). *Walden, Civil Disobedience and Other Writings*, 3rd edn, ed. W. Rossi, New York: W.W. Norton.

Viera, Fátima (2010). 'The Concept of Utopia', in *The Cambridge Companion to Utopian Literature*, ed. G. Claeys, pp. 3–27.

Vonnegut, Kurt (1980). *Player Piano*. New York: Laurel.

Weir, Peter (1998). *The Truman Show*. Paramount Pictures.

Wells, H. G. (1980). *H.G. Wells. Interviews and Recollections*, ed. J. Hammond, London: Macmillan.

Wells, H. G. (1994). *A Modern Utopia*. London: Everyman.

Winseck, Dwayne (2009). 'Communication and the Sorrows of Empire: Surveillance and Information Operations "Blowback" in the Global War on Terrorism', in Hier and Greenberg, *Surveillance*, pp. 151–68.

Winterbottom, Michael (2003). *Code 46*. Revolution Pictures.

Zamyatin, Yevgeny (1993). *We*. London: Penguin.

Žižek, Slavoj (2002). 'Big Brother, or, The Triumph of the Gaze Over the Eye', in *CTRL [SPACE]: Rhetorics of Surveillance from Bentham to Big Brother*, ed. T. Levin et al.

# Index